# CHARLEY'S
# WAR

## HITLER'S YOUTH

*CHARLEY'S WAR:* HITLER'S YOUTH
ISBN: 9780857682994

Published by
Titan Books
A division of Titan Publishing Group Ltd.
144 Southwark St.
London SE1 0UP

A CIP catalogue record for this title is available from the British Library.

This edition first published: October 2011
2 4 6 8 10 9 7 5 3 1

Printed in China.

Grateful thanks to Pat Mills, Moose Harris, Jane Colquhoun,
Steve White, Trucie Henderson, Yvonne Oliver and Chris Weston
for their help and support in the production of this book.

Poppy artwork © 2005 Trucie Henderson.
*Black Max* © 2011 Egmont UK Ltd. All rights reserved.
Illustration kindly provided by the artist.

'And All Hell Followed' feature © 2011 Steve White.
Strip commentary © 2011 Pat Mills.

Photo credits: Photographs sourced from the public domain except
where indicated. Cover photograph via the US Archival Research Catalog
(ARC); first issued by the Office for Emergency Management.

Page 4: US Archival Research Catalog. Page 5: First published in
*Vier Jahre Westfront: Geschite des Regiments List R.I.R.* (1932)
Page 8: German Federal Archive. Page 89: Crossbow: From *With the
American Ambulance Field Service in France, Personal Letters of Driver at the
Front* (1916). Gas mask: National Photo Company Collection.

What did you think of this book? We love to hear from our readers. Please email
us at: readerfeedback@titanemail.com or write to us at the above address.

To receive advance information, news, competitions, and exclusive Titan offers
online, please sign up for the Titan newletter on our website: **www.titanbooks.com**

**Much of the comic strip source material used by Titan Books in this
edition is exceedingly rare. As such, we hope that readers appreciate
that the quality of reproduction achievable can vary.**

# CHARLEY'S WAR

## HITLER'S YOUTH

### PAT MILLS
### JOE COLQUHOUN

Titan Books

# AND ALL HELL FOLLOWED...

## Hitler and the First World War

### *by Steve White*

I t's very hard to define Hitler's participation in the First World War with any degree of accuracy. Nazi propaganda, Gestapo record burnings, sympathetic apologists and the understandable efforts to destroy any shred of credibility he may have had has meant his military record has been obscured by the fog of war, although recent academic research has shed new light upon it.

But just how profoundly did Hitler's wartime experiences help formulate the views that, twenty years later, led to the most destructive war in history and with it the industrialised genocide of the Jews, Slavs and so many other unfortunate recipients of Nazi hatred? His time on the Western Front almost certainly helped crystalise his political and nationalist ethos but the road to the Third Reich was paved considerably earlier.

## HITLER: THE EARLY YEARS

Adolph Hitler was born in Braunau am Inn, Austria, on 20 April 1889. Whilst not a tale of woe – he had a loving mother and comfortable home – his father was, by some accounts, a strict disciplinarian and infant mortality took three of five siblings.

Hitler's artistic tendencies appeared at an early age but academically he far from excelled. His poor showing educationally was exacerbated by a lung infection that forced him to leave school at sixteen. By then his father was dead. To compound his suffering, he failed to be accepted into a prestigious Vienna art school after moving to the city with his mother. She then died a protracted, painful death of breast cancer, despite operations and radical drug treatment. Her attending doctor was Edward Block; he was Jewish.

**ABOVE:** Adolf Hitler (far left) poses for the camera with other German soldiers.

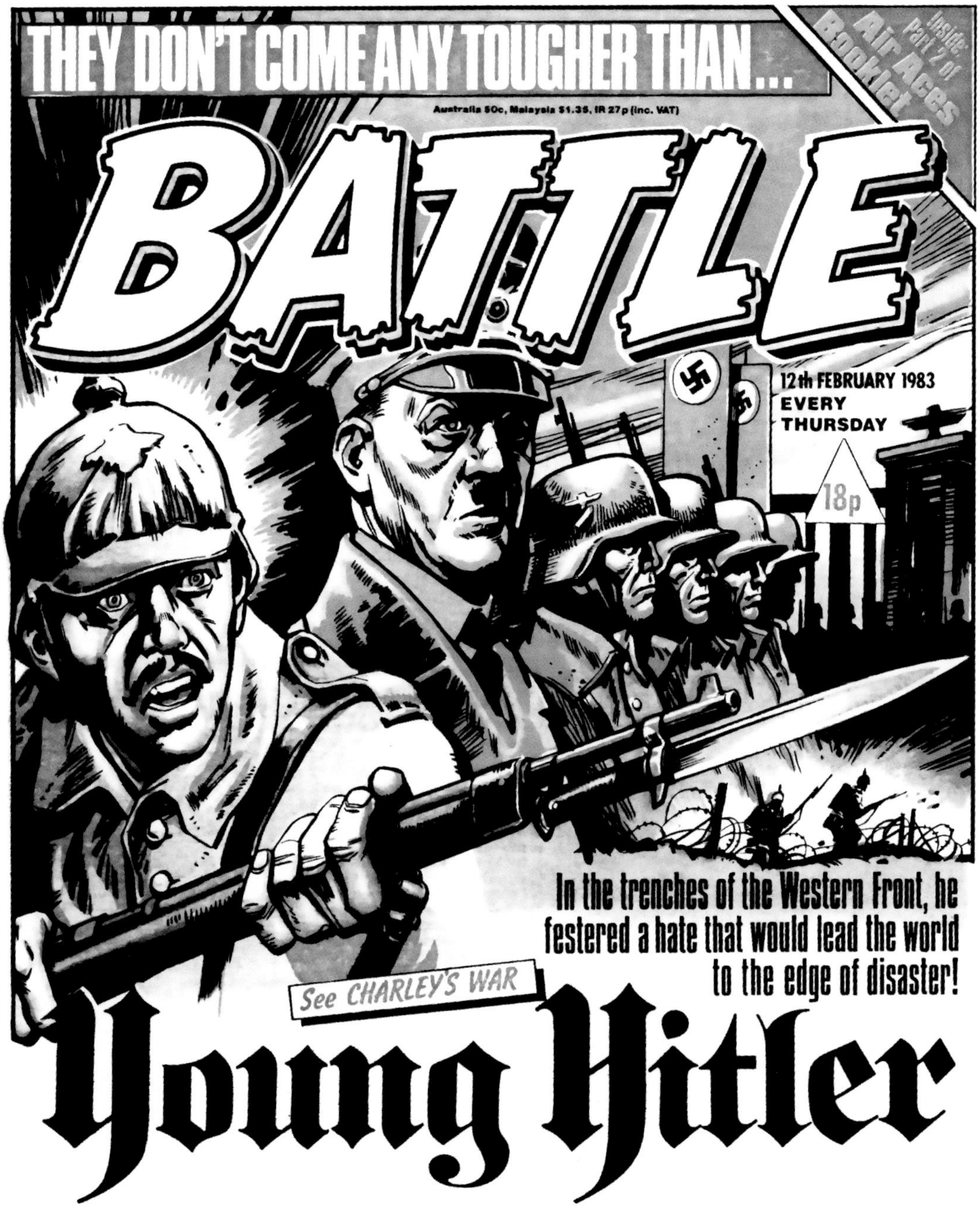
THEY DON'T COME ANY TOUGHER THAN...
Inside: Part 2 of Air Aces Booklet
Australia 50c, Malaysia $1.35, IR 27p (inc. VAT)
BATTLE
12th FEBRUARY 1983
EVERY THURSDAY
18p
In the trenches of the Western Front, he festered a hate that would lead the world to the edge of disaster!
See CHARLEY'S WAR
Young Hitler

**LEFT:** The 12 February 1983 issue of Battle announcing the 'Young Hitler' storyline.
**BELOW:** A rare photograph of Hitler on patrol.

Hitler soon exhausted the inheritance left to him and he became a virtual vagrant. He slept in bars and homeless shelters, did odd jobs and was infested with lice. When not hunting for work, food and money, Hitler spent his time in Vienna's libraries and it was here that his ideals and ethics, and his skill with rhetoric, really took shape.

Despite Jewish friends and an admiration for Jewish performers and artisans, Vienna's festering anti-Semitism increasingly influenced Hitler. This attitude fused with an awareness of what he saw as the negative impact of immigrant populations, especially Slavs and other Eastern Europeans. He became an increasing advocate of social Darwinism; that the weak should be expunged from society in any form; racial, medical, national.

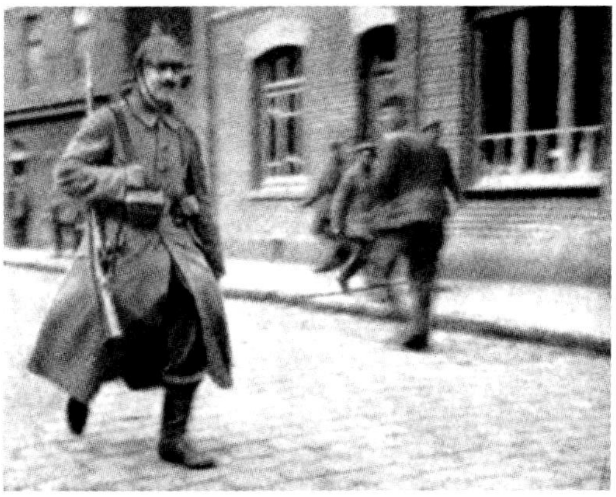

This firmament of political extremism was very

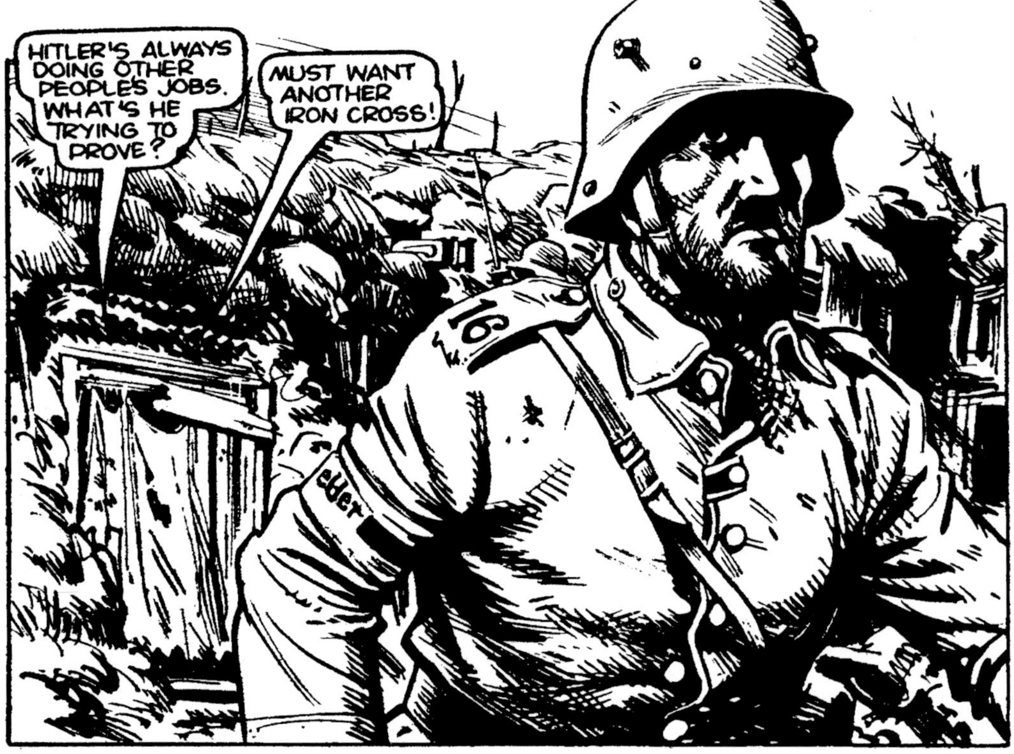
HITLER'S ALWAYS DOING OTHER PEOPLE'S JOBS. WHAT'S HE TRYING TO PROVE?
MUST WANT ANOTHER IRON CROSS!

much at odds with Vienna's cultural sophistication and elegance, but it was a potent brew that Hitler became increasingly intoxicated by. It fuelled his growing belief in Austria as a diseased, corrupt and anachronistic nation, and convinced him that the time had come for *Anschluss* – the unification of Austria and the country he had become an ardent admirer of: Germany. These were views he was happy to stridently expound to anyone happy to listen – and many who weren't.

## HITLER INVADES GERMANY

If he is to be believed, it was Hitler's disenchantment with his home nation that led him to travel to Munich in May 1913. History, however, reveals that he was actually seeking to avoid enlistment in the Austrian army and in January the following year, Austrian police tracked him down and arrested him. Shipped back to Salzburg, he was sent before a draft board but, ironically, while fighting for the Austrian empire was repugnant to him, he never got the chance. He was declared too weak to carry a weapon and discharged. It was said that after Germany seized control of Austria in 1938, Hitler ordered all files pertaining to this incident destroyed by the Gestapo. Luckily for history, they failed.

Fate intervened on Hitler's behalf when Archduke Franz Ferdinand was assassinated in Sarajevo; it was the spark that ignited the First World War. Hitler was still loath to fight for his home nation, but seized with a nationalist zeal, he personally petitioned Kaiser Wilhelm II to ask that his disabilities be overlooked so he could join a Bavarian regiment. He was overjoyed when he was accepted. His Austrian roots now lay shrivelled and dying behind him. Hitler was now German.

His Germanic identity was further reinforced on 8 October 1914 when he took the oath of allegiance with the 1st Company, 16th Bavarian Reserve Infantry Regiment. Boot camp had restored Hitler's health and fitness and, on 21 October, he and the regiment, nicknamed "the List Regiment" after its commanding officer, set off for the Western Front.

They joined German forces engaging British and Belgian units in what was to become known as "the First Battle of Ypres". The German units were made up largely of reserves and inexperienced troops; they were thrown against seasoned British regulars. Both sides suffered heavily but for the Germans, the battle became known as "Kindermord bey Ypern" or "the massacre of the innocents".

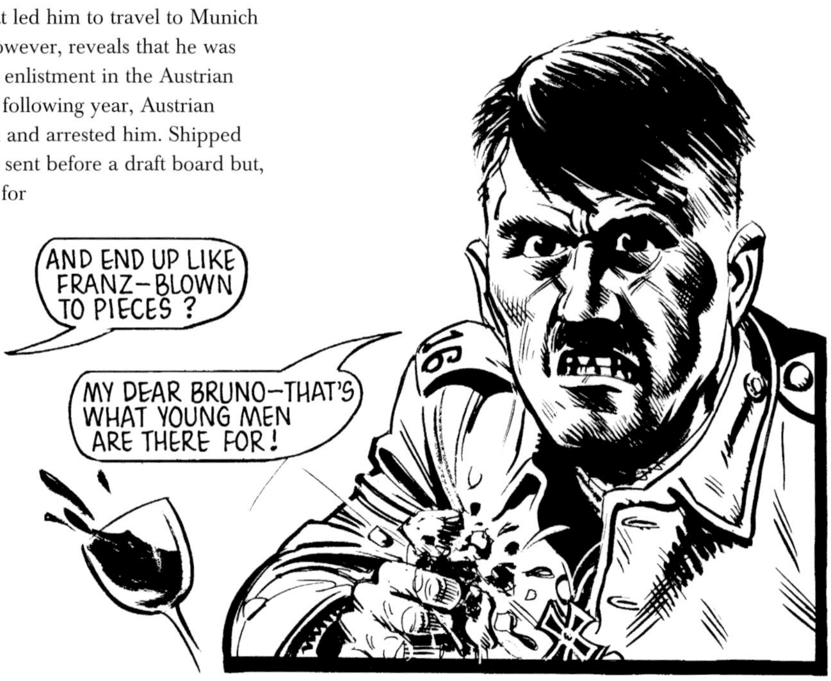
AND END UP LIKE FRANZ–BLOWN TO PIECES?
MY DEAR BRUNO–THAT'S WHAT YOUNG MEN ARE THERE FOR!

## CROSS OF IRON

By the end of the First Battle of Ypres, Hitler, according to letters he sent at the time, believed only 600 men remained in his Regiment out of an original roll call of over 3,000. He had by now won his first Iron Cross after he and another soldier pulled a wounded comrade to safety while under heavy fire.

But what was Hitler like as a soldier? Here, history becomes unclear. His medal and a promotion to Lance Corporal during the battle hint at a brave and dedicated infantryman. He was also tasked as a dispatch runner – a dangerous assignment at best as runners were targeted as often as possible to ensure their message died with them.

Yet Hitler never rose above Lance Corporal. He seems to have never shied away from combat but was also apparently a sloppy, unkempt soldier who, during pauses in the fighting, would break out his watercolours. He seems to have never indulged in a soldier's favourite pastime: complaining. He never questioned orders, received little in the way of personal mail and never asked for leave.

Recently uncovered records by Aberdeen University historian Dr. Thomas Weber for his controversial book, *Hitler's First War*, suggest that far from taking on the dangerous role of regimental runner between the trenches, his job was to deliver messages between regimental HQ and battalions or the HQs of other units, and not companies – which means he would have been between three and five kilometres behind the front line. Weber notes that Hitler's distance from the front line led one soldier to describe him as "a rear area pig", or *etappenschwein* in German.

He also seems to have been something of a loner. But was he shunned because he was a toadying rear-echelon malcontent as has been suggested? Or was it simply because of his odd manners? Any man like Hitler who did not drink, smoke and have little interest in women must indeed have seemed strange, especially as he seemed content to lecture fellow soldiers on their moral and ethical lapses.

His own crisis of faith seems to have occurred in October 1916 as the Battle of the Somme was winding down. Hitler's luck failed him at last, when he suffered a serious splinter wound to the leg. He was evacuated back to Beelitz, near Berlin, and after recovering moved to Munich where he performed light duties at the regiment's reserve barracks.

It was during his time back in Germany that he saw what the war had done to his beloved adopted nation. The Allied naval blockade had been very effective and rationing was now a way of life. Even the most basic of food items were in critically short supply. Germany's economy was also in a shambles; the work force was largely women and men too young, too old or unfit to fight. Long hours and poor nutrition added to a collapse in morale; there was a growing anti-war sentiment and even strikes by disaffected industrial workers; many of these were communist-inspired. Hitler was also aware that some of the Bolshevik leaders were Jewish.

Hitler was growing rapidly disenchanted with the defeatism and apathy of the civilian populations. It was here that he began to suspect that not just communists but Jews were orchestrating the anti-war movement. Dispirited and increasingly anti-Semitic, he requested a return to the Front line.

## RED OR DEAD

He was soon back in the thick of the fighting, but Hitler's real concern was the insidious enemies back home, describing to his fellow soldiers what he had seen whilst convalescing in no uncertain terms. He was increasingly convinced that any hope of a German victory would be undermined by the machinations of communists and Jews.

However, it was Bolshevism that changed the course of the war for the Germans. In February 1917, the Russian Revolution toppled the Tsarist monarchy and led to the cessation of hostilities between Germany and Russia, soon to be the Soviet Union. This released thousands of experienced troops and tonnes of arms and equipment to reinforce exhausted German units on the Western Front.

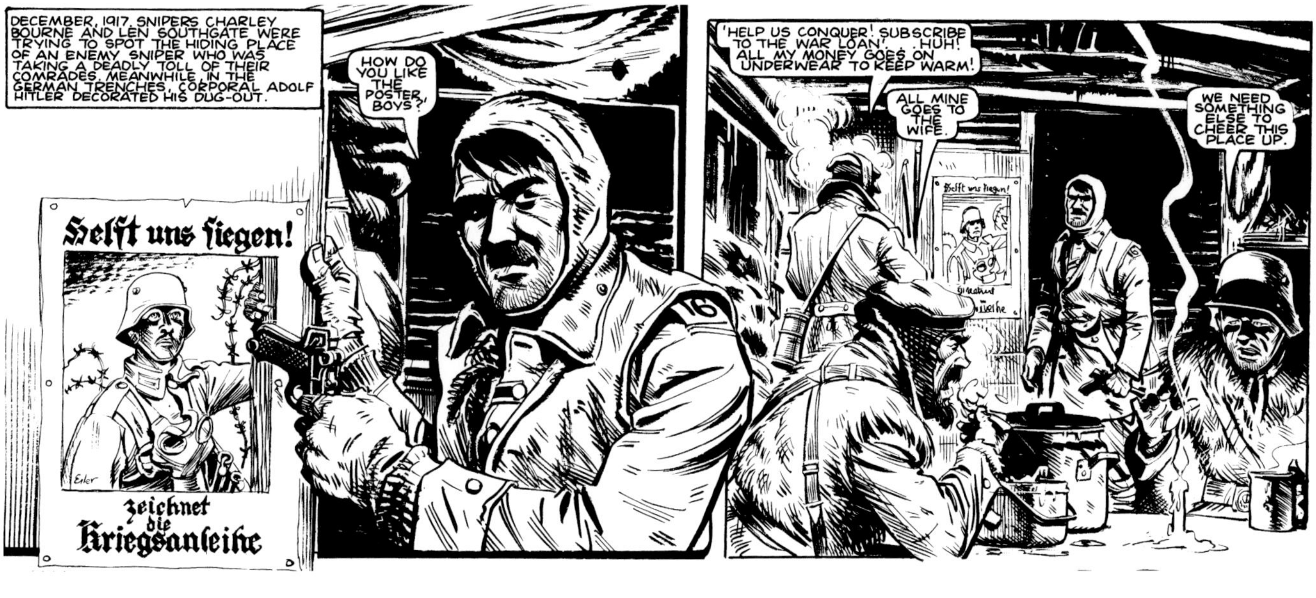

DECEMBER, 1917. SNIPERS CHARLEY BOURNE AND LEN SOUTHGATE WERE TRYING TO SPOT THE HIDING PLACE OF AN ENEMY SNIPER WHO WAS TAKING A DEADLY TOLL OF THEIR COMRADES. MEANWHILE, IN THE GERMAN TRENCHES, CORPORAL ADOLF HITLER DECORATED HIS DUG-OUT.
HOW DO YOU LIKE THE POSTER BOYS?'
Helft uns siegen!
zeichnet die Kriegsanleihe
'HELP US CONQUER! SUBSCRIBE TO THE WAR LOAN'. . . HUH! ALL MY MONEY GOES ON UNDERWEAR TO KEEP WARM!
ALL MINE GOES TO THE WIFE.
WE NEED SOMETHING ELSE TO CHEER THIS PLACE UP.

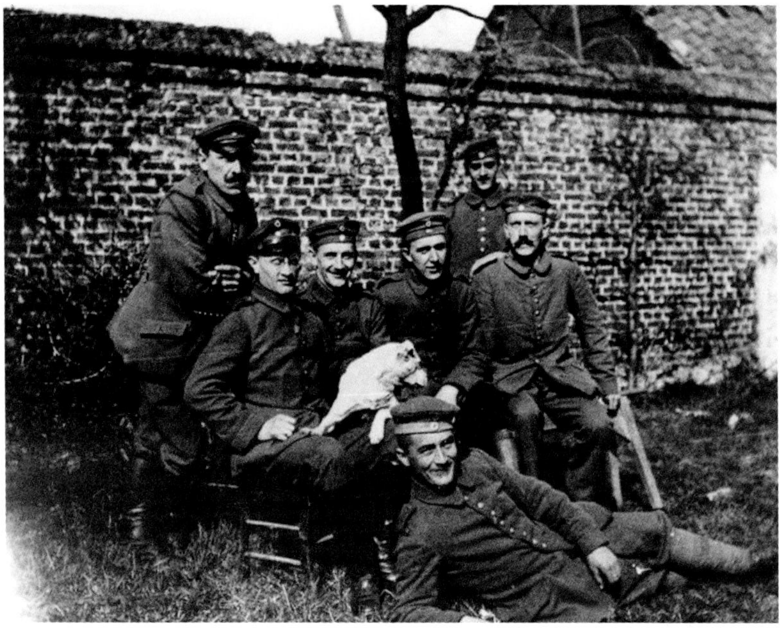

**ABOVE:** Hitler (sitting to the far right) in the German Army, 1914.

But the German High Command knew they were on a tight deadline. America's entry into the war had similarly boosted Allied strength. If the Germans could not deliver a knock-out blow against their enemies, they faced economic and military strangulation by the newly empowered Allies. This haste became the 1918 Spring Offensive.

Hitler was among those whose confidence in the German Military Machine was at an all-time high, believing that the new offensive would be the final one, and was proud to be a part of it. The attack, launched in March, initially went brilliantly for the Germans; they made sweeping advances into France, finally breaking the stultifying deadlock of trench warfare, and by June were within miles of Paris itself.

But the German Army had overstretched itself. Whilst Allied losses were easily replaced, the economic ruination of Germany meant the destruction of manpower and materials were permanent. Exposed and exhausted, the Germans found themselves on the receiving end of furious Allied counterattacks and it was in August 1918, as the German offensive was grinding to a halt, that Hitler won his second Iron Cross.

Whilst Nazi propaganda exaggerated the incident, it seems very clear that Hitler did manage to capture a group of French soldiers, leading them to believe they were surrounded when he was in fact alone. For this act, he received an Iron Cross First Class. This in and of itself indicates that Hitler's actions were highly regarded; the distinction of a First Class was very rarely bestowed on a lowly Lance Corporal. Interestingly, it was the regiment's Jewish Adjutant that recommended him for the award, a fact later hidden by the Nazi propaganda machine.

## THE END

October 1918 was a seminal moment in the war for Hitler. Early in the month, it became apparent that Germany's leaders were looking at a negotiated peace with the Allies. As news of this spread, it became clear, as is so often the way in wartime, that propaganda and reality were far removed from each other; that the much-vaunted successes described in newspapers were in fact masking the inevitable defeat of the German army. On the front and at home, morale collapsed.

Hitler was distraught – but his troubles were made far worse when, on the night of 13 October, he was caught in British mustard gas attack and temporarily blinded. Crippled, he was evacuated to Pasewalk, in Germany, where he convalesced amidst rumours that the country was on the verge of collapse – very much at odds with the headlines announcing the continued success of the German Army.

Hitler learned of Germany's surrender on 10 November 1918, when the hospital chaplain announced the abdication of the Kaiser and the Allied victory to the recovering patients. Hitler was stunned and sunk into a deep depression. This was fuelled by a mounting rage against those he said were responsible for the defeat: communist and Jewish-inspired anti-war movements, and betrayal by the German monarchy – what he referred to as the "stab in the back". The Kaiser and his government had accepted Armistice terms that were to cripple the already savaged German economy.

The war had cost the country nearly 25 billion pounds – what equates to around £1,275 billion today. Meanwhile, economic output had dropped some forty

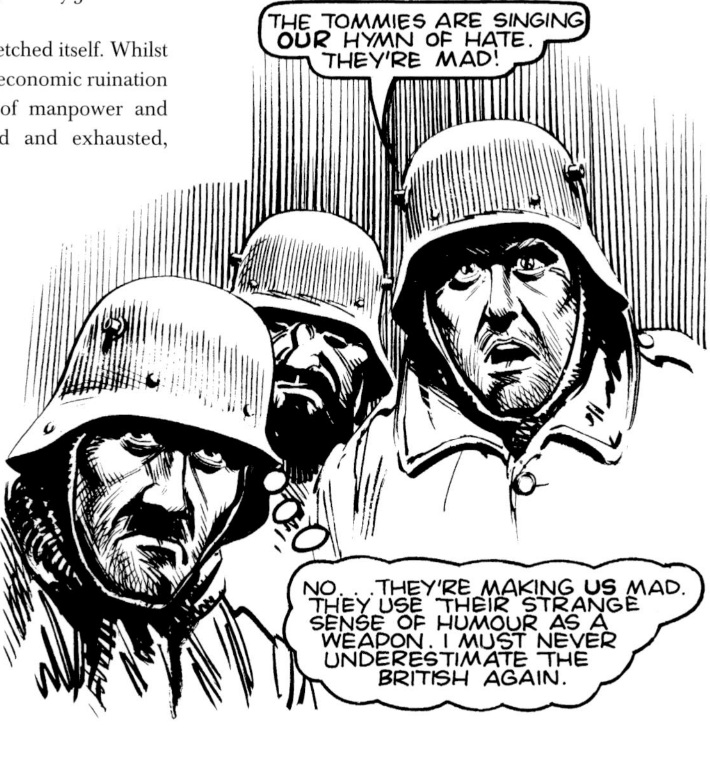
THE TOMMIES ARE SINGING OUR HYMN OF HATE. THEY'RE MAD!
NO... THEY'RE MAKING US MAD. THEY USE THEIR STRANGE SENSE OF HUMOUR AS A WEAPON. I MUST NEVER UNDERESTIMATE THE BRITISH AGAIN.

per cent during the course of the war. The work force had been stripped of young men to fill out the Front line fighting units, leaving behind the poorly trained and ill-equipped. Rationing led to a rise in crime and racketeering; and to poor health amongst the workers, who had resorted to eating dogs, cats, rats and horses.

The harsh repayments demanded by the Allies could hardly be met by an economy bled of manpower. Germany lost 1.7 million men in the war; another 4.3 million were injured.

With the country in chaos, a political vacuum emerged and political extremists were given the opportunity to expose people to their ideologies against a background of mistrust and a desperate desire for self-preservation. Hitler's belief that Bolshevism and "International Jewry" were the reasons for the country's current state crystallised in this crucible and thus the rise of National Socialism became an inevitability. Scapegoating allowed an angry, starving and bitter population to vent its discontent and gave Hitler the power he sought. The Third Reich was no longer the idle whim of a man who had learned the lessons of war but a deep-rooted philosophy that transformed the fortunes of a nation, and with it, the World. ✛

**Further Reading:**
*Hitler's First War* by Thomas Weber, Oxford University Press, 2010. ISBN: 9780199233205.
A radical revision of the period of Hitler's early life through the stories of the veterans of the regiment: an

officer who became Hitler's personal adjutant in the 1930s but then offered himself to British intelligence; a soldier-turned-Concentration Camp Commander; Jewish veterans who fell victim to the Holocaust; and veterans who simply returned to their lives in Bavaria. Thomas Weber presents a Private Hitler very different from the one portrayed in his own mythical accounts.

*Hitler's Vienna: A Dictator's Apprenticeship* by Brigitte Hamann, Taurus Parke, 2010. ISBN: 9781848852778.
What turned Adolf Hitler, a relatively normal and apparently unexceptional young man, into the very personification of evil? Acclaimed historian Brigitte Hamann reveals the critical formative years that the young Hitler spent in Vienna.

**Online:**
*Hitler's War Service*
www.worldwar1.com/heritage/hitler.htm
A brief timeline of Hitler's First World War experience.

*The Hitler Pages*
www.hitlerpages.com
A detailed non-political online guide to Hitler's life, including detailed notes on his WWI activities.

*The Bavarian War Archives*
www.gda.bayern.de/enp1.htm
Source of recently uncovered documentation about Hitler's war record.

YOU WILL HEAR MUCH ABOUT ME. JUST WAIT UNTIL MY TIME COMES.

# PREVIOUSLY IN *CHARLEY'S WAR*

**2 June 1916:** Under the age of conscription, Charley Bourne joins the Army is sent to France, several weeks before the Battle of the Somme.

**1 July 1916:** The Battle of the Somme begins. Charley and his comrades spare a German soldier they find, but he is shot in cold blood by Lieutenant Snell.

**1 August 1916:** On Charley's seventeenth birthday, British forces accidentally begin shelling their own side.

**October 1916:** Shortly after Ginger is killed by a stray shell, Charley is wounded during the battle against the "Judgement Troopers" and sent back to the lines.

**March 1917:** In London, Charley meets a French Foreign Legion deserter, "Blue", and helps him hide as he tells him the grim story of the Battle of Verdun.

**April 1917:** 17-year-old Charley rejoins his regiment and is reunited with Weeper and his longtime sergeant, "Old Bill", as it moves up to Flanders to Ypres. The company's duties in the face of snipers and gas attacks are made all the more miserable by Snell's interference.

**May 1917:** After weeks in reserve trenches, Charley begins a 20-mile march out of the line to billets, led by Snell. Old Bill loses his sergeant's stripes after the march, and even life away from the Front proves harsh. But worse is to come, as Snell is ordered to take charge of a tunnel intended to undermine German guns at Messines.

**June 1917:** The mines are exploded – except Snell's, who shoots Charley's fellow 'Claykicker' Budgie, believing he is a saboteur, and heads into the mine to set it off – even though the delay means blowing up the advancing British troops. Charley goes after Snell to kill him but Snell is hit in the head by a ricochet from his own gun and although still alive, is invalided out.

**August 1917:** Charley is caught up in the Third Battle of Ypres, rescuing his brother, Wilf, whom he discovers has joined the Royal Flying Corps. Later, Charley arrives at the Étaples training camp and meets the sandbaggers – army deserters led by Gunboat and a disguised Blue. He's also reunited with Weeper, who's arrested as a deserter.

**September 1917:** Charley takes an injured Weeper to Sanctuary, the deserters' hideout, but it's discovered by a Special Branch man and Military Police. The traitorous Gunboat kills Weeper but is in turn killed by Blue when his treachery is revealed. The deserters escape and the Bullring is closed down. Charley returns to the front and becomes a stretcher bearer.

**9 September 1917:** The Mutiny begins after a popular Scottish corporal, Wood, is shot and wounded by a Military Policeman. Charley and a platoon of loyal soldiers are sent to guard a bridge into town.

**10 September 1917:** As the mutiny continues and even the Sarge joins it, cavalry refuse to come to officers' help and the mutineers' demands are met.

**9 October 1917:** Charley is accused of stealing from the dead but a German prisoner, Kat, vouches for him. Ordered to work with Kat, he and Charley are caught in a gas attack and they fight for Charley's gas helmet.

**October 1917:** Kat takes shelter from gas in a pillbox and is unharmed, but the Germans take the trench, shooting the British out of hand. Charley survives – but only if he licks Kat's boots first. After the German stuffs a grenade down his battle tunic, which is luckily a dud, an enraged Charley picks up a rifle and bayonets Kat. Later, Douglas Haig visits the front and inspects the wounded – but is not shown any bad injuries, in case they might upset him. Shortly after this, Charley is thrown out of the stretcher bearers by an American surgeon, but will do one final tour of duty.

**November 1917:** The tank battle of Cambrai begins, but the generals do not exploit the breach and the attack falters. The Bantams fight the Prussian Guards at Bourlon Wood – the Cambrai offensive fails.

**6 November 1917:** A British plane is downed in No Man's Land and Charley goes to rescue the observer, Fred. After his comrades are killed, Charley has to carry by himself – and is caught in a shell explosion on Hellfire Corner.

**December 1917:** Scholar returns as platoon commander. Charley becomes number two to sniper Len Southgate and meets the wily Corporal Hitler. ✣

**BELOW:** The first appearance of Corporal Hitler in the strip.

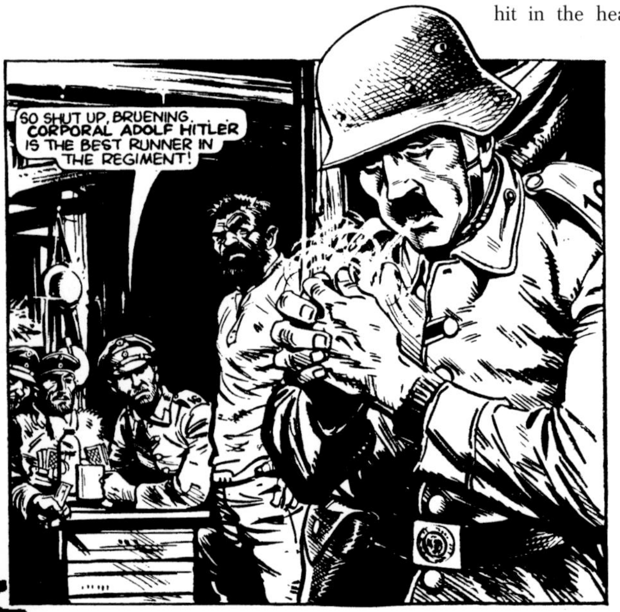
SO SHUT UP, BRUENING. CORPORAL ADOLF HITLER IS THE BEST RUNNER IN THE REGIMENT!

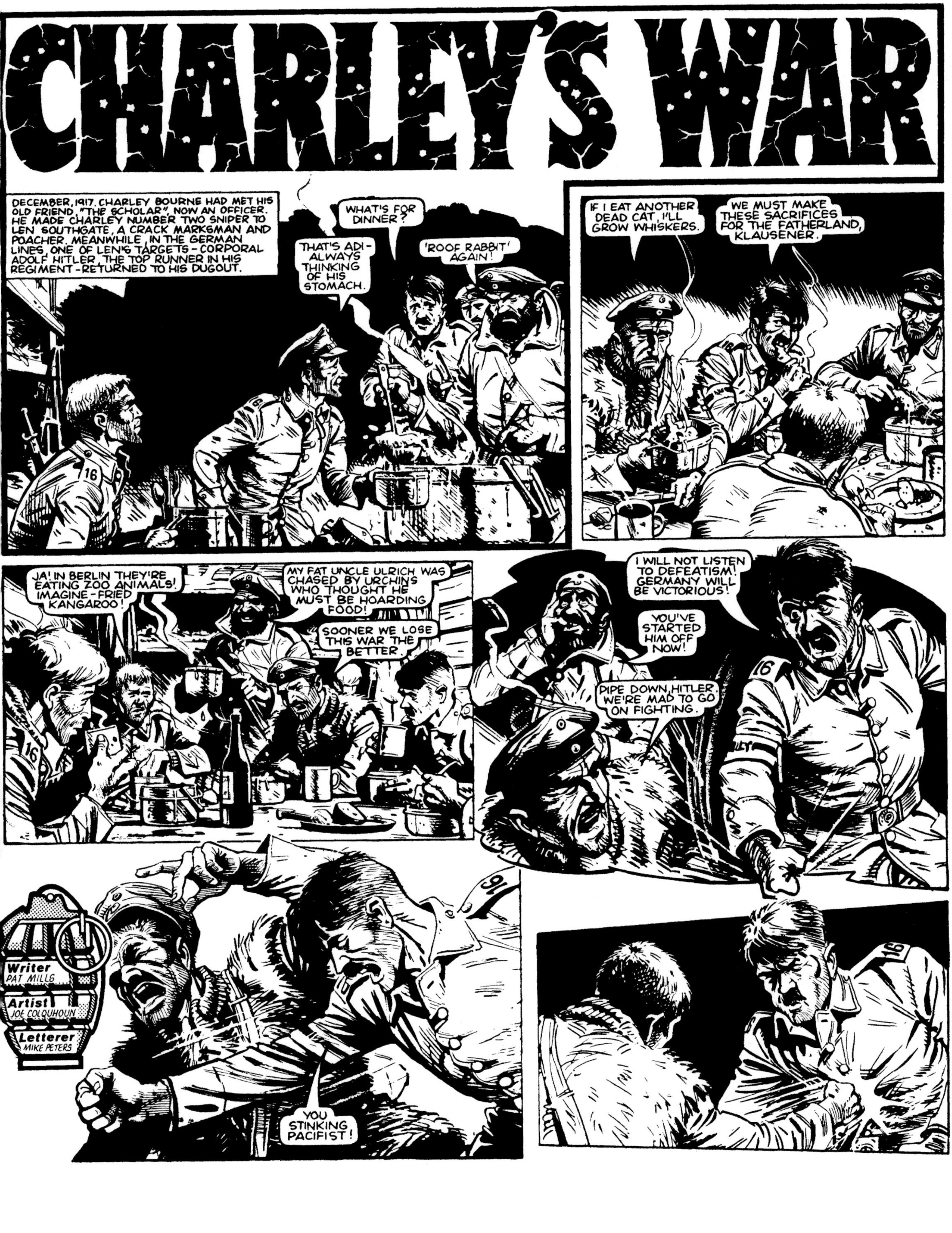
CHARLEY'S WAR
DECEMBER, 1917. CHARLEY BOURNE HAD MET HIS OLD FRIEND, "THE SCHOLAR", NOW AN OFFICER. HE MADE CHARLEY NUMBER TWO SNIPER TO LEN SOUTHGATE, A CRACK MARKSMAN AND POACHER. MEANWHILE, IN THE GERMAN LINES, ONE OF LEN'S TARGETS - CORPORAL ADOLF HITLER, THE TOP RUNNER IN HIS REGIMENT - RETURNED TO HIS DUGOUT.
WHAT'S FOR DINNER?
THAT'S ADI - ALWAYS THINKING OF HIS STOMACH.
'ROOF RABBIT' AGAIN!
IF I EAT ANOTHER DEAD CAT, I'LL GROW WHISKERS.
WE MUST MAKE THESE SACRIFICES FOR THE FATHERLAND, KLAUSENER.
JA! IN BERLIN THEY'RE EATING ZOO ANIMALS! IMAGINE - FRIED KANGAROO!
MY FAT UNCLE ULRICH WAS CHASED BY URCHINS WHO THOUGHT HE MUST BE HOARDING FOOD!
SOONER WE LOSE THIS WAR THE BETTER.
I WILL NOT LISTEN TO DEFEATISM! GERMANY WILL BE VICTORIOUS!
YOU'VE STARTED HIM OFF NOW!
PIPE DOWN, HITLER. WE'RE MAD TO GO ON FIGHTING.
Writer PAT MILLS
Artist JOE COLQUHOUN
Letterer MIKE PETERS
YOU STINKING PACIFIST!

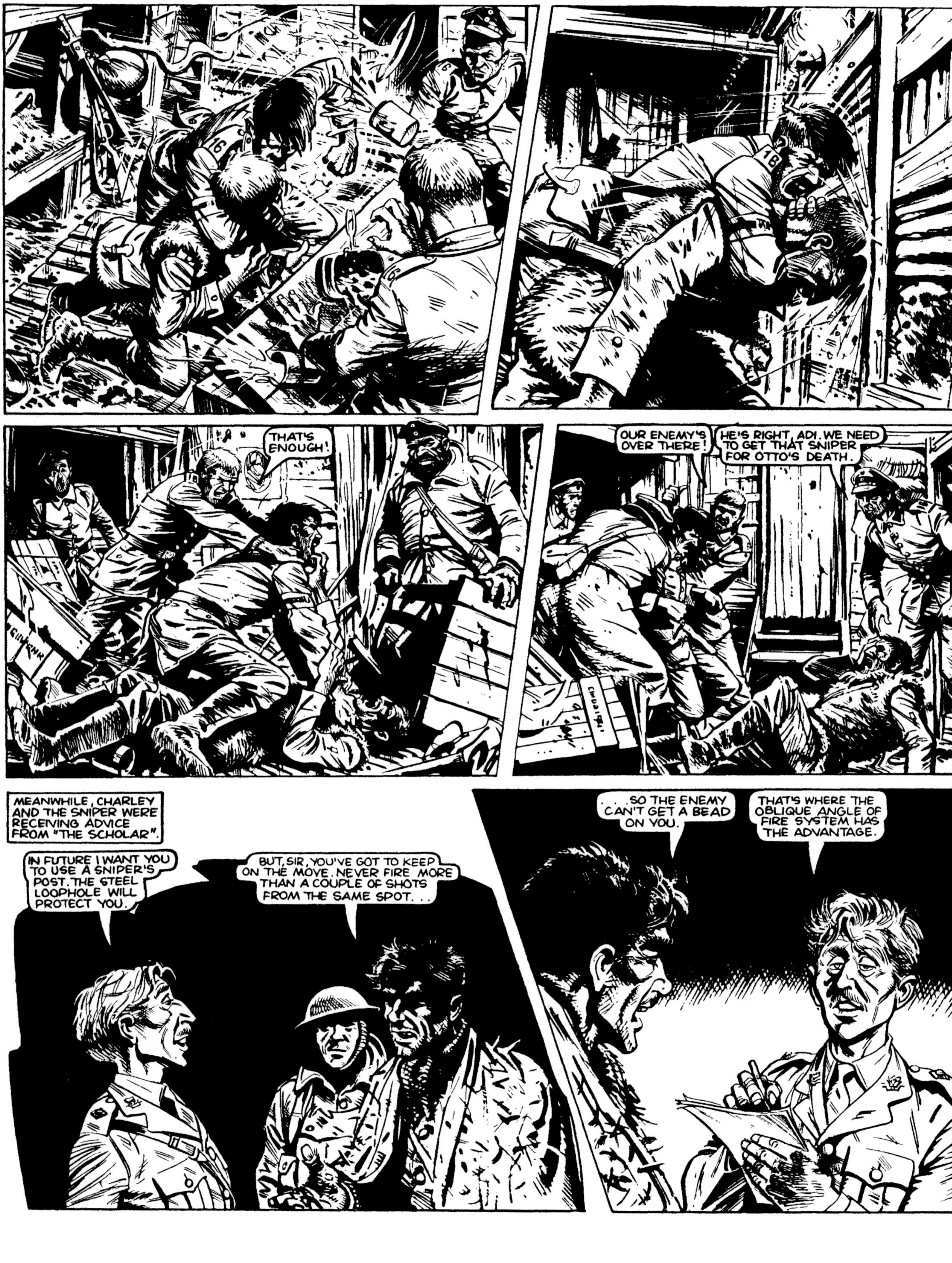
THAT'S ENOUGH!
OUR ENEMY'S OVER THERE!
HE'S RIGHT, ADI. WE NEED TO GET THAT SNIPER FOR OTTO'S DEATH.
MEANWHILE, CHARLEY AND THE SNIPER WERE RECEIVING ADVICE FROM "THE SCHOLAR".
IN FUTURE I WANT YOU TO USE A SNIPER'S POST. THE STEEL LOOPHOLE WILL PROTECT YOU.
BUT, SIR, YOU'VE GOT TO KEEP ON THE MOVE. NEVER FIRE MORE THAN A COUPLE OF SHOTS FROM THE SAME SPOT...
...SO THE ENEMY CAN'T GET A BEAD ON YOU.
THAT'S WHERE THE OBLIQUE ANGLE OF FIRE SYSTEM HAS THE ADVANTAGE.

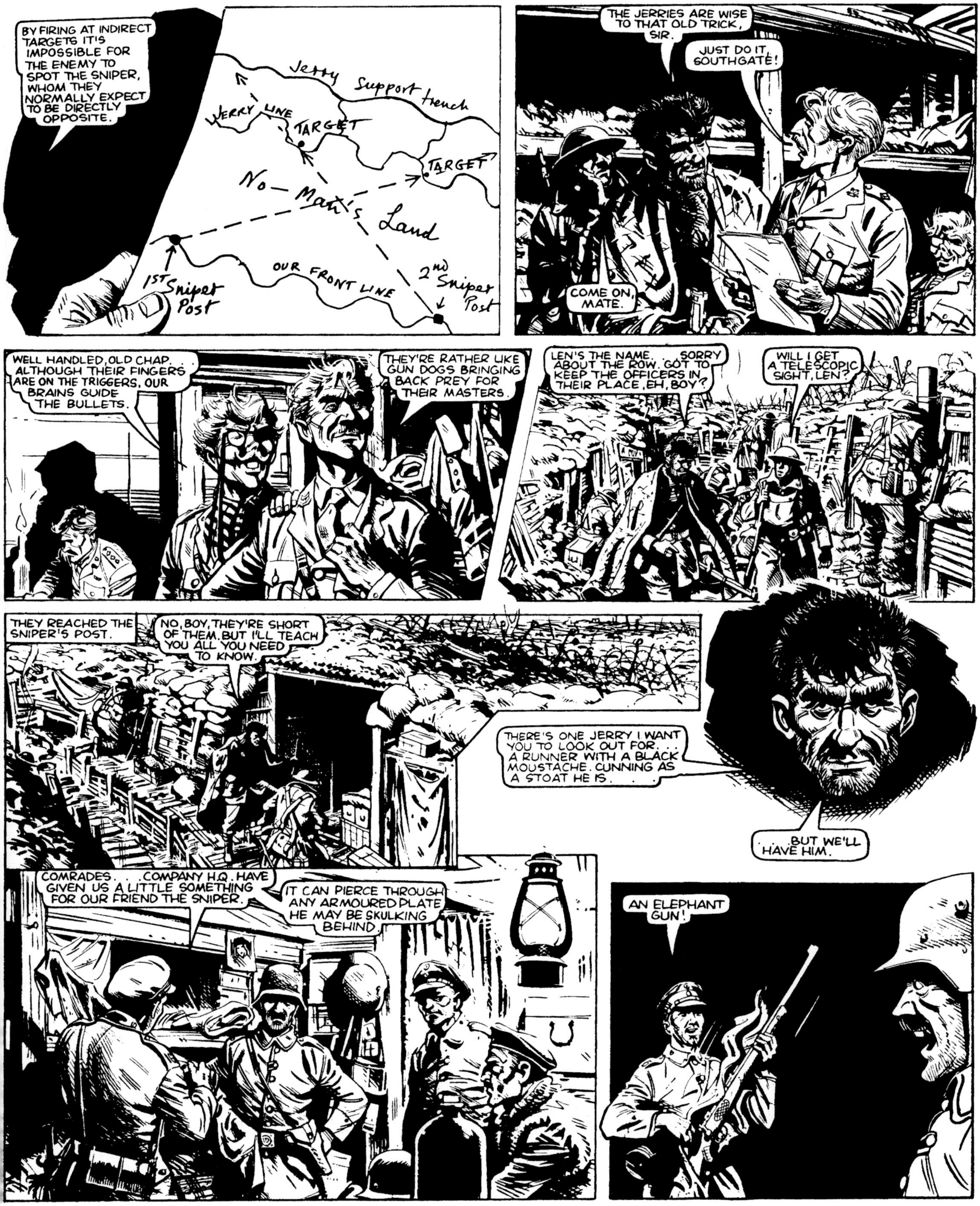
BY FIRING AT INDIRECT TARGETS IT'S IMPOSSIBLE FOR THE ENEMY TO SPOT THE SNIPER, WHOM THEY NORMALLY EXPECT TO BE DIRECTLY OPPOSITE.
Jerry Support trench
JERRY LINE
TARGET
TARGET
No-Man's Land
OUR FRONT LINE
1ST Sniper Post
2ND Sniper Post
THE JERRIES ARE WISE TO THAT OLD TRICK, SIR.
JUST DO IT, SOUTHGATE!
COME ON, MATE.
WELL HANDLED, OLD CHAP. . . ALTHOUGH THEIR FINGERS ARE ON THE TRIGGERS, OUR BRAINS GUIDE THE BULLETS.
THEY'RE RATHER LIKE GUN DOGS BRINGING BACK PREY FOR THEIR MASTERS.
LEN'S THE NAME. . . SORRY ABOUT THE ROW. GOT TO KEEP THE OFFICERS IN THEIR PLACE, EH, BOY?
WILL I GET A TELESCOPIC SIGHT, LEN?
THEY REACHED THE SNIPER'S POST.
NO, BOY, THEY'RE SHORT OF THEM. BUT I'LL TEACH YOU ALL YOU NEED TO KNOW.
THERE'S ONE JERRY I WANT YOU TO LOOK OUT FOR. . . A RUNNER WITH A BLACK MOUSTACHE. CUNNING AS A STOAT HE IS. . .
. . . BUT WE'LL HAVE HIM.
COMRADES. . . COMPANY H.Q. HAVE GIVEN US A LITTLE SOMETHING FOR OUR FRIEND THE SNIPER.
IT CAN PIERCE THROUGH ANY ARMOURED PLATE HE MAY BE SKULKING BEHIND.
AN ELEPHANT GUN!

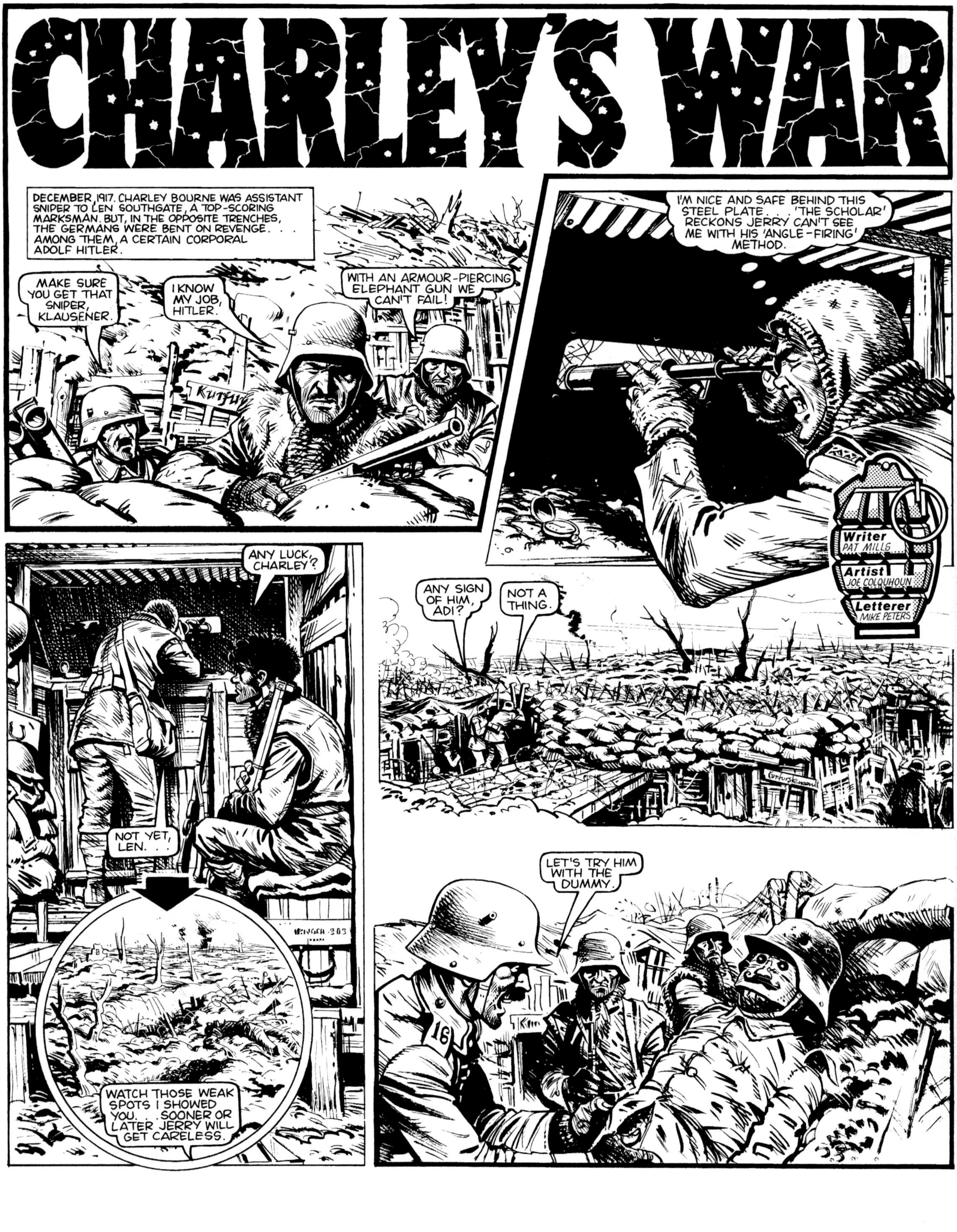
CHARLEY'S WAR
DECEMBER 1917. CHARLEY BOURNE WAS ASSISTANT SNIPER TO LEN SOUTHGATE, A TOP-SCORING MARKSMAN. BUT, IN THE OPPOSITE TRENCHES, THE GERMANS WERE BENT ON REVENGE. . . AMONG THEM, A CERTAIN CORPORAL ADOLF HITLER.
MAKE SURE YOU GET THAT SNIPER, KLAUSENER.
I KNOW MY JOB, HITLER.
WITH AN ARMOUR-PIERCING ELEPHANT GUN WE CAN'T FAIL!
I'M NICE AND SAFE BEHIND THIS STEEL PLATE. . . 'THE SCHOLAR' RECKONS JERRY CAN'T SEE ME WITH HIS 'ANGLE-FIRING' METHOD.
Writer PAT MILLS
Artist JOE COLQUHOUN
Letterer MIKE PETERS
ANY LUCK, CHARLEY?
NOT YET, LEN. . .
WATCH THOSE WEAK SPOTS I SHOWED YOU. . . SOONER OR LATER JERRY WILL GET CARELESS.
ANY SIGN OF HIM, ADI?
NOT A THING.
LET'S TRY HIM WITH THE DUMMY.

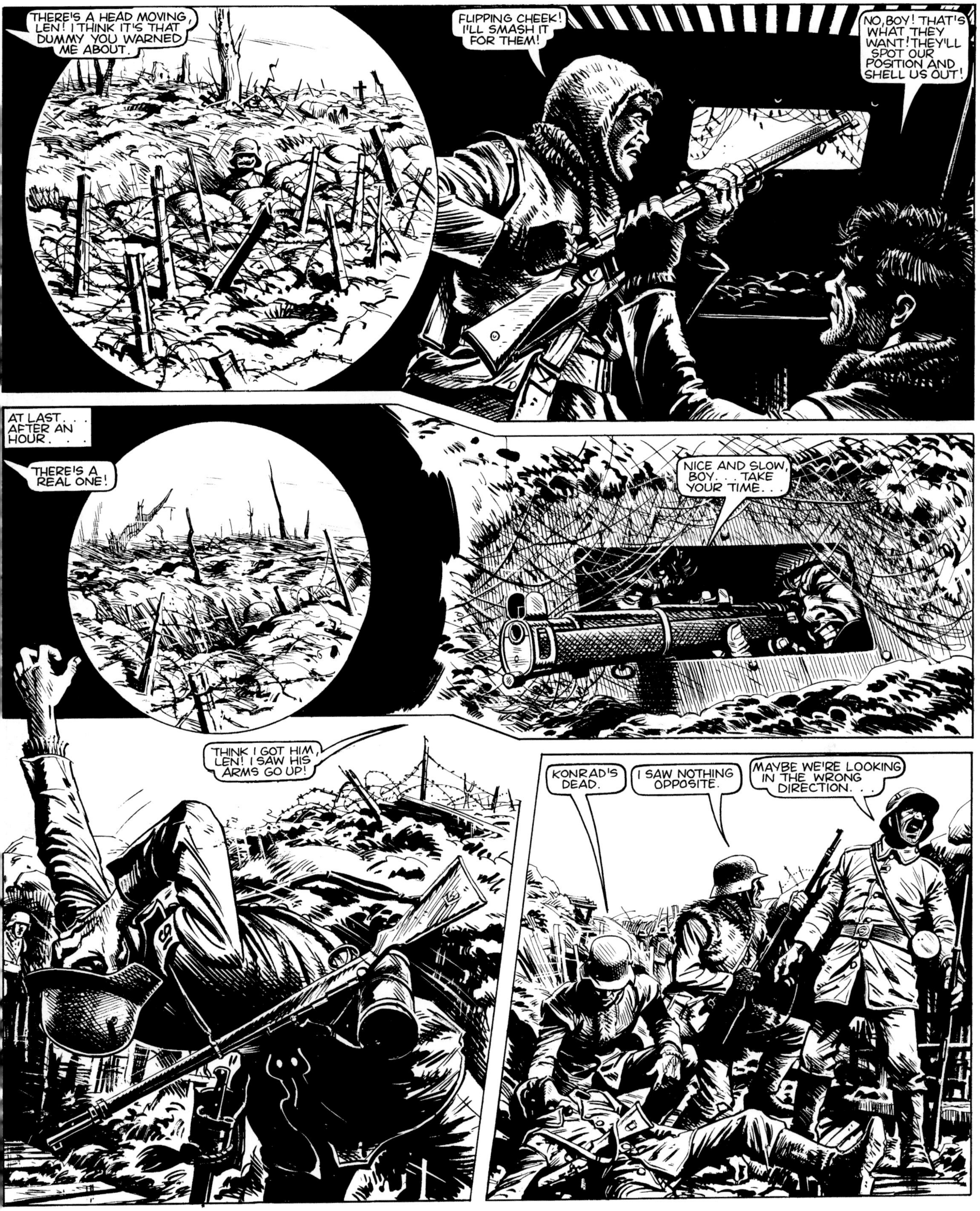
THERE'S A HEAD MOVING, LEN! I THINK IT'S THAT DUMMY YOU WARNED ME ABOUT.
FLIPPING CHEEK! I'LL SMASH IT FOR THEM!
NO, BOY! THAT'S WHAT THEY WANT! THEY'LL SPOT OUR POSITION AND SHELL US OUT!
AT LAST. . . AFTER AN HOUR. . .
THERE'S A REAL ONE!
NICE AND SLOW, BOY. . . TAKE YOUR TIME. . .
THINK I GOT HIM, LEN! I SAW HIS ARMS GO UP!
KONRAD'S DEAD.
I SAW NOTHING OPPOSITE.
MAYBE WE'RE LOOKING IN THE WRONG DIRECTION. . .

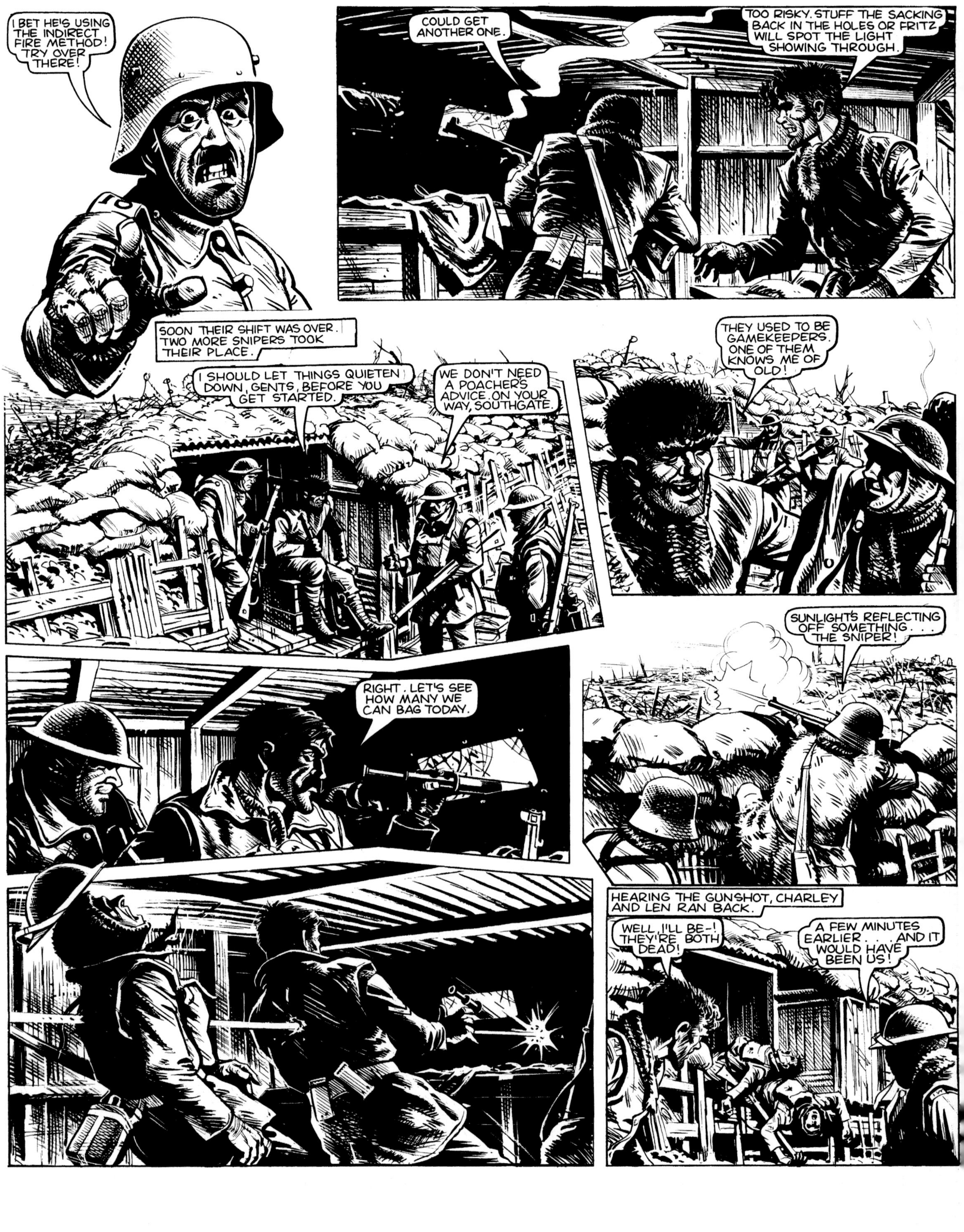
I BET HE'S USING THE INDIRECT FIRE METHOD! TRY OVER THERE!
COULD GET ANOTHER ONE.
TOO RISKY. STUFF THE SACKING BACK IN THE HOLES OR FRITZ WILL SPOT THE LIGHT SHOWING THROUGH.
SOON THEIR SHIFT WAS OVER. TWO MORE SNIPERS TOOK THEIR PLACE.
I SHOULD LET THINGS QUIETEN DOWN, GENTS, BEFORE YOU GET STARTED.
WE DON'T NEED A POACHER'S ADVICE. ON YOUR WAY, SOUTHGATE.
THEY USED TO BE GAMEKEEPERS. ONE OF THEM KNOWS ME OF OLD!
RIGHT. LET'S SEE HOW MANY WE CAN BAG TODAY.
SUNLIGHT'S REFLECTING OFF SOMETHING . . . THE SNIPER!
HEARING THE GUNSHOT, CHARLEY AND LEN RAN BACK.
WELL, I'LL BE-! THEY'RE BOTH DEAD!
A FEW MINUTES EARLIER . . . AND IT WOULD HAVE BEEN US!

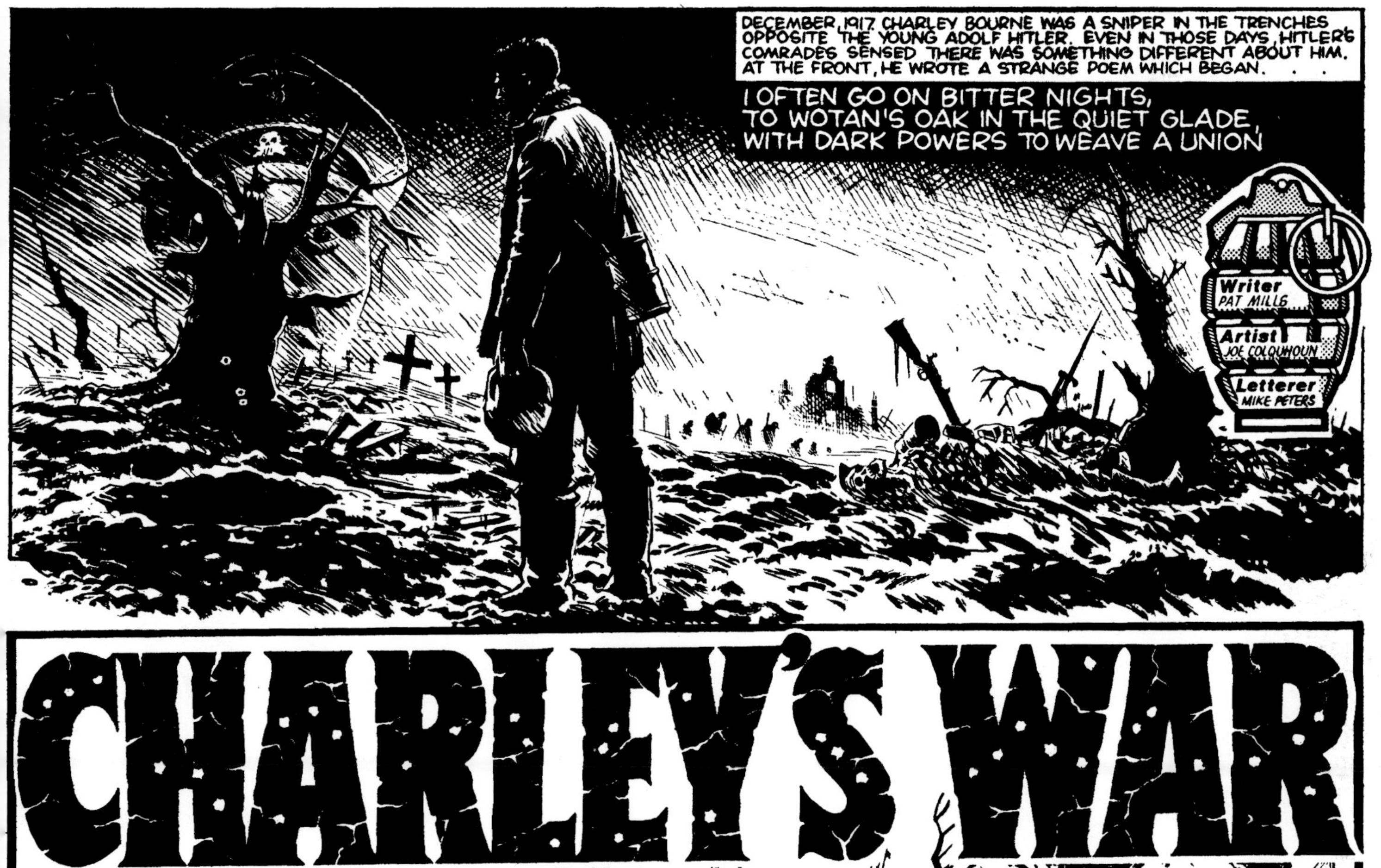
DECEMBER, 1917 CHARLEY BOURNE WAS A SNIPER IN THE TRENCHES OPPOSITE THE YOUNG ADOLF HITLER. EVEN IN THOSE DAYS, HITLER'S COMRADES SENSED THERE WAS SOMETHING DIFFERENT ABOUT HIM. AT THE FRONT, HE WROTE A STRANGE POEM WHICH BEGAN. . .
I OFTEN GO ON BITTER NIGHTS, TO WOTAN'S OAK IN THE QUIET GLADE, WITH DARK POWERS TO WEAVE A UNION
Writer PAT MILLS
Artist JOE COLQUHOUN
Letterer MIKE PETERS

# CHARLEY'S WAR

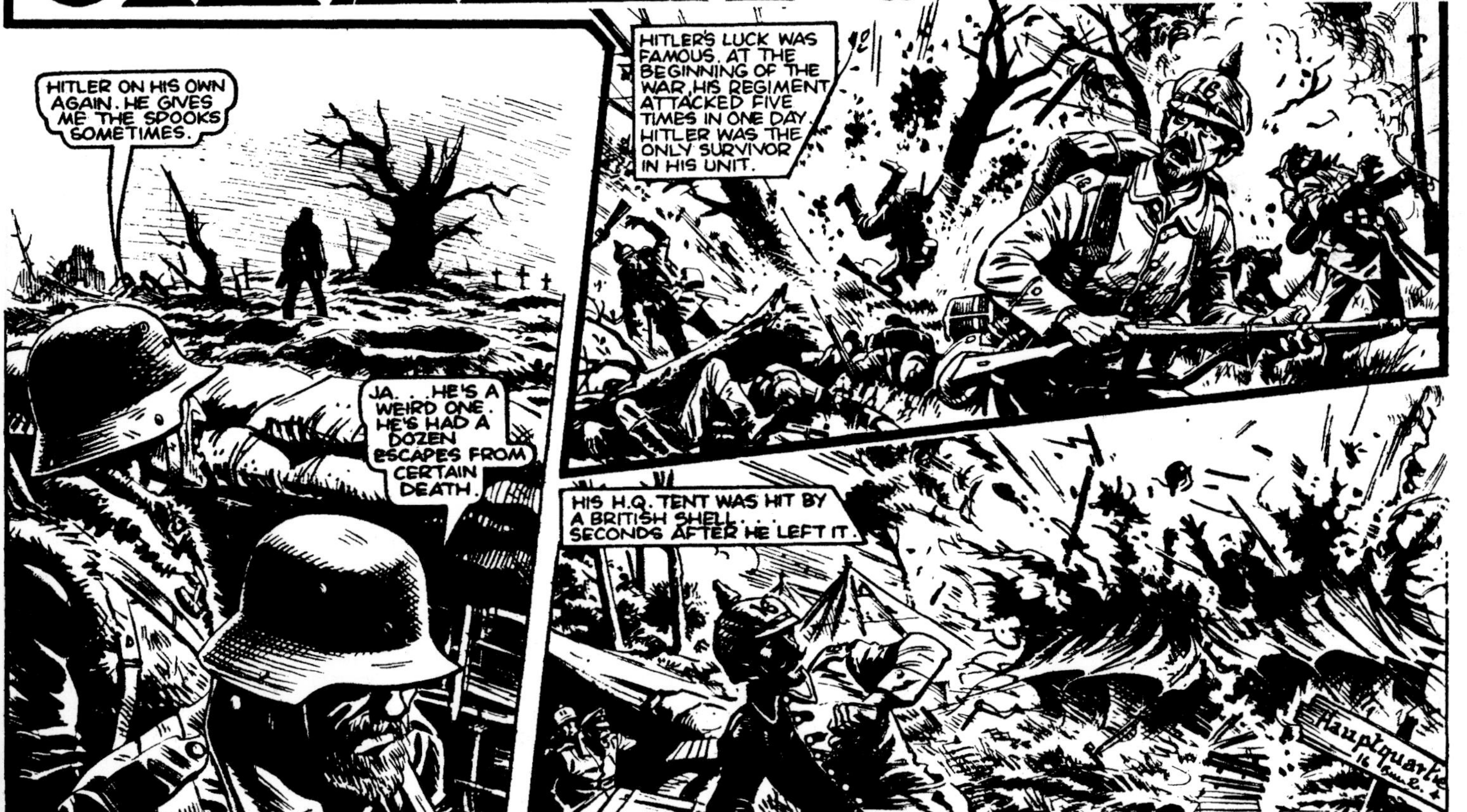
HITLER ON HIS OWN AGAIN. HE GIVES ME THE SPOOKS SOMETIMES.
JA. . . HE'S A WEIRD ONE. HE'S HAD A DOZEN ESCAPES FROM CERTAIN DEATH.
HITLER'S LUCK WAS FAMOUS. AT THE BEGINNING OF THE WAR, HIS REGIMENT ATTACKED FIVE TIMES IN ONE DAY. HITLER WAS THE ONLY SURVIVOR IN HIS UNIT.
HIS H.Q. TENT WAS HIT BY A BRITISH SHELL. . . SECONDS AFTER HE LEFT IT.

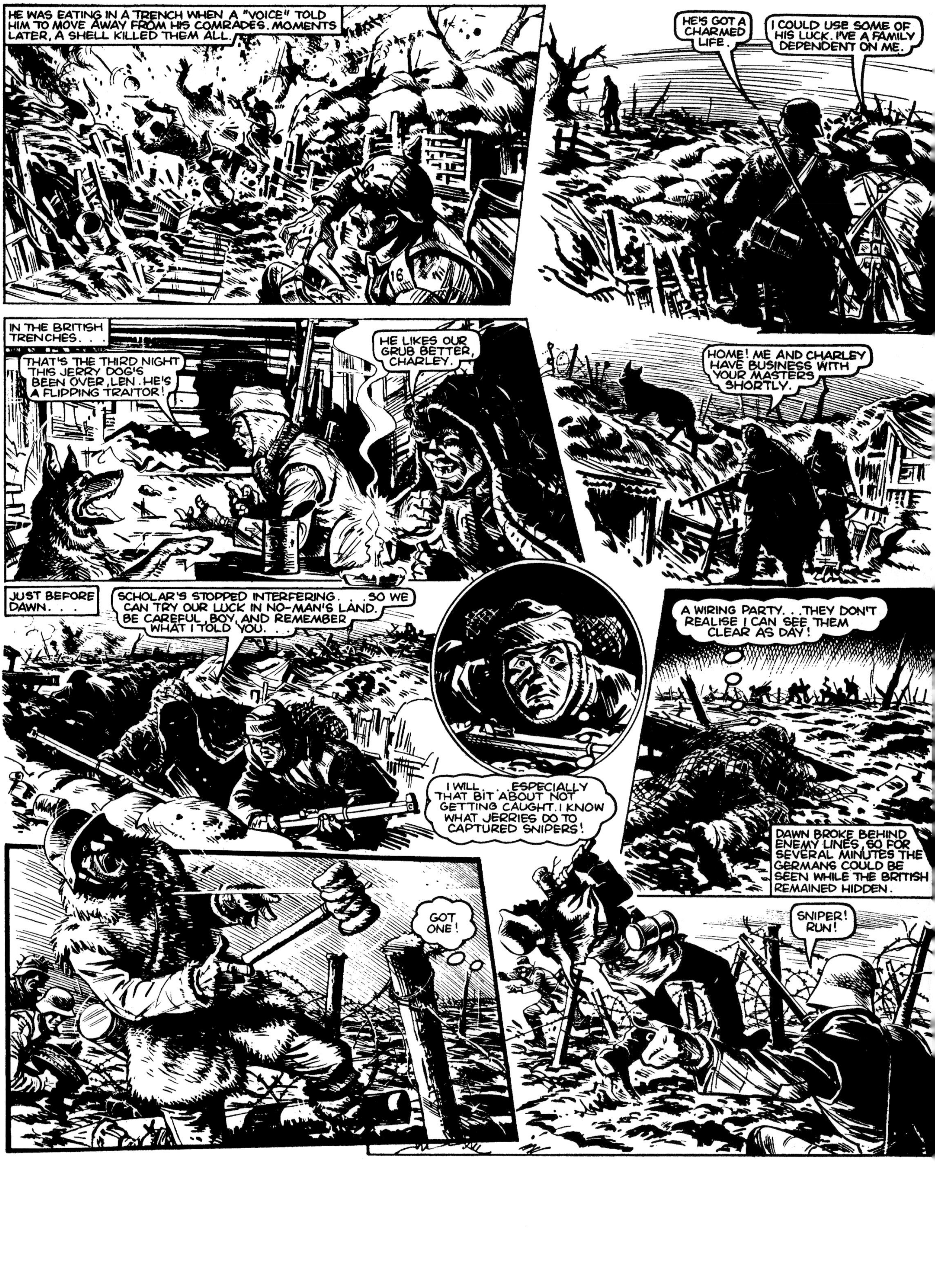
HE WAS EATING IN A TRENCH WHEN A "VOICE" TOLD HIM TO MOVE AWAY FROM HIS COMRADES. MOMENTS LATER, A SHELL KILLED THEM ALL.
HE'S GOT A CHARMED LIFE.
I COULD USE SOME OF HIS LUCK. I'VE A FAMILY DEPENDENT ON ME.
IN THE BRITISH TRENCHES. . .
THAT'S THE THIRD NIGHT THIS JERRY DOG'S BEEN OVER, LEN. HE'S A FLIPPING TRAITOR!
HE LIKES OUR GRUB BETTER, CHARLEY.
HOME! ME AND CHARLEY HAVE BUSINESS WITH YOUR MASTERS SHORTLY.
JUST BEFORE DAWN. . .
SCHOLAR'S STOPPED INTERFERING. . . SO WE CAN TRY OUR LUCK IN NO-MAN'S LAND. BE CAREFUL, BOY, AND REMEMBER WHAT I TOLD YOU. . .
I WILL. . . ESPECIALLY THAT BIT ABOUT NOT GETTING CAUGHT. I KNOW WHAT JERRIES DO TO CAPTURED SNIPERS!
A WIRING PARTY. . . THEY DON'T REALISE I CAN SEE THEM CLEAR AS DAY!
DAWN BROKE BEHIND ENEMY LINES, SO FOR SEVERAL MINUTES THE GERMANS COULD BE SEEN WHILE THE BRITISH REMAINED HIDDEN.
GOT ONE!
SNIPER! RUN!

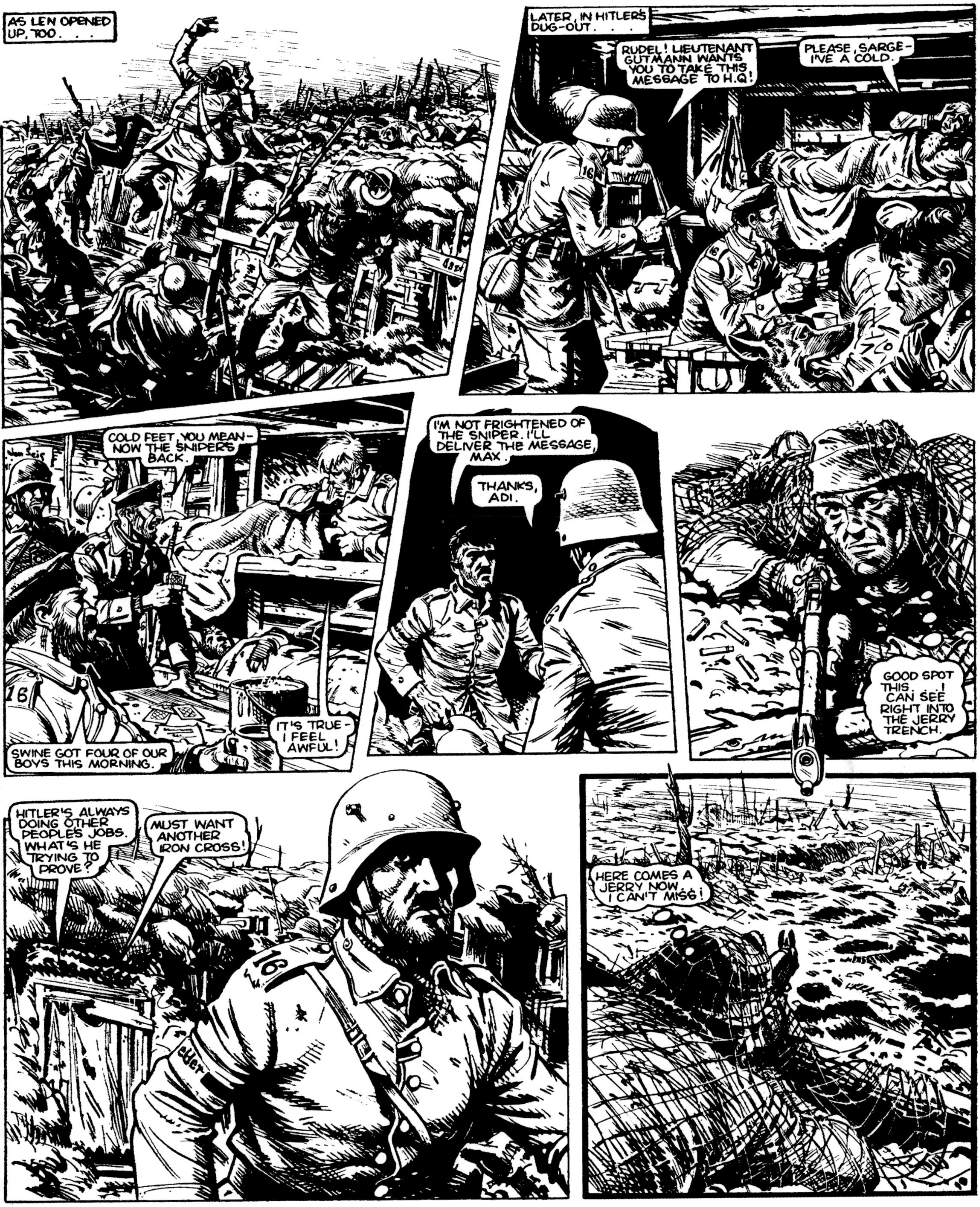
AS LEN OPENED UP, TOO . . .
LATER, IN HITLER'S DUG-OUT . . .
RUDEL! LIEUTENANT GUTMANN WANTS YOU TO TAKE THIS MESSAGE TO H.Q!
PLEASE, SARGE - I'VE A COLD.
COLD FEET, YOU MEAN - NOW THE SNIPER'S BACK.
SWINE GOT FOUR OF OUR BOYS THIS MORNING.
IT'S TRUE - I FEEL AWFUL!
I'M NOT FRIGHTENED OF THE SNIPER. I'LL DELIVER THE MESSAGE, MAX.
THANKS, ADI.
GOOD SPOT THIS . . . I CAN SEE RIGHT INTO THE JERRY TRENCH.
HITLER'S ALWAYS DOING OTHER PEOPLE'S JOBS. WHAT'S HE TRYING TO PROVE?
MUST WANT ANOTHER IRON CROSS!
HERE COMES A JERRY NOW. I CAN'T MISS!

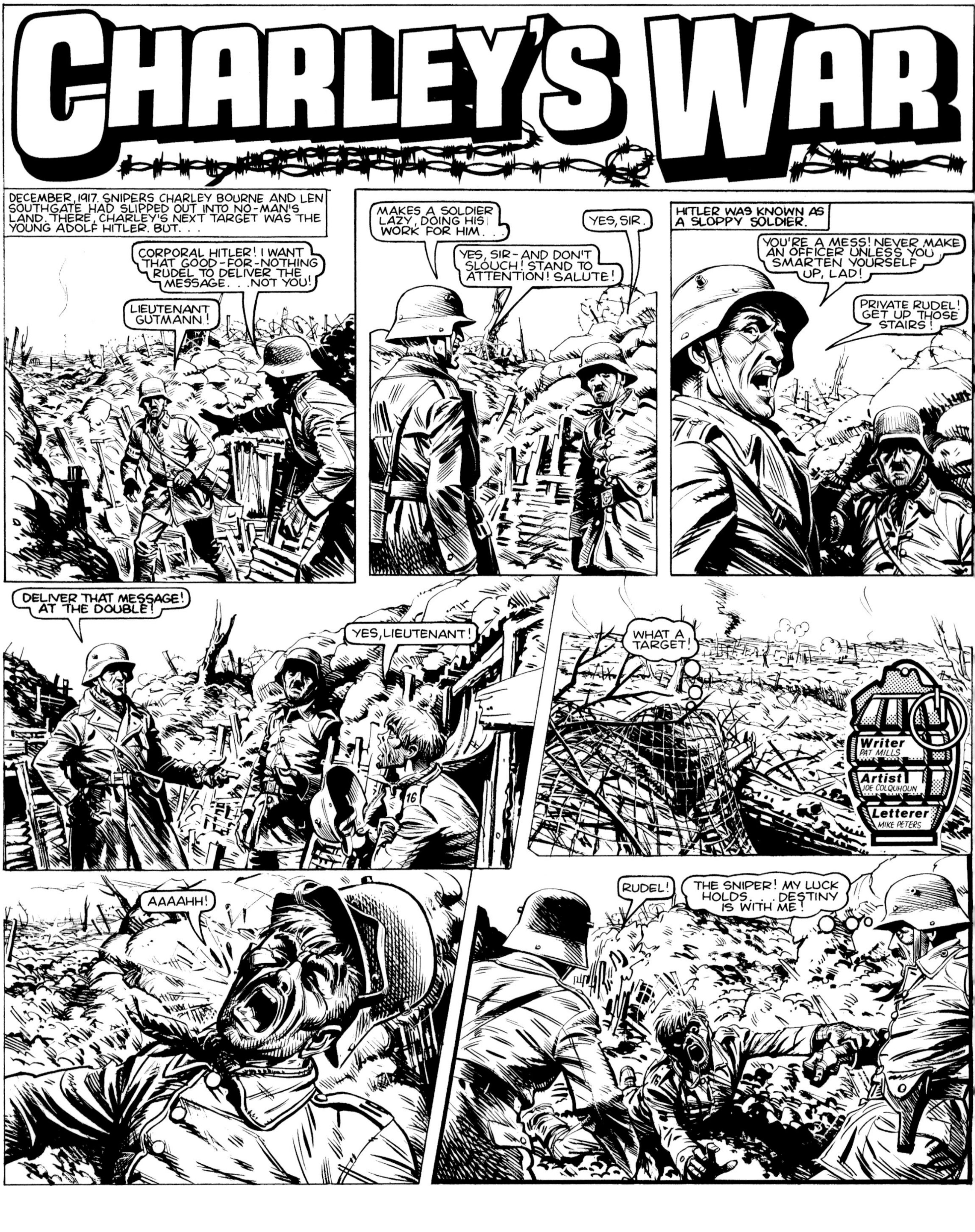
CHARLEY'S WAR
DECEMBER, 1917. SNIPERS CHARLEY BOURNE AND LEN SOUTHGATE HAD SLIPPED OUT INTO NO-MAN'S LAND. THERE, CHARLEY'S NEXT TARGET WAS THE YOUNG ADOLF HITLER. BUT. . .
CORPORAL HITLER! I WANT THAT GOOD-FOR-NOTHING RUDEL TO DELIVER THE MESSAGE. . .NOT YOU!
LIEUTENANT GUTMANN!
MAKES A SOLDIER LAZY, DOING HIS WORK FOR HIM. . .
YES, SIR-AND DON'T SLOUCH! STAND TO ATTENTION! SALUTE!
YES, SIR.
HITLER WAS KNOWN AS A SLOPPY SOLDIER.
YOU'RE A MESS! NEVER MAKE AN OFFICER UNLESS YOU SMARTEN YOURSELF UP, LAD!
PRIVATE RUDEL! GET UP THOSE STAIRS!
DELIVER THAT MESSAGE! AT THE DOUBLE!
YES, LIEUTENANT!
WHAT A TARGET!
Writer PAT MILLS
Artist JOE COLQUHOUN
Letterer MIKE PETERS
AAAAHH!
RUDEL!
THE SNIPER! MY LUCK HOLDS. . . DESTINY IS WITH ME!

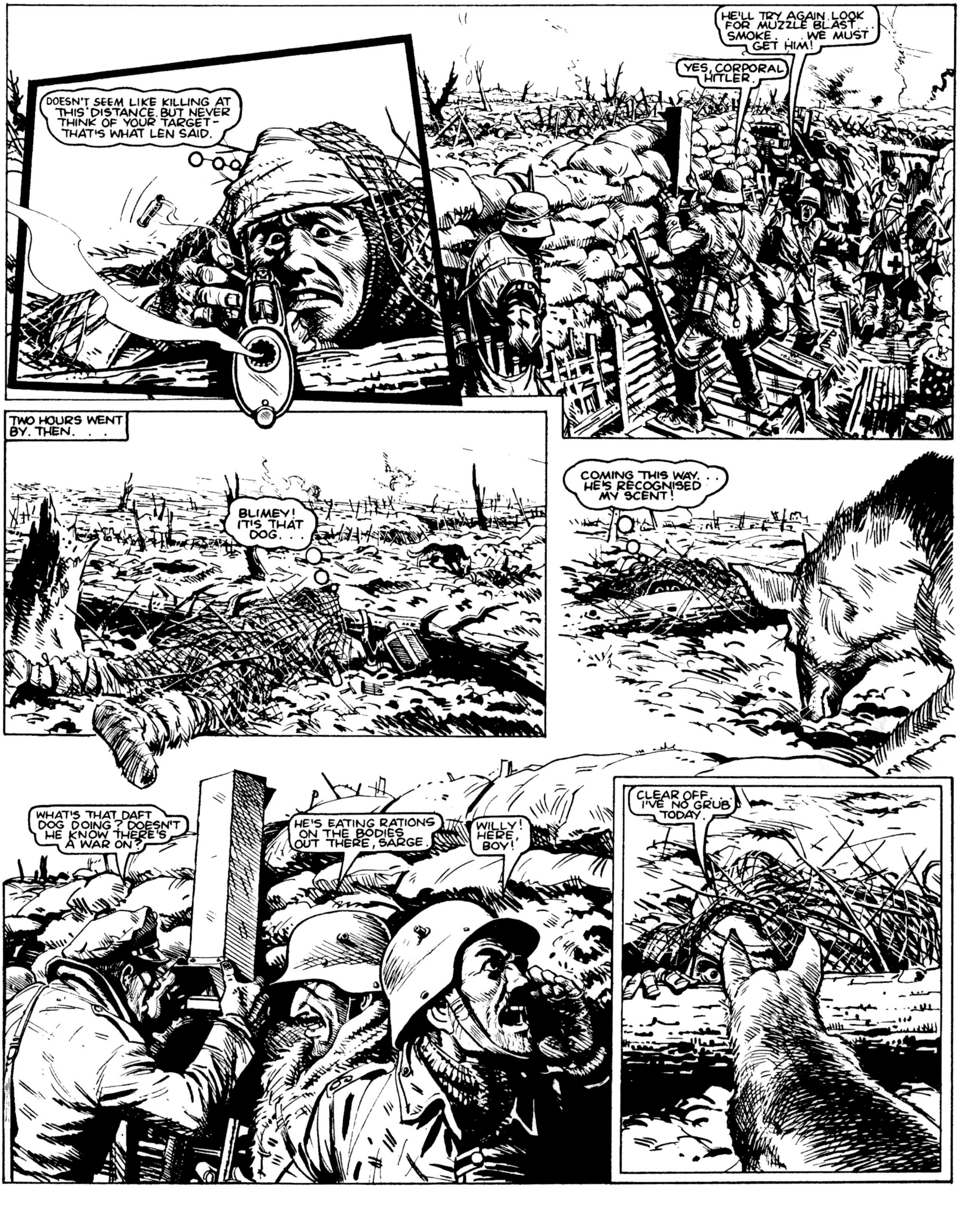
DOESN'T SEEM LIKE KILLING AT THIS DISTANCE. BUT NEVER THINK OF YOUR TARGET - THAT'S WHAT LEN SAID.
HE'LL TRY AGAIN. LOOK FOR MUZZLE BLAST... SMOKE... WE MUST GET HIM!
YES, CORPORAL HITLER.
TWO HOURS WENT BY. THEN...
BLIMEY! IT'S THAT DOG...
COMING THIS WAY. HE'S RECOGNISED MY SCENT!
WHAT'S THAT DAFT DOG DOING? DOESN'T HE KNOW THERE'S A WAR ON?
HE'S EATING RATIONS ON THE BODIES OUT THERE, SARGE.
WILLY! HERE, BOY!
CLEAR OFF... I'VE NO GRUB TODAY.

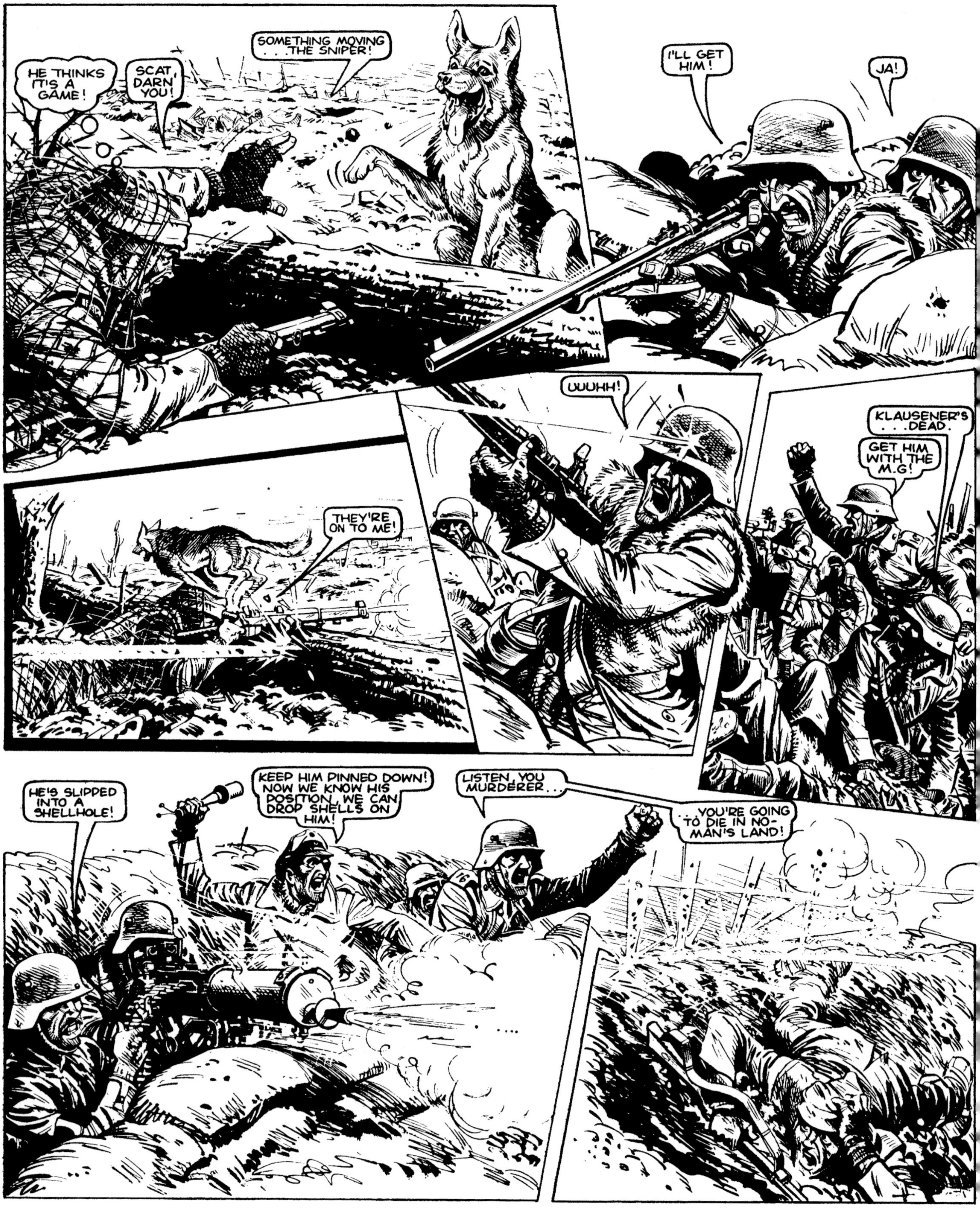
HE THINKS IT'S A GAME!
SCAT, DARN YOU!
SOMETHING MOVING . . . THE SNIPER!
I'LL GET HIM!
JA!
THEY'RE ON TO ME!
UUUHH!
KLAUSENER'S . . . DEAD.
GET HIM WITH THE M.G!
HE'S SLIPPED INTO A SHELLHOLE!
KEEP HIM PINNED DOWN! NOW WE KNOW HIS POSITION, WE CAN DROP SHELLS ON HIM!
LISTEN, YOU MURDERER . . .
. . . YOU'RE GOING TO DIE IN NO-MAN'S LAND!

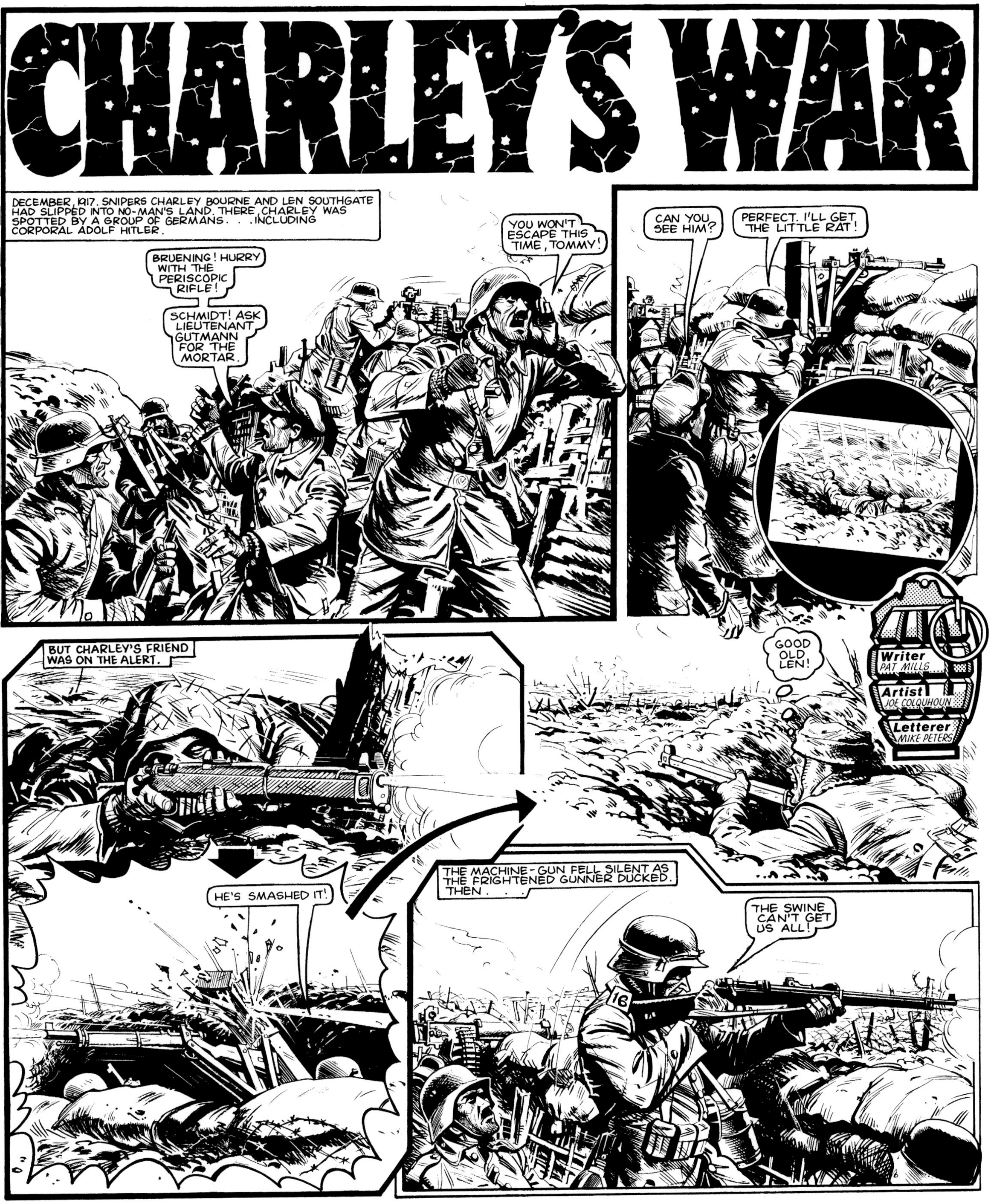
CHARLEY'S WAR
DECEMBER, 1917. SNIPERS CHARLEY BOURNE AND LEN SOUTHGATE HAD SLIPPED INTO NO-MAN'S LAND. THERE, CHARLEY WAS SPOTTED BY A GROUP OF GERMANS. . . INCLUDING CORPORAL ADOLF HITLER.
YOU WON'T ESCAPE THIS TIME, TOMMY!
BRUENING! HURRY WITH THE PERISCOPIC RIFLE!
SCHMIDT! ASK LIEUTENANT GUTMANN FOR THE MORTAR.
CAN YOU SEE HIM?
PERFECT. I'LL GET THE LITTLE RAT!
Writer PAT MILLS
Artist JOE COLQUHOUN
Letterer MIKE PETERS
BUT CHARLEY'S FRIEND WAS ON THE ALERT.
GOOD OLD LEN!
HE'S SMASHED IT!
THE MACHINE-GUN FELL SILENT AS THE FRIGHTENED GUNNER DUCKED. THEN. . .
THE SWINE CAN'T GET US ALL!

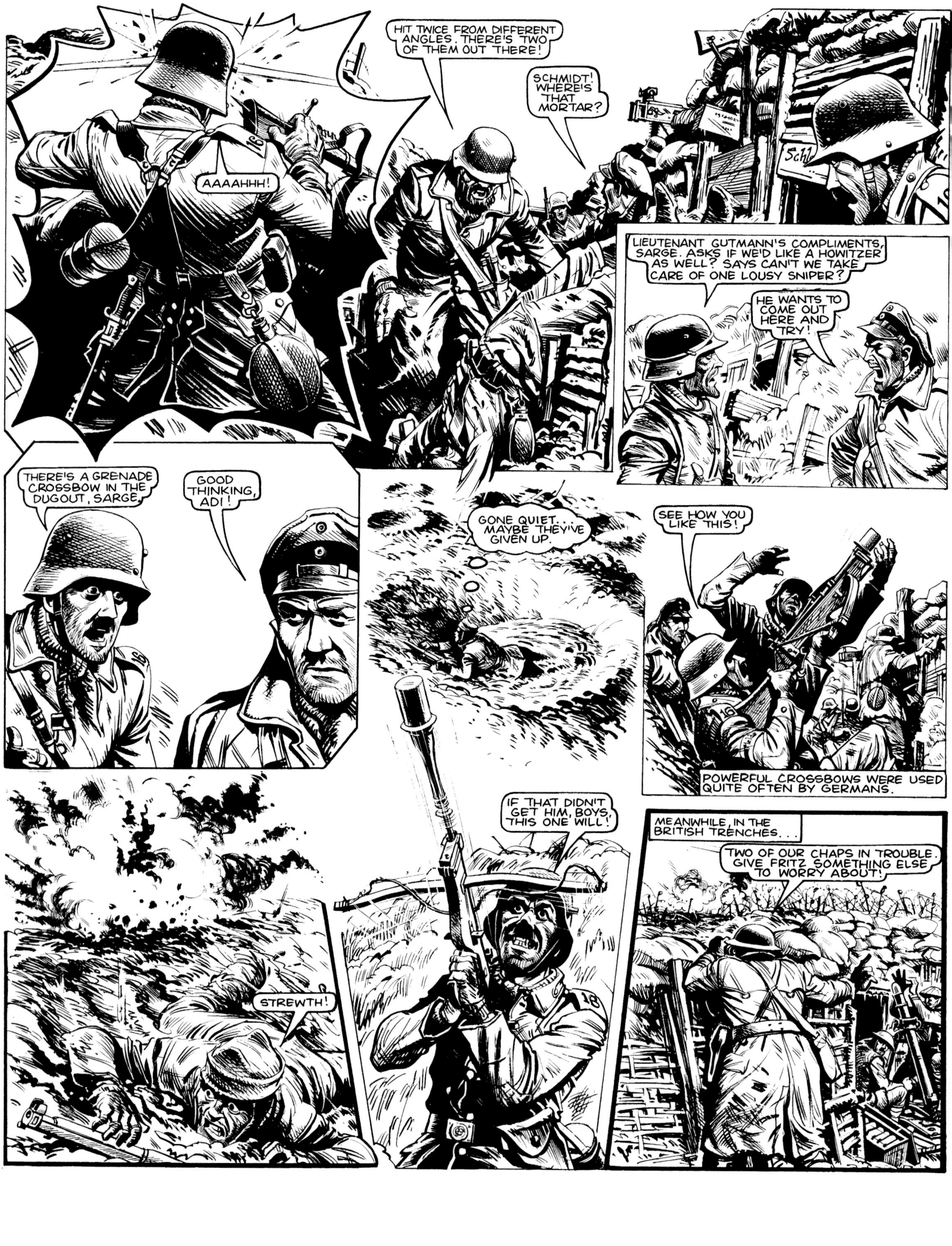
AAAAHHH!
HIT TWICE FROM DIFFERENT ANGLES. THERE'S TWO OF THEM OUT THERE!
SCHMIDT! WHERE'S THAT MORTAR?
LIEUTENANT GUTMANN'S COMPLIMENTS, SARGE. ASKS IF WE'D LIKE A HOWITZER AS WELL? SAYS CAN'T WE TAKE CARE OF ONE LOUSY SNIPER?
HE WANTS TO COME OUT HERE AND TRY!
THERE'S A GRENADE CROSSBOW IN THE DUGOUT, SARGE.
GOOD THINKING, ADI!
GONE QUIET... MAYBE THEY'VE GIVEN UP.
SEE HOW YOU LIKE THIS!
POWERFUL CROSSBOWS WERE USED QUITE OFTEN BY GERMANS.
STREWTH!
IF THAT DIDN'T GET HIM, BOYS, THIS ONE WILL!
MEANWHILE, IN THE BRITISH TRENCHES...
TWO OF OUR CHAPS IN TROUBLE. GIVE FRITZ SOMETHING ELSE TO WORRY ABOUT!

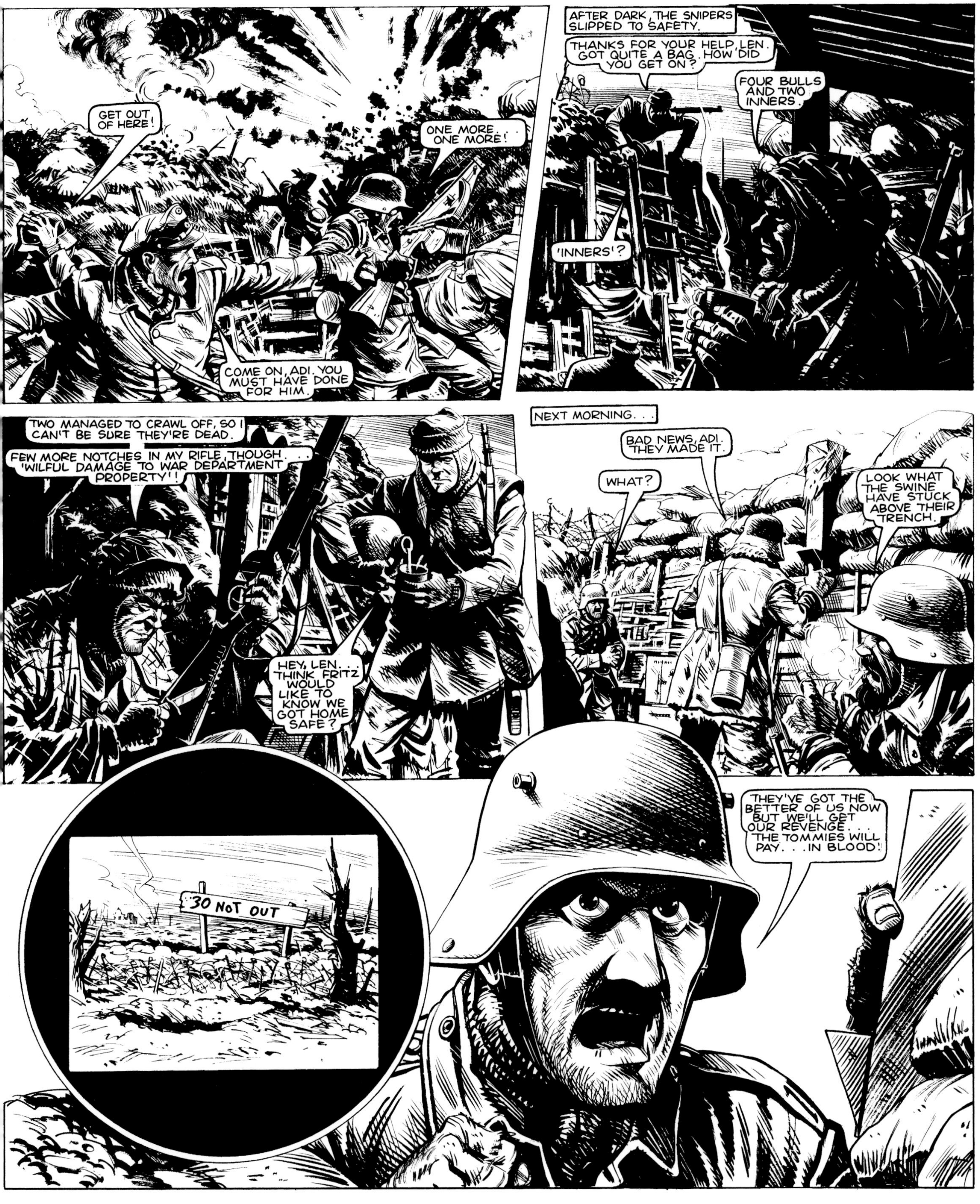

GET OUT OF HERE!
ONE MORE. ONE MORE!
COME ON, ADI. YOU MUST HAVE DONE FOR HIM.
AFTER DARK, THE SNIPERS SLIPPED TO SAFETY.
THANKS FOR YOUR HELP, LEN. GOT QUITE A BAG. HOW DID YOU GET ON?
FOUR BULLS AND TWO INNERS.
'INNERS'?
TWO MANAGED TO CRAWL OFF, SO I CAN'T BE SURE THEY'RE DEAD.
FEW MORE NOTCHES IN MY RIFLE, THOUGH. . . 'WILFUL DAMAGE TO WAR DEPARTMENT PROPERTY'!
HEY, LEN. . . THINK FRITZ WOULD LIKE TO KNOW WE GOT HOME SAFE?
NEXT MORNING. . .
BAD NEWS, ADI. THEY MADE IT.
WHAT?
LOOK WHAT THE SWINE HAVE STUCK ABOVE THEIR TRENCH.
30 NOT OUT
THEY'VE GOT THE BETTER OF US NOW BUT WE'LL GET OUR REVENGE. . . THE TOMMIES WILL PAY. . . IN BLOOD!

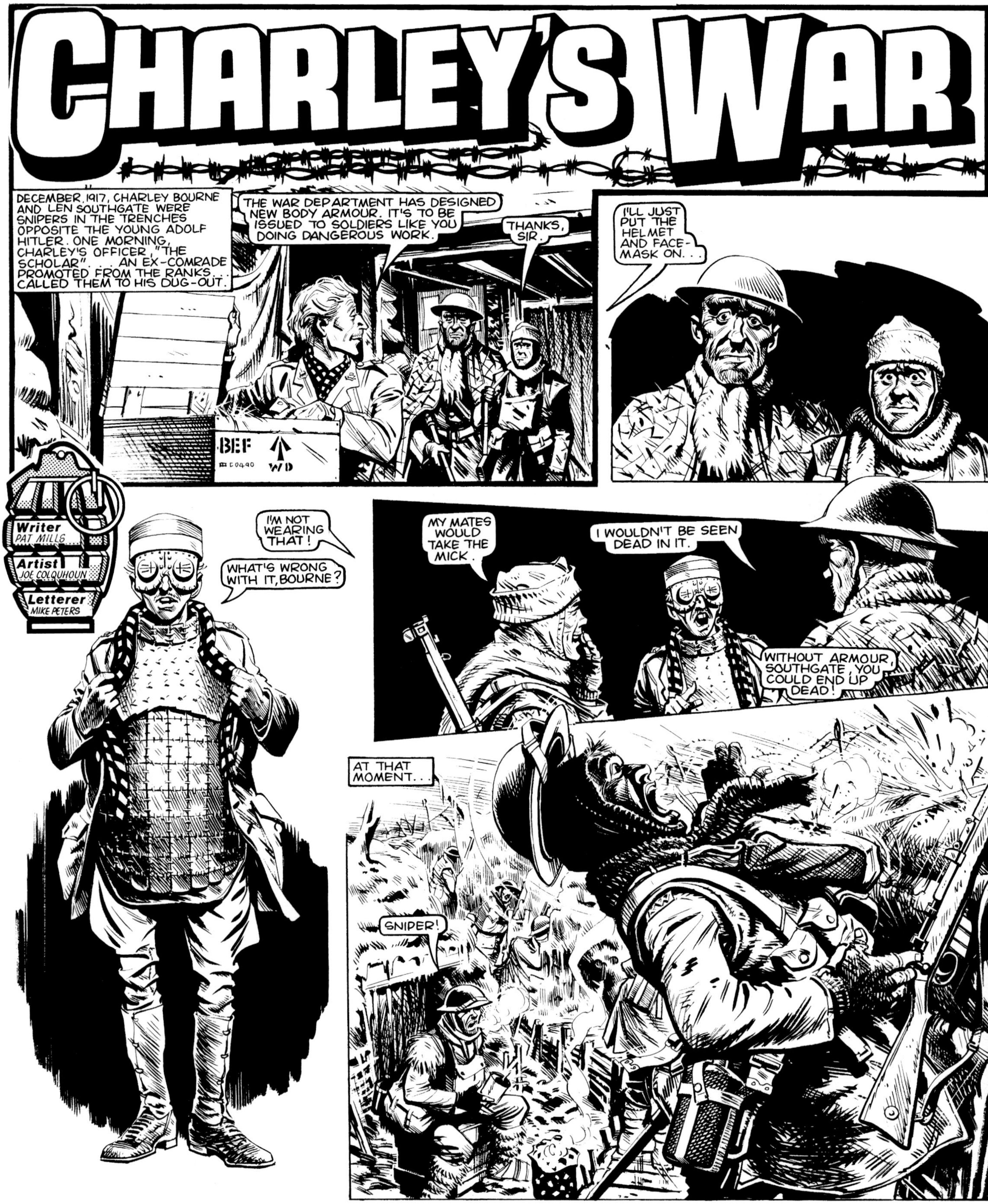
CHARLEY'S WAR
DECEMBER, 1917, CHARLEY BOURNE AND LEN SOUTHGATE WERE SNIPERS IN THE TRENCHES OPPOSITE THE YOUNG ADOLF HITLER. ONE MORNING, CHARLEY'S OFFICER, "THE SCHOLAR"... AN EX-COMRADE PROMOTED FROM THE RANKS... CALLED THEM TO HIS DUG-OUT.
THE WAR DEPARTMENT HAS DESIGNED NEW BODY ARMOUR. IT'S TO BE ISSUED TO SOLDIERS LIKE YOU DOING DANGEROUS WORK.
THANKS, SIR.
BEF
WD
I'LL JUST PUT THE HELMET AND FACE-MASK ON...
Writer PAT MILLS
Artist JOE COLQUHOUN
Letterer MIKE PETERS
I'M NOT WEARING THAT!
WHAT'S WRONG WITH IT, BOURNE?
MY MATES WOULD TAKE THE MICK.
I WOULDN'T BE SEEN DEAD IN IT.
WITHOUT ARMOUR, SOUTHGATE, YOU COULD END UP DEAD!
AT THAT MOMENT...
SNIPER!

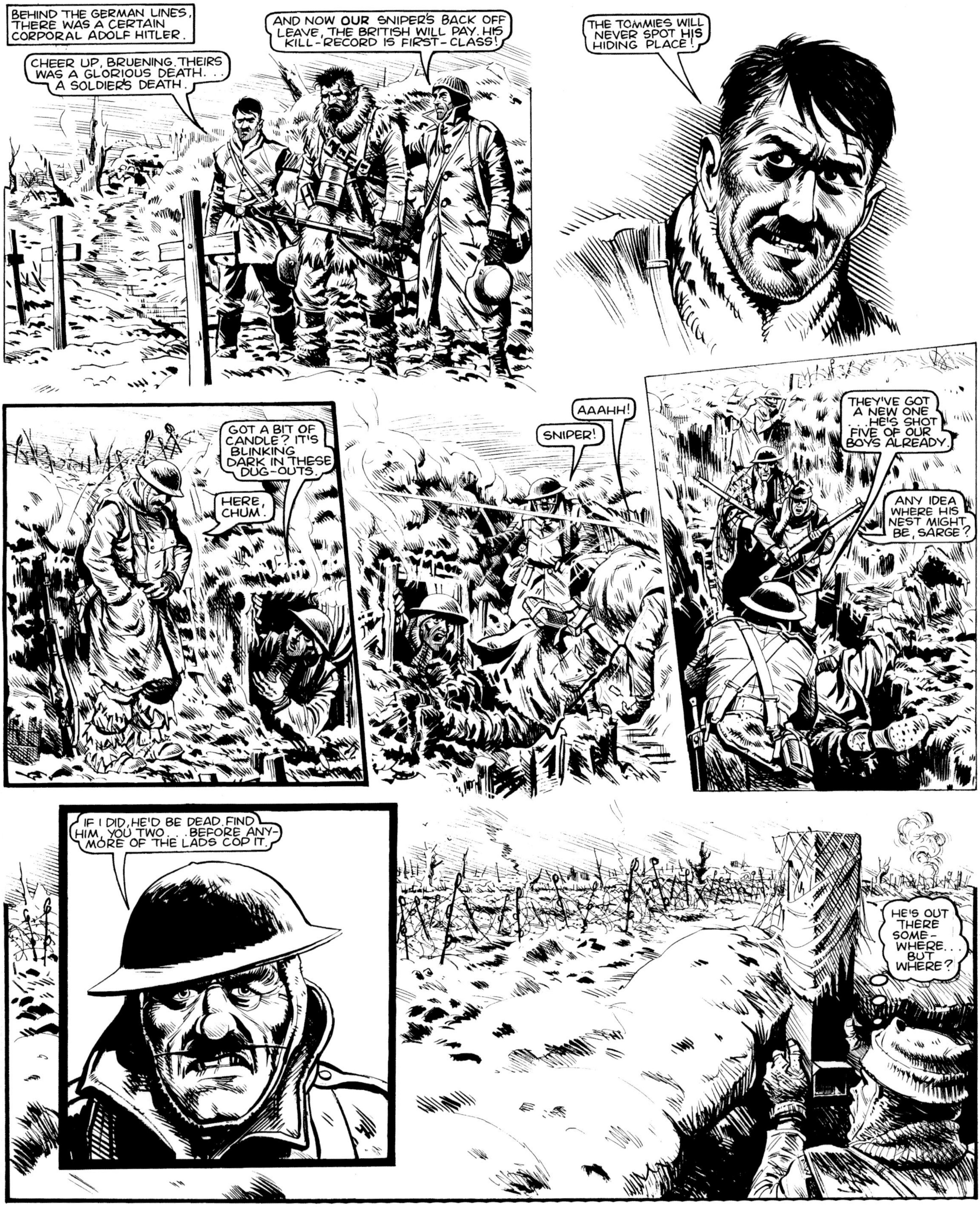

BEHIND THE GERMAN LINES, THERE WAS A CERTAIN CORPORAL ADOLF HITLER.
CHEER UP, BRUENING. THEIRS WAS A GLORIOUS DEATH. . . A SOLDIER'S DEATH.
AND NOW **OUR** SNIPER'S BACK OFF LEAVE, THE BRITISH WILL PAY. HIS KILL-RECORD IS FIRST-CLASS!
THE TOMMIES WILL NEVER SPOT **HIS** HIDING PLACE!
GOT A BIT OF CANDLE? IT'S BLINKING DARK IN THESE DUG-OUTS.
HERE, CHUM.
AAAHH!
SNIPER!
THEY'VE GOT A NEW ONE . . . HE'S SHOT FIVE OF OUR BOYS ALREADY.
ANY IDEA WHERE HIS NEST MIGHT BE, SARGE?
IF I DID, HE'D BE DEAD. FIND HIM, YOU TWO . . . BEFORE ANY-MORE OF THE LADS COP IT.
HE'S OUT THERE SOME-WHERE. . . BUT WHERE?

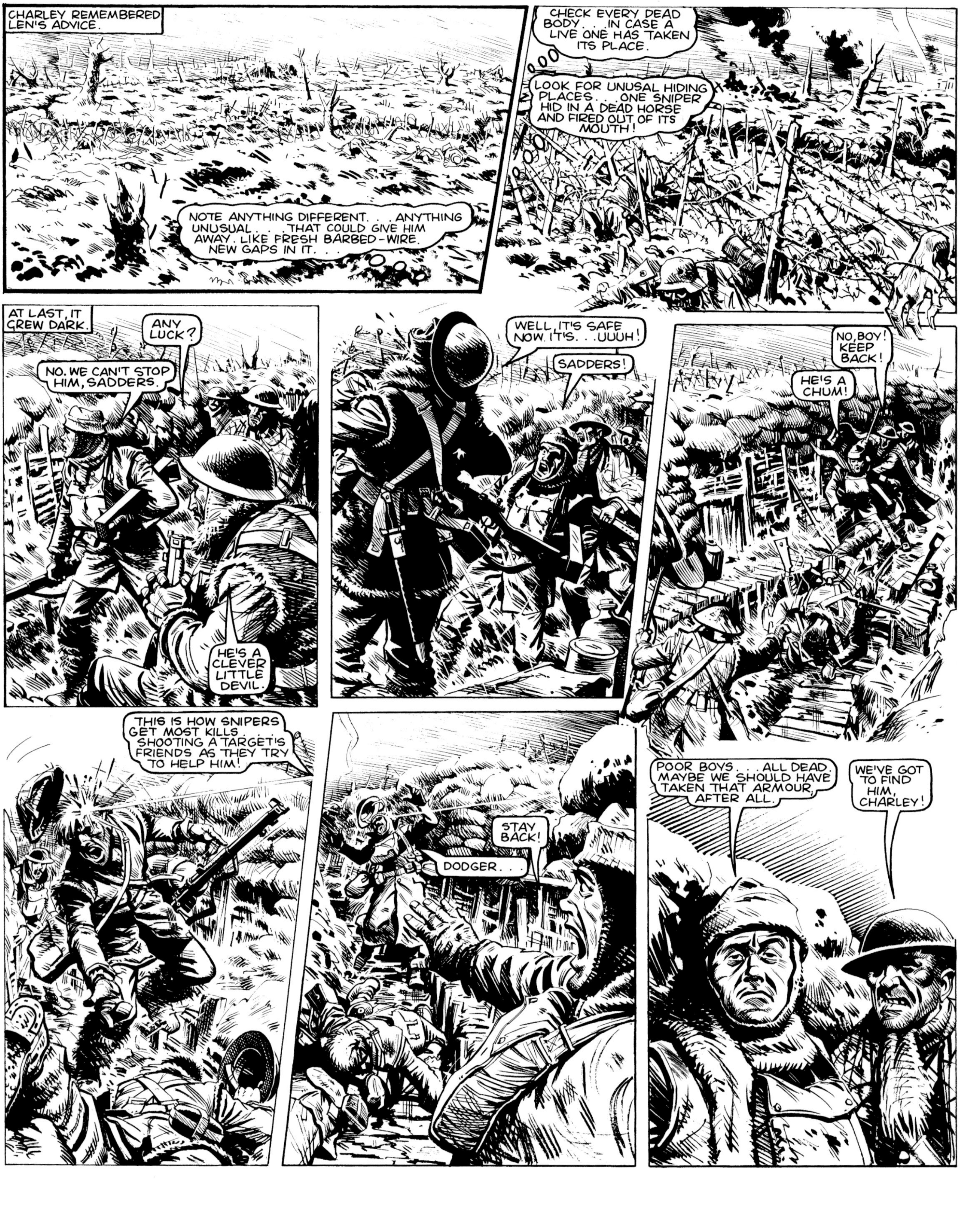
CHARLEY REMEMBERED LEN'S ADVICE.
NOTE ANYTHING DIFFERENT. . . ANYTHING UNUSUAL . . . THAT COULD GIVE HIM AWAY. LIKE FRESH BARBED-WIRE. NEW GAPS IN IT. . .
CHECK EVERY DEAD BODY. . . IN CASE A LIVE ONE HAS TAKEN ITS PLACE.
LOOK FOR UNUSAL HIDING PLACES. . . ONE SNIPER HID IN A DEAD HORSE AND FIRED OUT OF ITS MOUTH!
AT LAST, IT GREW DARK.
ANY LUCK?
NO. WE CAN'T STOP HIM, SADDERS.
HE'S A CLEVER LITTLE DEVIL.
WELL, IT'S SAFE NOW. IT'S. . . UUUH!
SADDERS!
NO, BOY! KEEP BACK!
HE'S A CHUM!
THIS IS HOW SNIPERS GET MOST KILLS . . . SHOOTING A TARGET'S FRIENDS AS THEY TRY TO HELP HIM!
STAY BACK!
DODGER. . .
POOR BOYS . . . ALL DEAD. MAYBE WE SHOULD HAVE TAKEN THAT ARMOUR, AFTER ALL.
WE'VE GOT TO FIND HIM, CHARLEY!

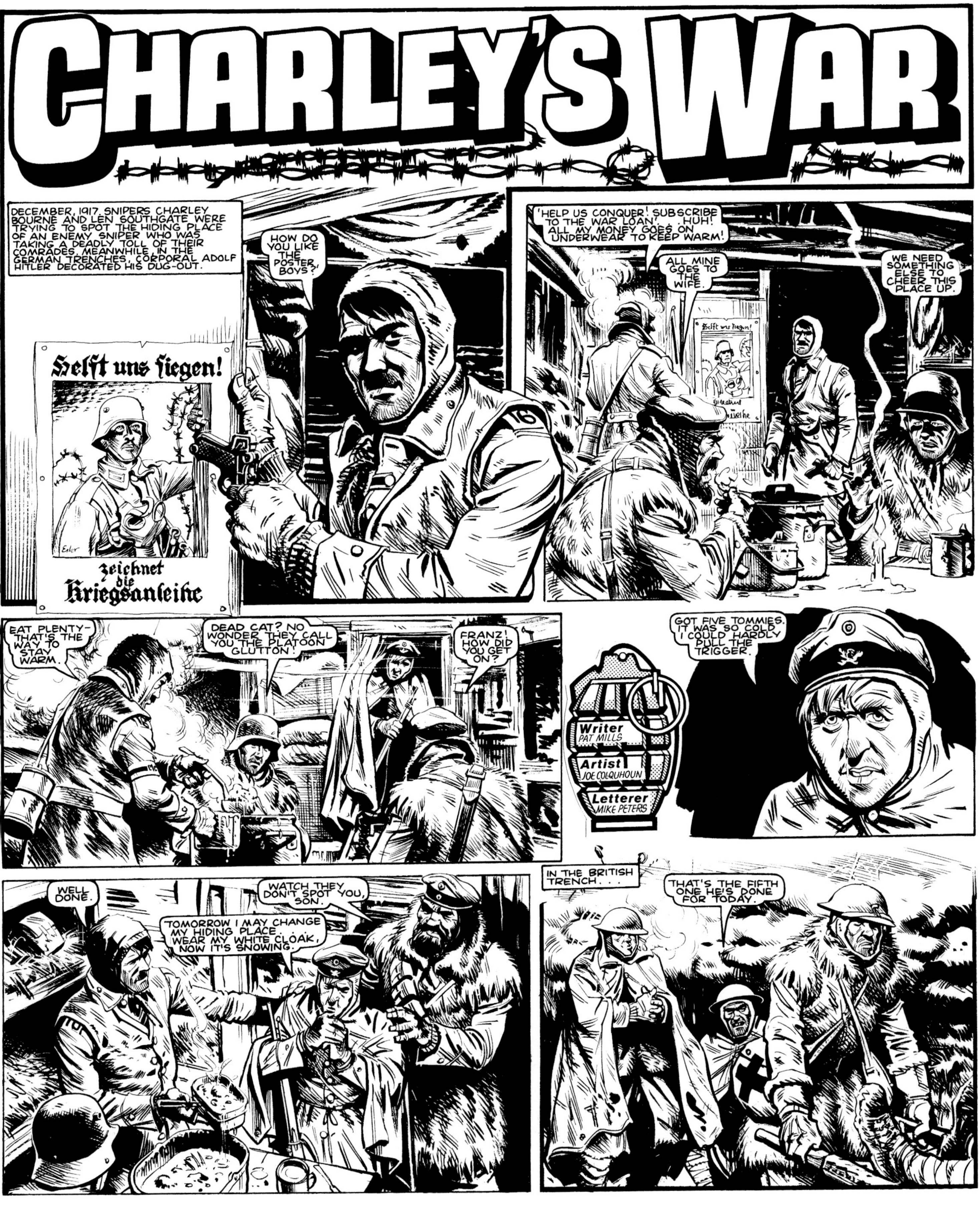
CHARLEY'S WAR
DECEMBER, 1917. SNIPERS CHARLEY BOURNE AND LEN SOUTHGATE WERE TRYING TO SPOT THE HIDING PLACE OF AN ENEMY SNIPER WHO WAS TAKING A DEADLY TOLL OF THEIR COMRADES. MEANWHILE, IN THE GERMAN TRENCHES, CORPORAL ADOLF HITLER DECORATED HIS DUG-OUT.
HOW DO YOU LIKE THE POSTER, BOYS?
Helft uns siegen!
zeichnet die Kriegsanleihe
'HELP US CONQUER! SUBSCRIBE TO THE WAR LOAN!' ...HUH! ALL MY MONEY GOES ON UNDERWEAR TO KEEP WARM!
ALL MINE GOES TO THE WIFE.
WE NEED SOMETHING ELSE TO CHEER THIS PLACE UP.
EAT PLENTY-THAT'S THE WAY TO STAY WARM.
DEAD CAT? NO WONDER THEY CALL YOU THE PLATOON GLUTTON!
FRANZ! HOW DID YOU GET ON?
Writer PAT MILLS
Artist JOE COLQUHOUN
Letterer MIKE PETERS
GOT FIVE TOMMIES. IT WAS SO COLD I COULD HARDLY PULL THE TRIGGER.
WELL DONE.
WATCH THEY DON'T SPOT YOU, SON.
TOMORROW I MAY CHANGE MY HIDING PLACE... WEAR MY WHITE CLOAK, NOW IT'S SNOWING.
IN THE BRITISH TRENCH...
THAT'S THE FIFTH ONE HE'S DONE FOR TODAY.

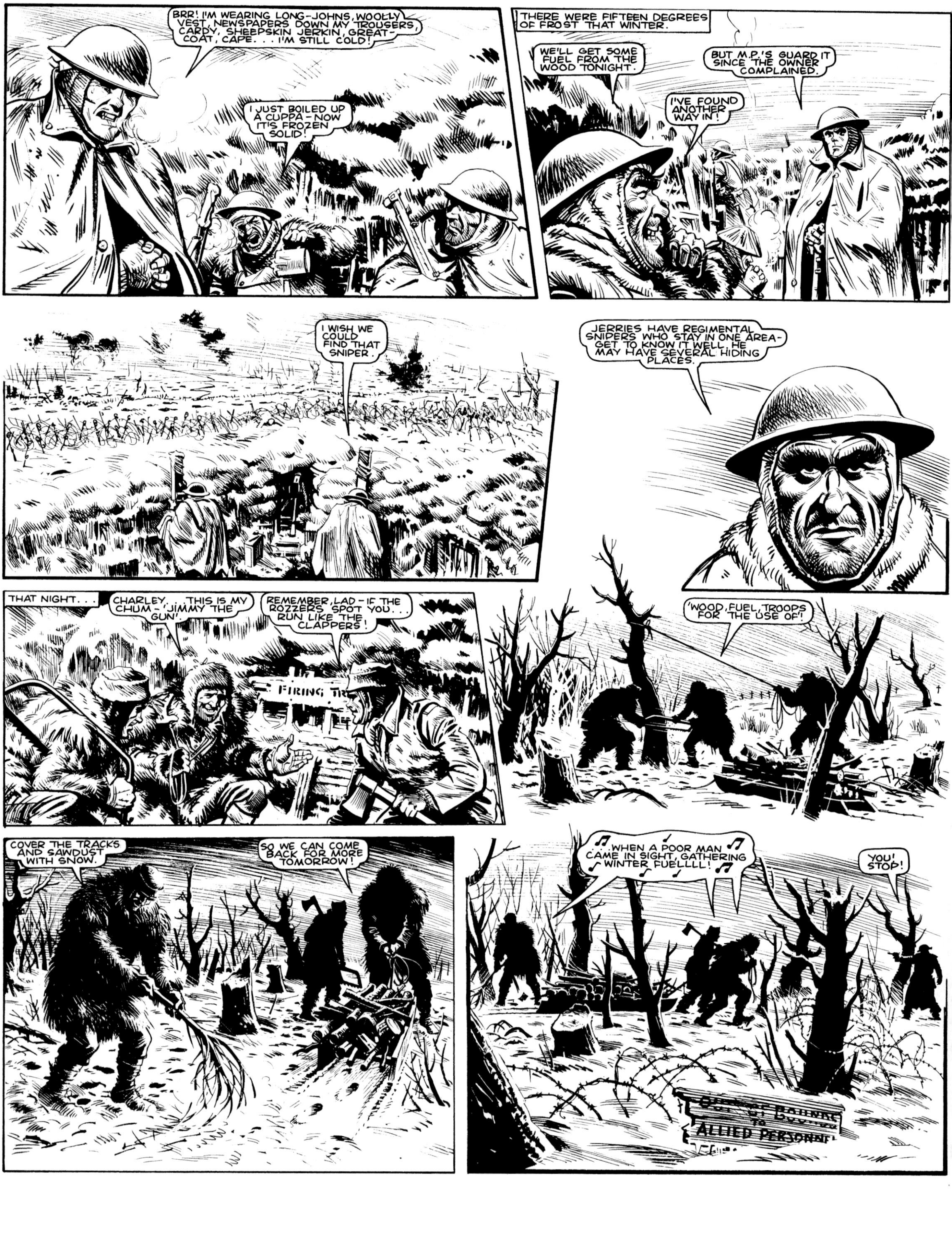
BRR! I'M WEARING LONG-JOHNS, WOOLLY VEST, NEWSPAPERS DOWN MY TROUSERS, CARDY, SHEEPSKIN JERKIN, GREAT-COAT, CAPE. . . I'M STILL COLD!
I JUST BOILED UP A CUPPA - NOW IT'S FROZEN SOLID!
THERE WERE FIFTEEN DEGREES OF FROST THAT WINTER.
WE'LL GET SOME FUEL FROM THE WOOD TONIGHT.
BUT M.P.'S GUARD IT SINCE THE OWNER COMPLAINED.
I'VE FOUND ANOTHER WAY IN!
I WISH WE COULD FIND THAT SNIPER.
JERRIES HAVE REGIMENTAL SNIPERS WHO STAY IN ONE AREA - GET TO KNOW IT WELL. HE MAY HAVE SEVERAL HIDING PLACES.
THAT NIGHT. . .
CHARLEY. . . THIS IS MY CHUM - 'JIMMY THE GUN'.
REMEMBER, LAD - IF THE ROZZERS SPOT YOU. . . RUN LIKE THE CLAPPERS!
FIRING
'WOOD, FUEL, TROOPS FOR THE USE OF'!
COVER THE TRACKS AND SAWDUST WITH SNOW.
SO WE CAN COME BACK FOR MORE TOMORROW!
WHEN A POOR MAN CAME IN SIGHT, GATHERING WINTER FUELLLL!
YOU! STOP!
ALLIED PERSONN

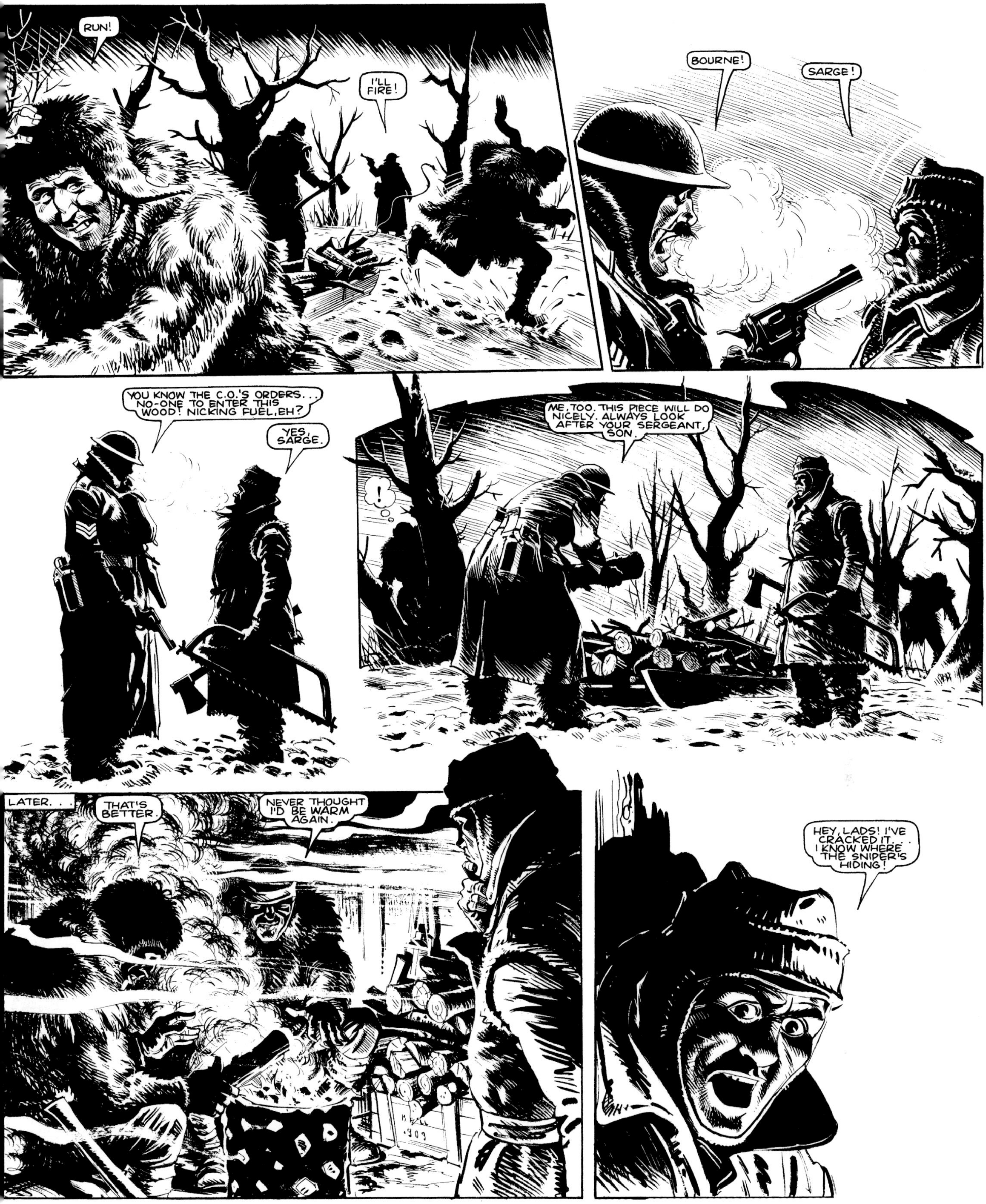
RUN!
I'LL FIRE!
BOURNE!
SARGE!
YOU KNOW THE C.O.'S ORDERS... NO-ONE TO ENTER THIS WOOD! NICKING FUEL, EH?
YES, SARGE.
!
ME, TOO. THIS PIECE WILL DO NICELY. ALWAYS LOOK AFTER YOUR SERGEANT, SON.
LATER...
THAT'S BETTER.
NEVER THOUGHT I'D BE WARM AGAIN.
HEY, LADS! I'VE CRACKED IT... I KNOW WHERE THE SNIPER'S HIDING!

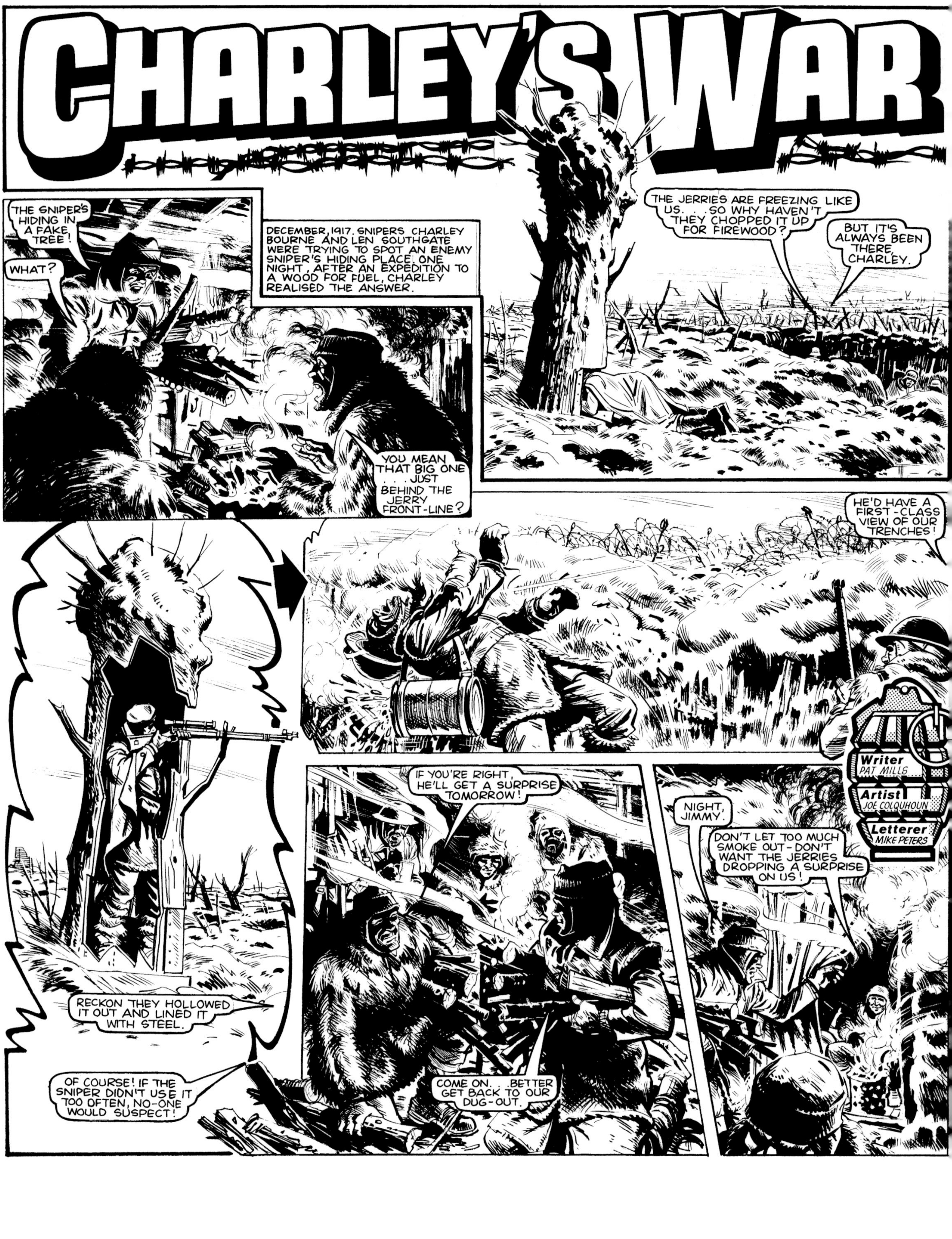
CHARLEY'S WAR
THE SNIPER'S HIDING IN A FAKE TREE!
WHAT?
DECEMBER, 1917. SNIPERS CHARLEY BOURNE AND LEN SOUTHGATE WERE TRYING TO SPOT AN ENEMY SNIPER'S HIDING PLACE. ONE NIGHT, AFTER AN EXPEDITION TO A WOOD FOR FUEL, CHARLEY REALISED THE ANSWER.
YOU MEAN THAT BIG ONE . . . JUST BEHIND THE JERRY FRONT-LINE?
THE JERRIES ARE FREEZING LIKE US. . . SO WHY HAVEN'T THEY CHOPPED IT UP FOR FIREWOOD?
BUT IT'S ALWAYS BEEN THERE, CHARLEY.
HE'D HAVE A FIRST-CLASS VIEW OF OUR TRENCHES!
RECKON THEY HOLLOWED IT OUT AND LINED IT WITH STEEL.
OF COURSE! IF THE SNIPER DIDN'T USE IT TOO OFTEN, NO-ONE WOULD SUSPECT!
IF YOU'RE RIGHT, HE'LL GET A SURPRISE TOMORROW!
COME ON. . .BETTER GET BACK TO OUR DUG-OUT.
NIGHT, JIMMY.
DON'T LET TOO MUCH SMOKE OUT - DON'T WANT THE JERRIES DROPPING A SURPRISE ON US!
Writer PAT MILLS
Artist JOE COLQUHOUN
Letterer MIKE PETERS

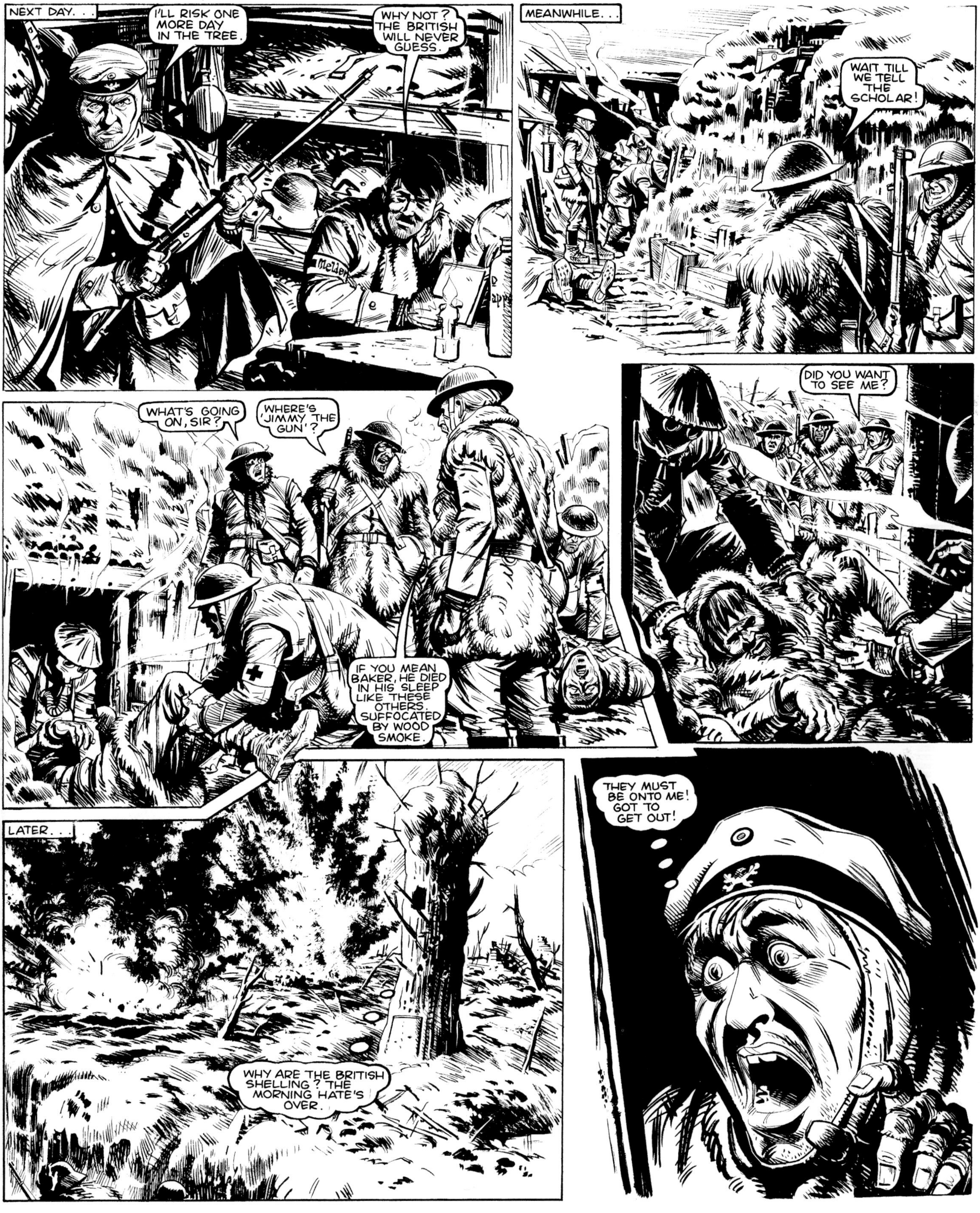
NEXT DAY. . .
I'LL RISK ONE MORE DAY IN THE TREE.
WHY NOT? THE BRITISH WILL NEVER GUESS.
MEANWHILE. . .
WAIT TILL WE TELL THE SCHOLAR!
WHAT'S GOING ON, SIR?
WHERE'S 'JIMMY THE GUN'?
IF YOU MEAN BAKER, HE DIED IN HIS SLEEP LIKE THESE OTHERS. SUFFOCATED BY WOOD SMOKE.
DID YOU WANT TO SEE ME?
LATER. . .
WHY ARE THE BRITISH SHELLING? THE MORNING HATE'S OVER.
THEY MUST BE ONTO ME! GOT TO GET OUT!

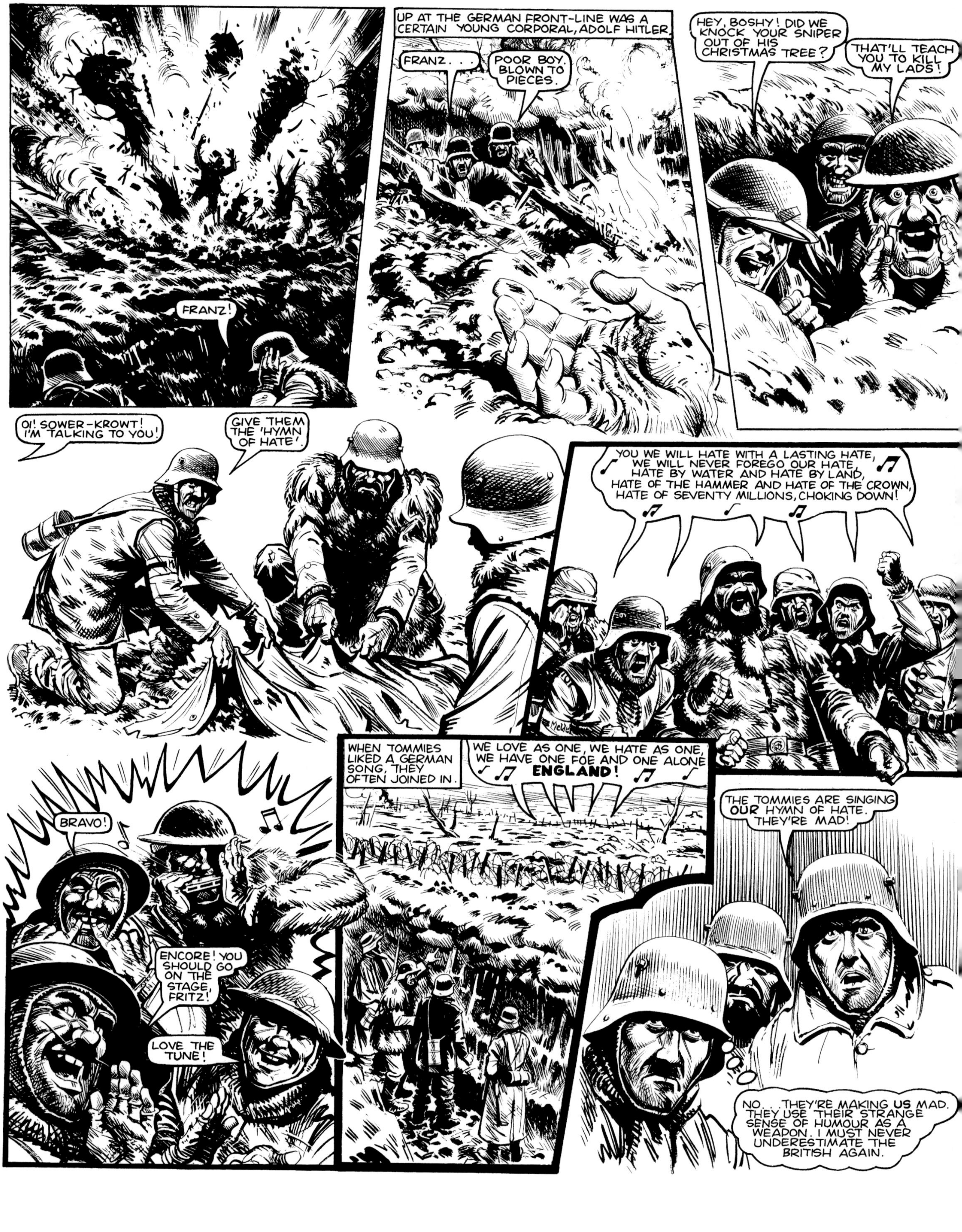
FRANZ!
UP AT THE GERMAN FRONT-LINE WAS A CERTAIN YOUNG CORPORAL, ADOLF HITLER.
FRANZ. . .
POOR BOY. BLOWN TO PIECES.
HEY, BOSHY! DID WE KNOCK YOUR SNIPER OUT OF HIS CHRISTMAS TREE?
THAT'LL TEACH YOU TO KILL MY LADS!
OI! SOWER-KROWT! I'M TALKING TO YOU!
GIVE THEM THE 'HYMN OF HATE'.
YOU WE WILL HATE WITH A LASTING HATE, WE WILL NEVER FOREGO OUR HATE, HATE BY WATER AND HATE BY LAND, HATE OF THE HAMMER AND HATE OF THE CROWN, HATE OF SEVENTY MILLIONS, CHOKING DOWN!
WHEN TOMMIES LIKED A GERMAN SONG, THEY OFTEN JOINED IN.
WE LOVE AS ONE, WE HATE AS ONE, WE HAVE ONE FOE AND ONE ALONE ENGLAND!
BRAVO!
ENCORE! YOU SHOULD GO ON THE STAGE, FRITZ!
LOVE THE TUNE!
THE TOMMIES ARE SINGING OUR HYMN OF HATE. THEY'RE MAD!
NO. . . THEY'RE MAKING US MAD. THEY USE THEIR STRANGE SENSE OF HUMOUR AS A WEAPON. I MUST NEVER UNDERESTIMATE THE BRITISH AGAIN.

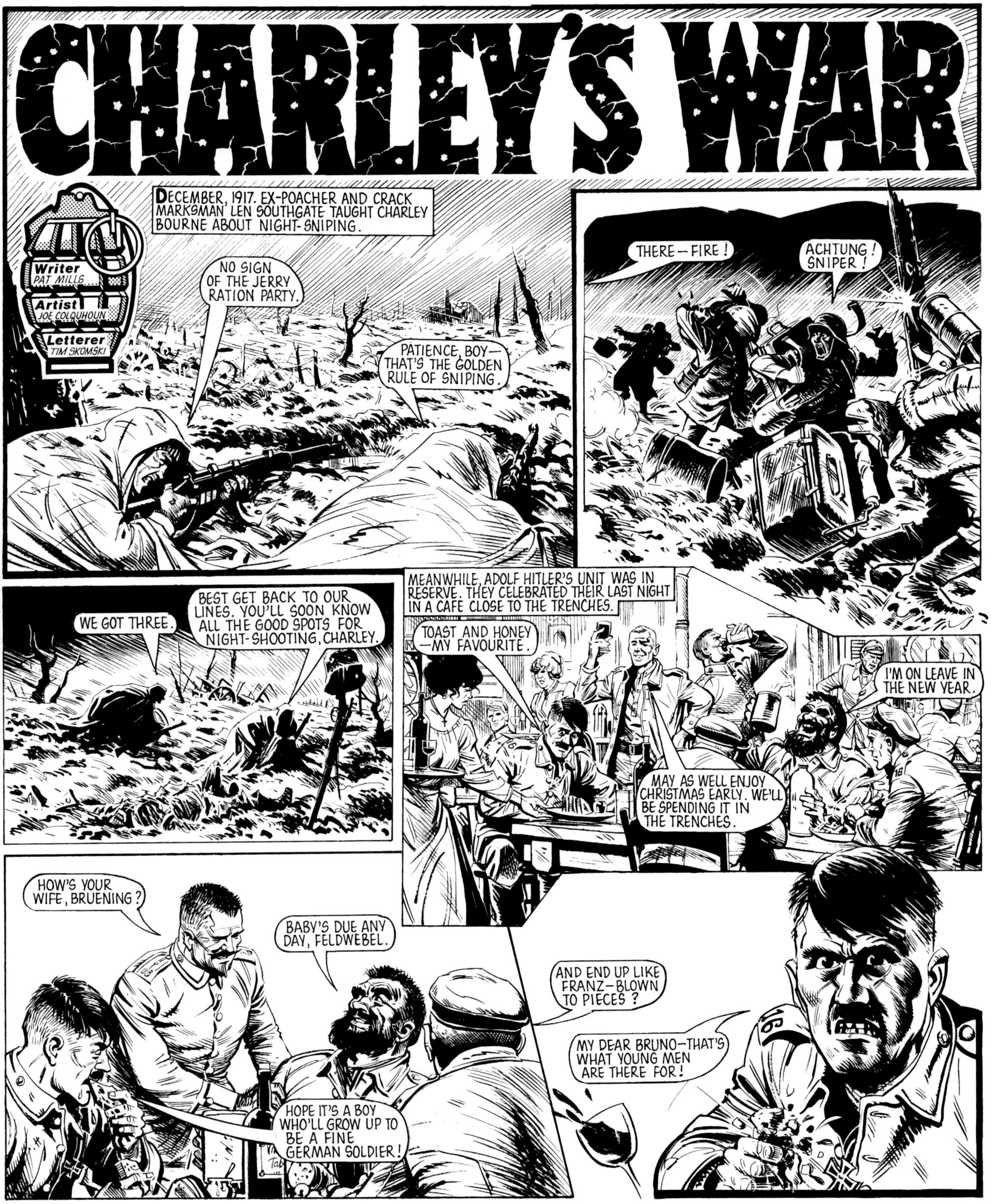
CHARLEY'S WAR
Writer PAT MILLS
Artist JOE COLQUHOUN
Letterer TIM SKOMSKI
DECEMBER, 1917. EX-POACHER AND CRACK MARKSMAN LEN SOUTHGATE TAUGHT CHARLEY BOURNE ABOUT NIGHT-SNIPING.
NO SIGN OF THE JERRY RATION PARTY.
PATIENCE, BOY— THAT'S THE GOLDEN RULE OF SNIPING.
THERE—FIRE!
ACHTUNG! SNIPER!
WE GOT THREE.
BEST GET BACK TO OUR LINES. YOU'LL SOON KNOW ALL THE GOOD SPOTS FOR NIGHT-SHOOTING, CHARLEY.
MEANWHILE, ADOLF HITLER'S UNIT WAS IN RESERVE. THEY CELEBRATED THEIR LAST NIGHT IN A CAFE CLOSE TO THE TRENCHES.
TOAST AND HONEY —MY FAVOURITE.
I'M ON LEAVE IN THE NEW YEAR.
MAY AS WELL ENJOY CHRISTMAS EARLY. WE'LL BE SPENDING IT IN THE TRENCHES.
HOW'S YOUR WIFE, BRUENING?
BABY'S DUE ANY DAY, FELDWEBEL.
HOPE IT'S A BOY WHO'LL GROW UP TO BE A FINE GERMAN SOLDIER!
AND END UP LIKE FRANZ—BLOWN TO PIECES?
MY DEAR BRUNO—THAT'S WHAT YOUNG MEN ARE THERE FOR!

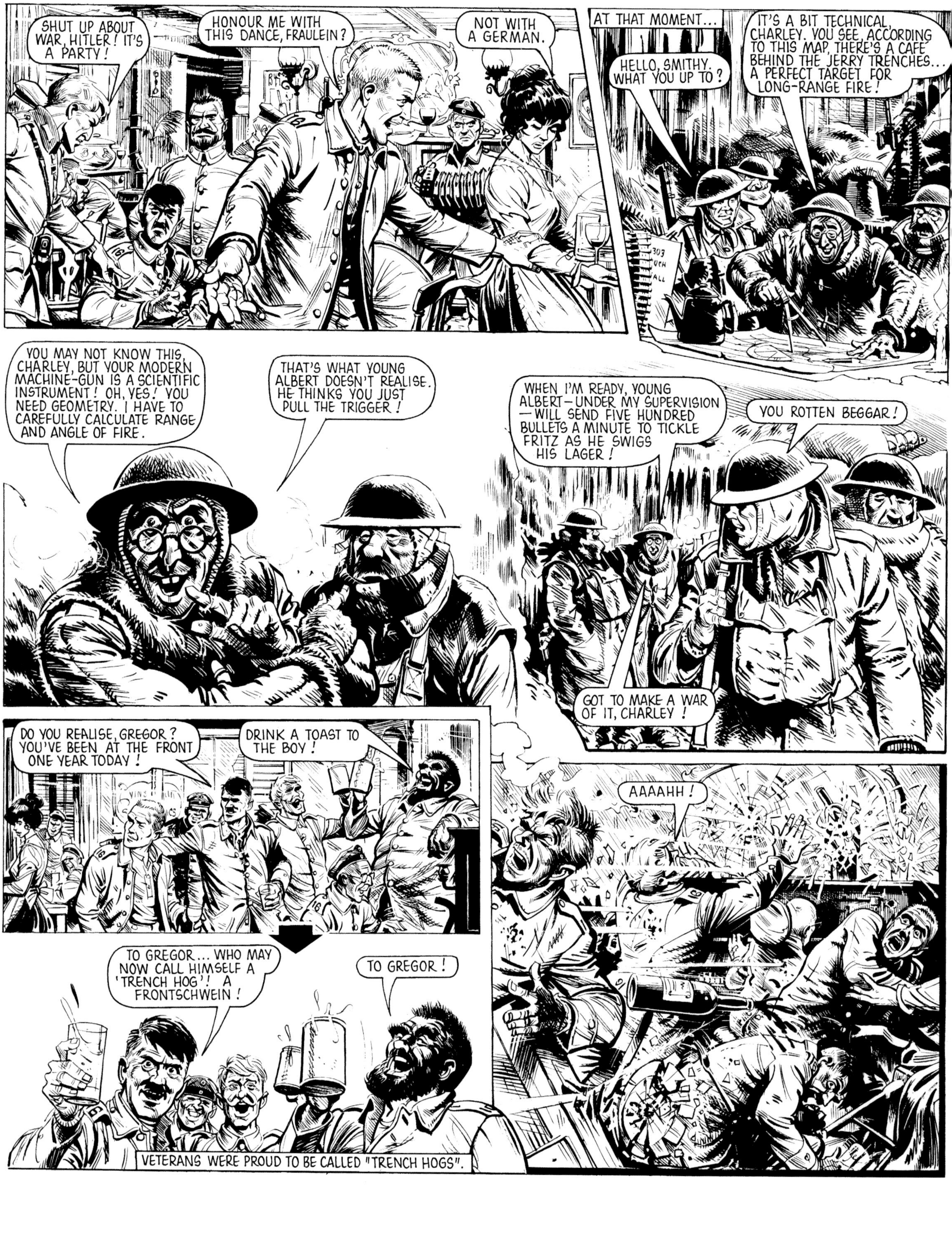
SHUT UP ABOUT WAR, HITLER! IT'S A PARTY!
HONOUR ME WITH THIS DANCE, FRAULEIN?
NOT WITH A GERMAN.
AT THAT MOMENT...
HELLO, SMITHY. WHAT YOU UP TO?
IT'S A BIT TECHNICAL, CHARLEY. YOU SEE, ACCORDING TO THIS MAP, THERE'S A CAFE BEHIND THE JERRY TRENCHES... A PERFECT TARGET FOR LONG-RANGE FIRE!
YOU MAY NOT KNOW THIS, CHARLEY, BUT YOUR MODERN MACHINE-GUN IS A SCIENTIFIC INSTRUMENT! OH, YES! YOU NEED GEOMETRY. I HAVE TO CAREFULLY CALCULATE RANGE AND ANGLE OF FIRE.
THAT'S WHAT YOUNG ALBERT DOESN'T REALISE. HE THINKS YOU JUST PULL THE TRIGGER!
WHEN I'M READY, YOUNG ALBERT—UNDER MY SUPERVISION—WILL SEND FIVE HUNDRED BULLETS A MINUTE TO TICKLE FRITZ AS HE SWIGS HIS LAGER!
YOU ROTTEN BEGGAR!
GOT TO MAKE A WAR OF IT, CHARLEY!
DO YOU REALISE, GREGOR? YOU'VE BEEN AT THE FRONT ONE YEAR TODAY!
DRINK A TOAST TO THE BOY!
TO GREGOR... WHO MAY NOW CALL HIMSELF A 'TRENCH HOG'! A FRONTSCHWEIN!
TO GREGOR!
VETERANS WERE PROUD TO BE CALLED "TRENCH HOGS".
AAAAHH!

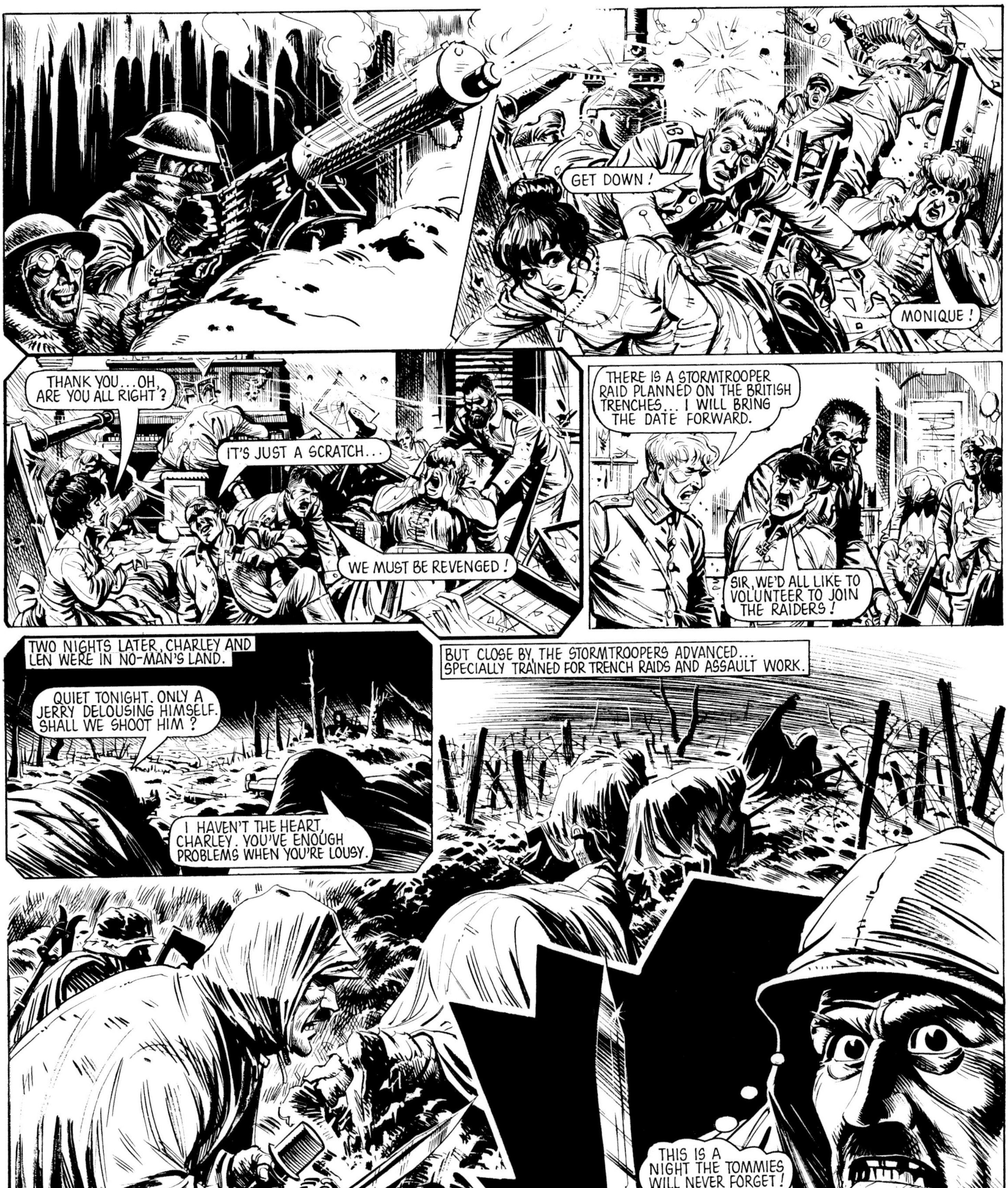
GET DOWN!
MONIQUE!
THANK YOU...OH, ARE YOU ALL RIGHT?
IT'S JUST A SCRATCH..
WE MUST BE REVENGED!
THERE IS A STORMTROOPER RAID PLANNED ON THE BRITISH TRENCHES... I WILL BRING THE DATE FORWARD.
SIR, WE'D ALL LIKE TO VOLUNTEER TO JOIN THE RAIDERS!
TWO NIGHTS LATER, CHARLEY AND LEN WERE IN NO-MAN'S LAND.
QUIET TONIGHT. ONLY A JERRY DELOUSING HIMSELF. SHALL WE SHOOT HIM?
I HAVEN'T THE HEART, CHARLEY. YOU'VE ENOUGH PROBLEMS WHEN YOU'RE LOUSY.
BUT CLOSE BY, THE STORMTROOPERS ADVANCED... SPECIALLY TRAINED FOR TRENCH RAIDS AND ASSAULT WORK.
THIS IS A NIGHT THE TOMMIES WILL NEVER FORGET!

# CHARLEY'S WAR

DECEMBER, 1917. CORPORAL ADOLF HITLER AND A SQUAD OF STORMTROOPERS BEGAN A RAID ON THE BRITISH TRENCHES. HITLER'S C.O. ONCE SAID NOTHING WOULD STOP HIM "VOLUNTEERING FOR THE MOST DIFFICULT, ARDUOUS AND DANGEROUS TASKS. . .HE WAS ALWAYS READY TO SACRIFICE LIFE FOR HIS FATHERLAND."

WHY DID HITLER HAVE TO RISK OUR LIVES? HOW WILL THE WIFE MANAGE IF I DIE?

HITLER'S GOING TO GET US ALL KILLED!

CHARLEY AND LEN SOUTHGATE WERE HIDING IN NO-MAN'S LAND.

NOTICE A WARM, DRY FLANNELY SMELL, CHARLEY?

NO.

IT'S FRITZ'S SMELL – I RECOGNISE IT FROM CAPTURED DUG-OUTS. HE'S OUT THERE SOMEWHERE!

SIR-I HEARD ICE CRACKING OVER THERE. MAYBE A BRITISH SNIPER.

TAKE SIX MEN AND FIND OUT. MAKE SURE HE DOESN'T GET BACK TO ALERT HIS COMRADES.

IT'S FRITZ! WHAT'LL WE DO?

IF WE MOVE OR FIRE THEY'LL SPOT OUR POSITION. . .AND WE MIGHT NOT HIT THEM ALL. LET'S LIE LOW, CHARLEY. THEY MAY NOT BE AFTER US.

**Writer**
PAT MILLS

**Artist**
JOE COLQUHOUN

**Letterer**
MIKE PETERS

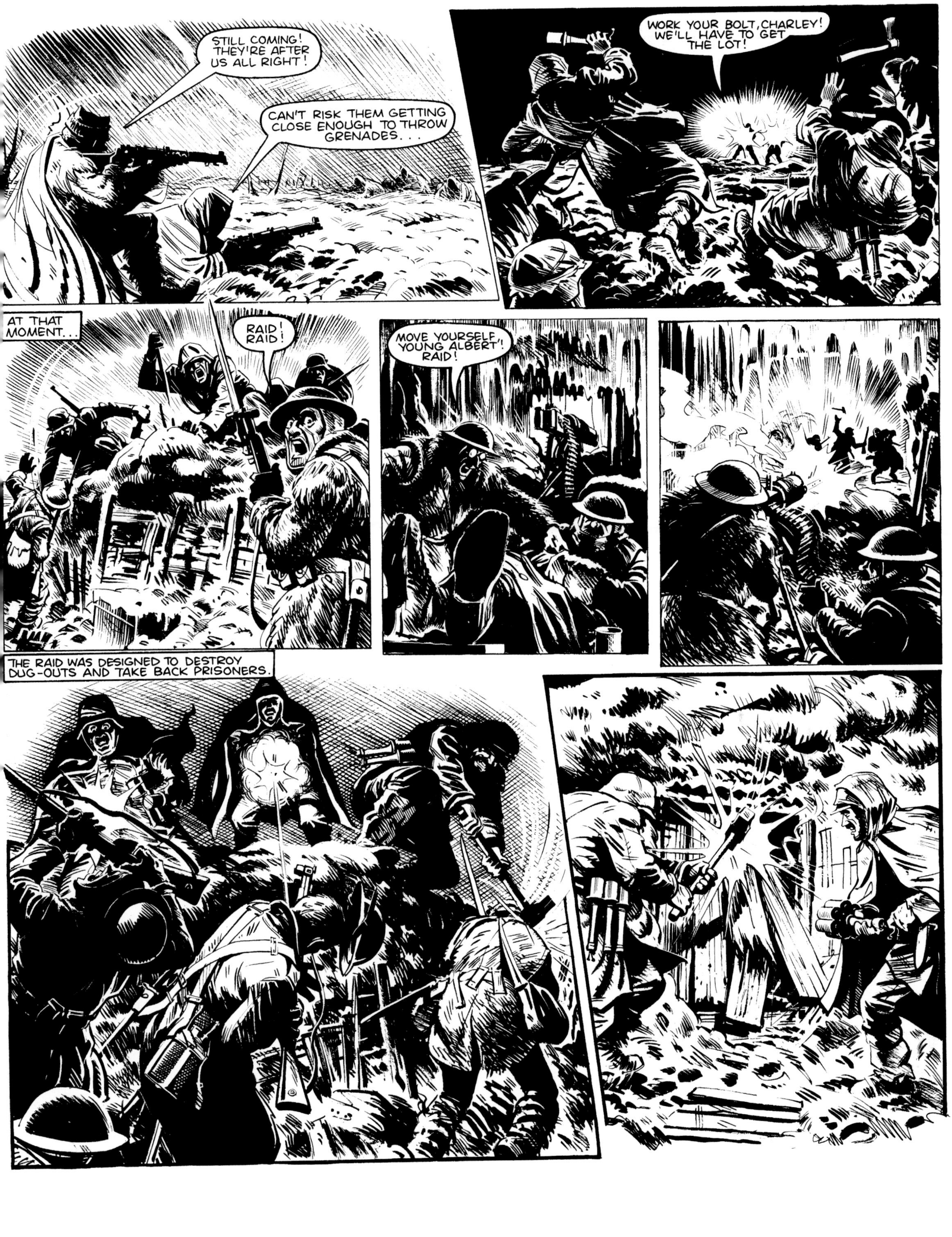
STILL COMING! THEY'RE AFTER US ALL RIGHT!
CAN'T RISK THEM GETTING CLOSE ENOUGH TO THROW GRENADES...
WORK YOUR BOLT, CHARLEY! WE'LL HAVE TO GET THE LOT!
AT THAT MOMENT...
RAID! RAID!
MOVE YOURSELF, YOUNG ALBERT! RAID!
THE RAID WAS DESIGNED TO DESTROY DUG-OUTS AND TAKE BACK PRISONERS.

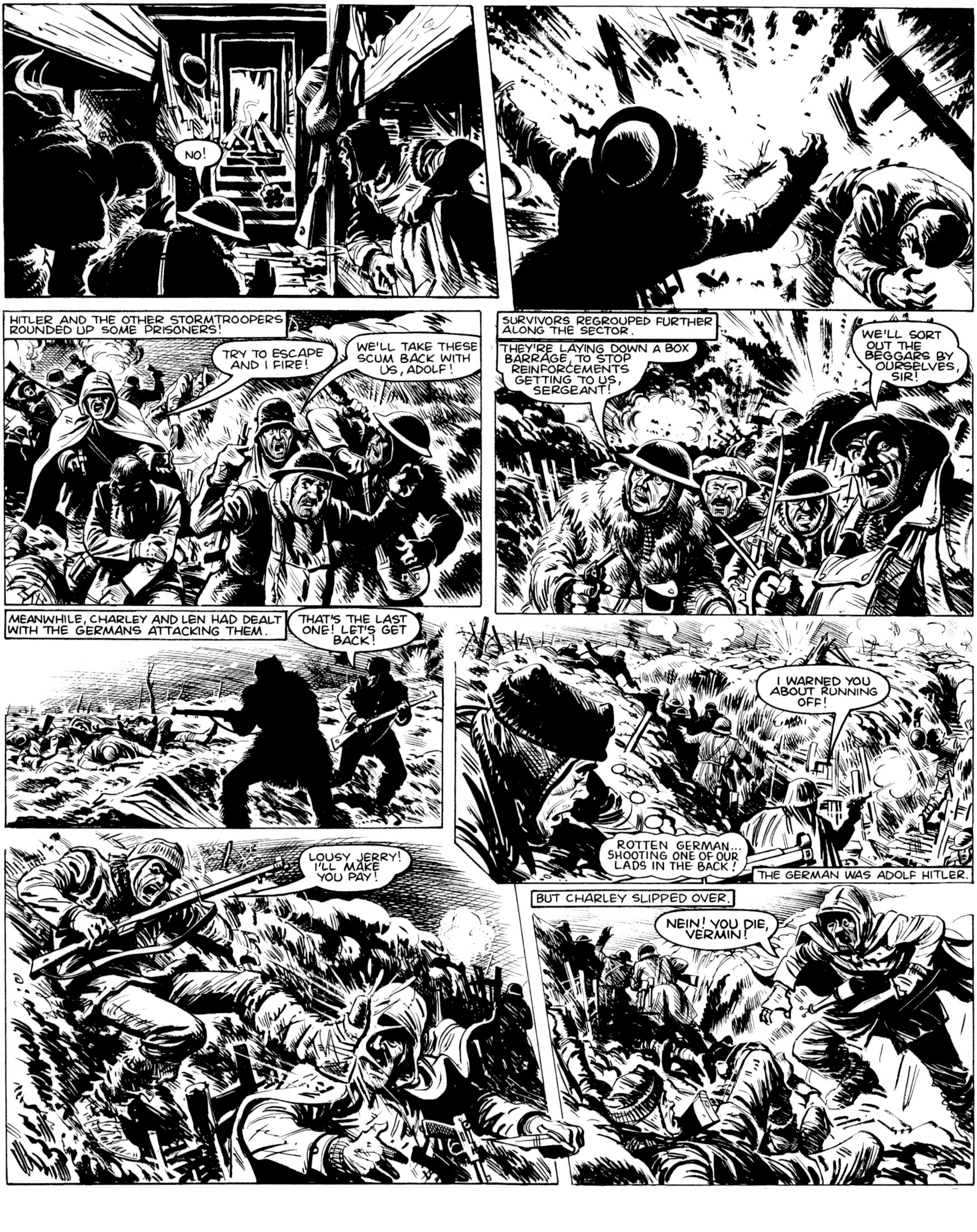
NO!
HITLER AND THE OTHER STORMTROOPERS ROUNDED UP SOME PRISONERS!
TRY TO ESCAPE AND I FIRE!
WE'LL TAKE THESE SCUM BACK WITH US, ADOLF!
SURVIVORS REGROUPED FURTHER ALONG THE SECTOR.
THEY'RE LAYING DOWN A BOX BARRAGE, TO STOP REINFORCEMENTS GETTING TO US, SERGEANT!
WE'LL SORT OUT THE BEGGARS BY OURSELVES, SIR!
MEANWHILE, CHARLEY AND LEN HAD DEALT WITH THE GERMANS ATTACKING THEM.
THAT'S THE LAST ONE! LET'S GET BACK!
I WARNED YOU ABOUT RUNNING OFF!
ROTTEN GERMAN... SHOOTING ONE OF OUR LADS IN THE BACK!
THE GERMAN WAS ADOLF HITLER.
LOUSY JERRY! I'LL MAKE YOU PAY!
BUT CHARLEY SLIPPED OVER.
NEIN! YOU DIE, VERMIN!

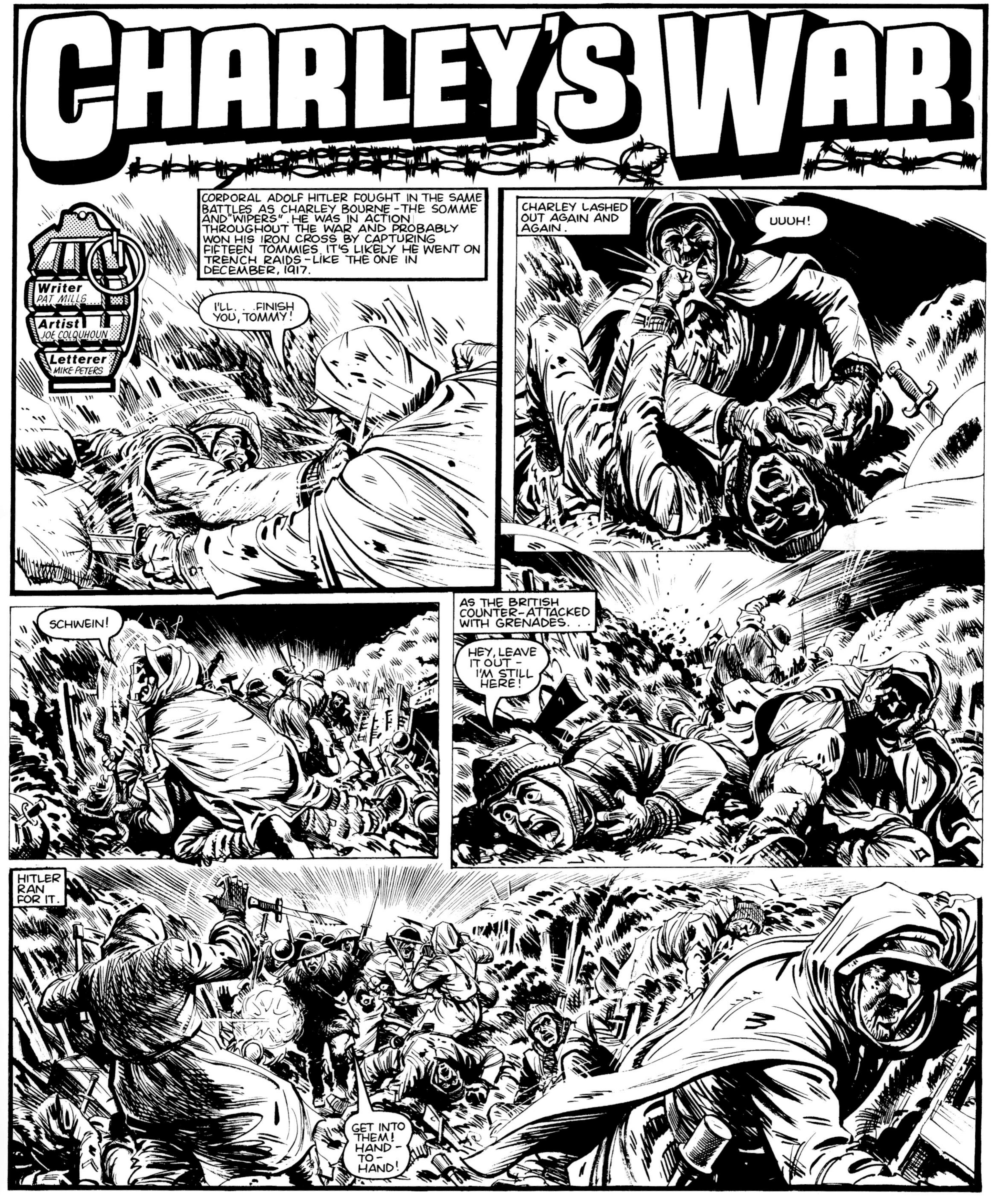
CHARLEY'S WAR
Writer PAT MILLS
Artist JOE COLQUHOUN
Letterer MIKE PETERS
CORPORAL ADOLF HITLER FOUGHT IN THE SAME BATTLES AS CHARLEY BOURNE - THE SOMME AND "WIPERS". HE WAS IN ACTION THROUGHOUT THE WAR AND PROBABLY WON HIS IRON CROSS BY CAPTURING FIFTEEN TOMMIES. IT'S LIKELY HE WENT ON TRENCH RAIDS - LIKE THE ONE IN DECEMBER, 1917.
I'LL. . .FINISH YOU, TOMMY!
CHARLEY LASHED OUT AGAIN AND AGAIN.
UUUH!
SCHWEIN!
AS THE BRITISH COUNTER-ATTACKED WITH GRENADES. . .
HEY, LEAVE IT OUT - I'M STILL HERE!
HITLER RAN FOR IT.
GET INTO THEM! HAND-TO-HAND!

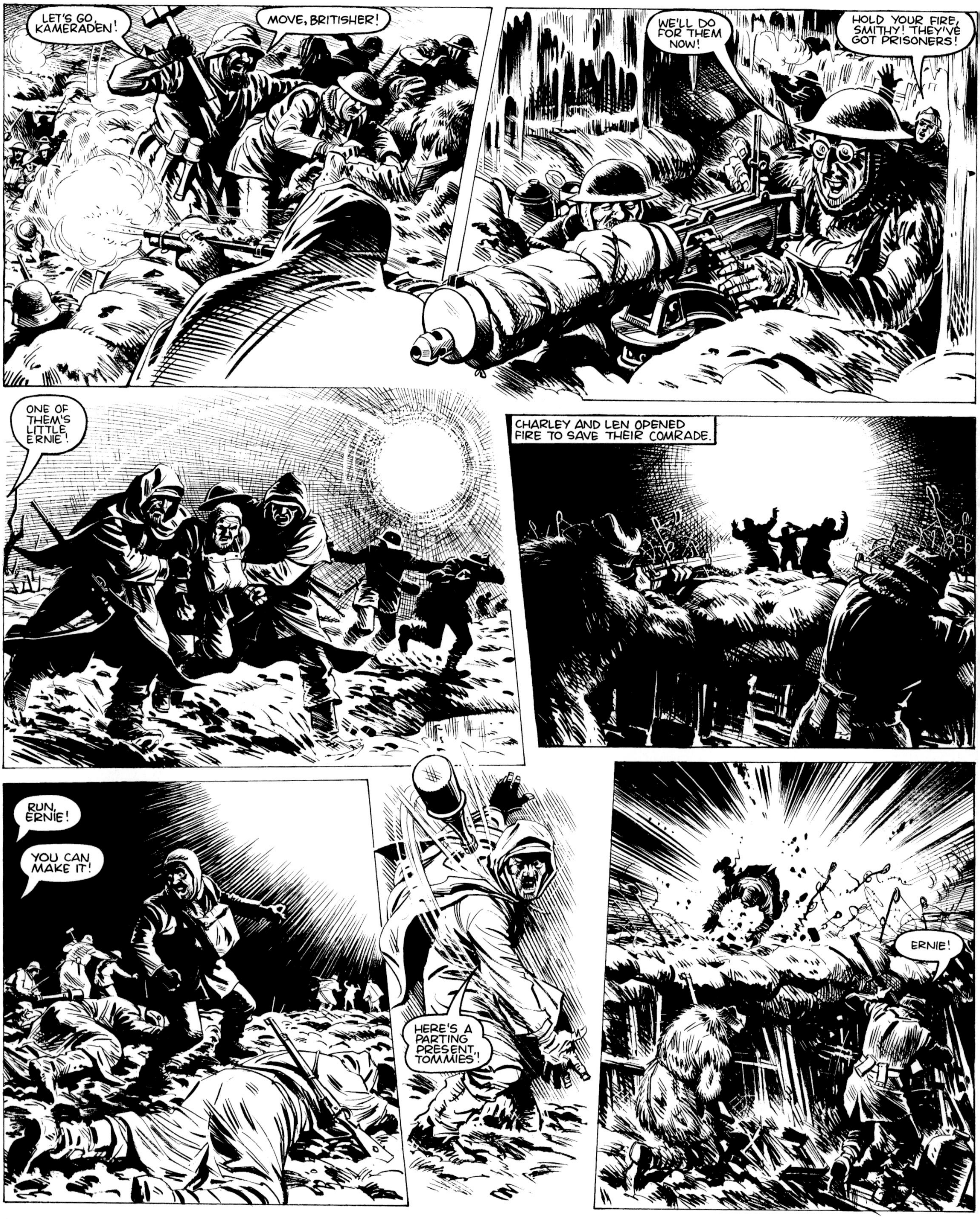
LET'S GO, KAMERADEN!
MOVE, BRITISHER!
WE'LL DO FOR THEM NOW!
HOLD YOUR FIRE, SMITHY! THEY'VE GOT PRISONERS!
ONE OF THEM'S LITTLE ERNIE!
CHARLEY AND LEN OPENED FIRE TO SAVE THEIR COMRADE.
RUN, ERNIE!
YOU CAN MAKE IT!
HERE'S A PARTING PRESENT, TOMMIES!
ERNIE!

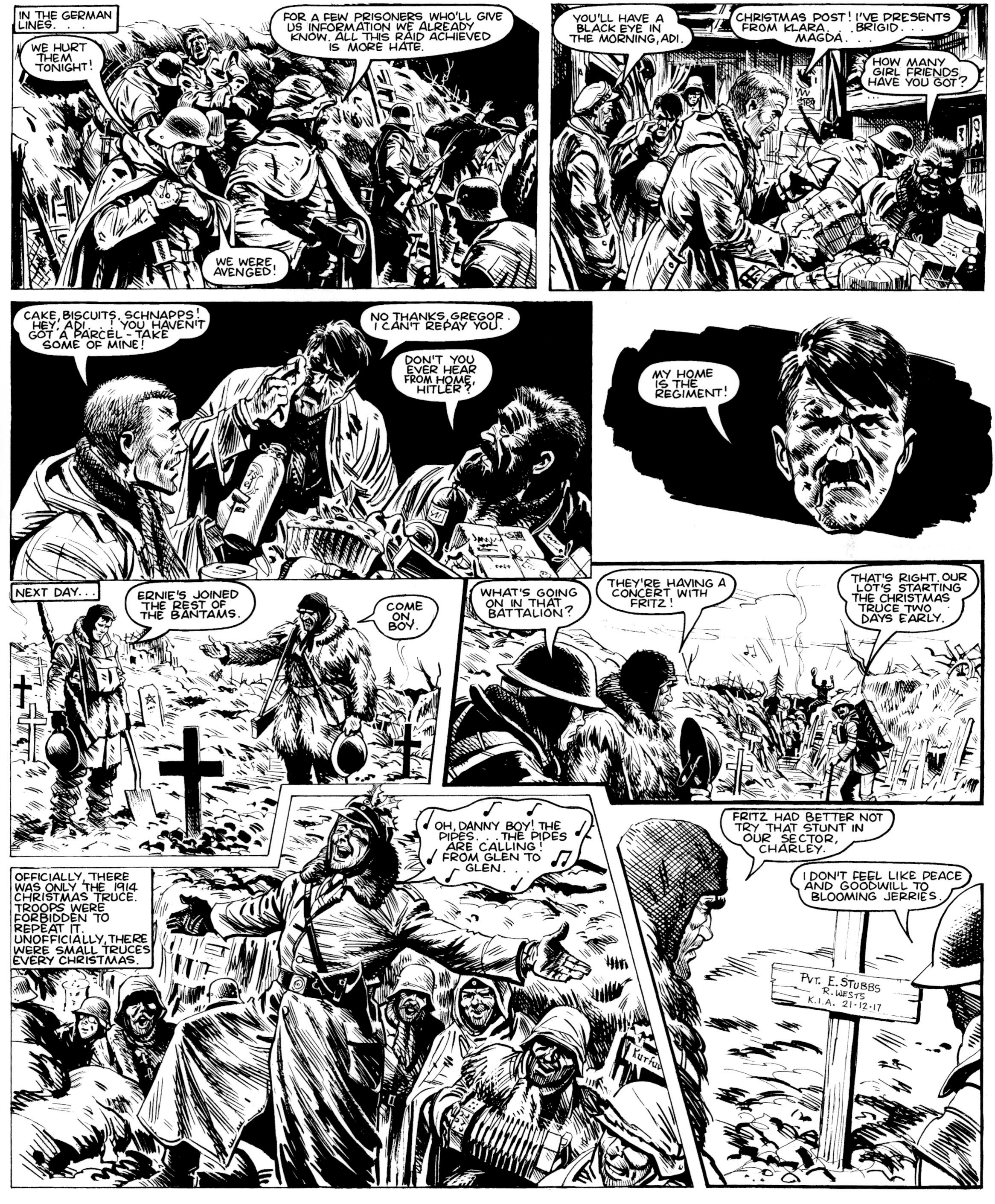
IN THE GERMAN LINES. . .
WE HURT THEM TONIGHT!
FOR A FEW PRISONERS WHO'LL GIVE US INFORMATION WE ALREADY KNOW. ALL THIS RAID ACHIEVED IS MORE HATE.
WE WERE AVENGED!
YOU'LL HAVE A BLACK EYE IN THE MORNING, ADI.
CHRISTMAS POST! I'VE PRESENTS FROM KLARA. . . BRIGID. . . MAGDA. . .
HOW MANY GIRL FRIENDS HAVE YOU GOT?
CAKE, BISCUITS, SCHNAPPS! HEY, ADI. . .! YOU HAVEN'T GOT A PARCEL - TAKE SOME OF MINE!
NO THANKS, GREGOR. I CAN'T REPAY YOU.
DON'T YOU EVER HEAR FROM HOME, HITLER?
MY HOME IS THE REGIMENT!
NEXT DAY. . .
ERNIE'S JOINED THE REST OF THE BANTAMS.
COME ON, BOY.
WHAT'S GOING ON IN THAT BATTALION?
THEY'RE HAVING A CONCERT WITH FRITZ!
THAT'S RIGHT. OUR LOT'S STARTING THE CHRISTMAS TRUCE TWO DAYS EARLY.
OFFICIALLY, THERE WAS ONLY THE 1914 CHRISTMAS TRUCE. TROOPS WERE FORBIDDEN TO REPEAT IT. UNOFFICIALLY, THERE WERE SMALL TRUCES EVERY CHRISTMAS.
OH, DANNY BOY! THE PIPES. . . THE PIPES ARE CALLING! FROM GLEN TO GLEN. . .
FRITZ HAD BETTER NOT TRY THAT STUNT IN OUR SECTOR, CHARLEY.
I DON'T FEEL LIKE PEACE AND GOODWILL TO BLOOMING JERRIES.
PVT. E. STUBBS
R. WESTS
K.I.A. 21·12·17

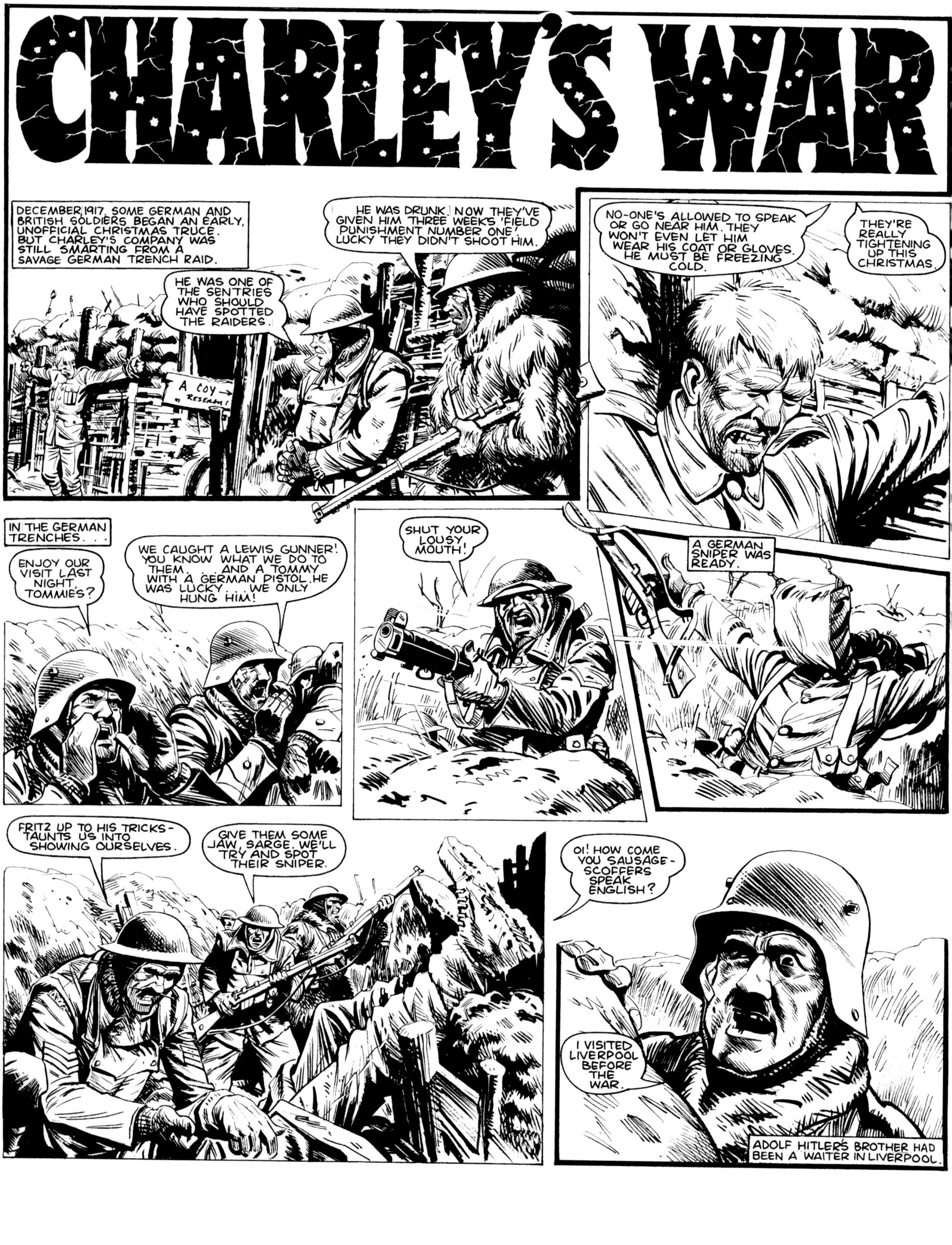
CHARLEY'S WAR
DECEMBER 1917. SOME GERMAN AND BRITISH SOLDIERS BEGAN AN EARLY, UNOFFICIAL CHRISTMAS TRUCE. BUT CHARLEY'S COMPANY WAS STILL SMARTING FROM A SAVAGE GERMAN TRENCH RAID.
HE WAS ONE OF THE SENTRIES WHO SHOULD HAVE SPOTTED THE RAIDERS.
HE WAS DRUNK! NOW THEY'VE GIVEN HIM THREE WEEKS 'FIELD PUNISHMENT NUMBER ONE'. LUCKY THEY DIDN'T SHOOT HIM.
A COY RESERVE!
NO-ONE'S ALLOWED TO SPEAK OR GO NEAR HIM. THEY WON'T EVEN LET HIM WEAR HIS COAT OR GLOVES. HE MUST BE FREEZING COLD.
THEY'RE REALLY TIGHTENING UP THIS CHRISTMAS.
IN THE GERMAN TRENCHES . . .
ENJOY OUR VISIT LAST NIGHT, TOMMIES?
WE CAUGHT A LEWIS GUNNER! YOU KNOW WHAT WE DO TO THEM. . . AND A TOMMY WITH A GERMAN PISTOL. HE WAS LUCKY . . . WE ONLY HUNG HIM!
SHUT YOUR LOUSY MOUTH!
A GERMAN SNIPER WAS READY.
FRITZ UP TO HIS TRICKS - TAUNTS US INTO SHOWING OURSELVES.
GIVE THEM SOME JAW, SARGE. WE'LL TRY AND SPOT THEIR SNIPER.
OI! HOW COME YOU SAUSAGE-SCOFFERS SPEAK ENGLISH?
I VISITED LIVERPOOL BEFORE THE WAR.
ADOLF HITLER'S BROTHER HAD BEEN A WAITER IN LIVERPOOL.

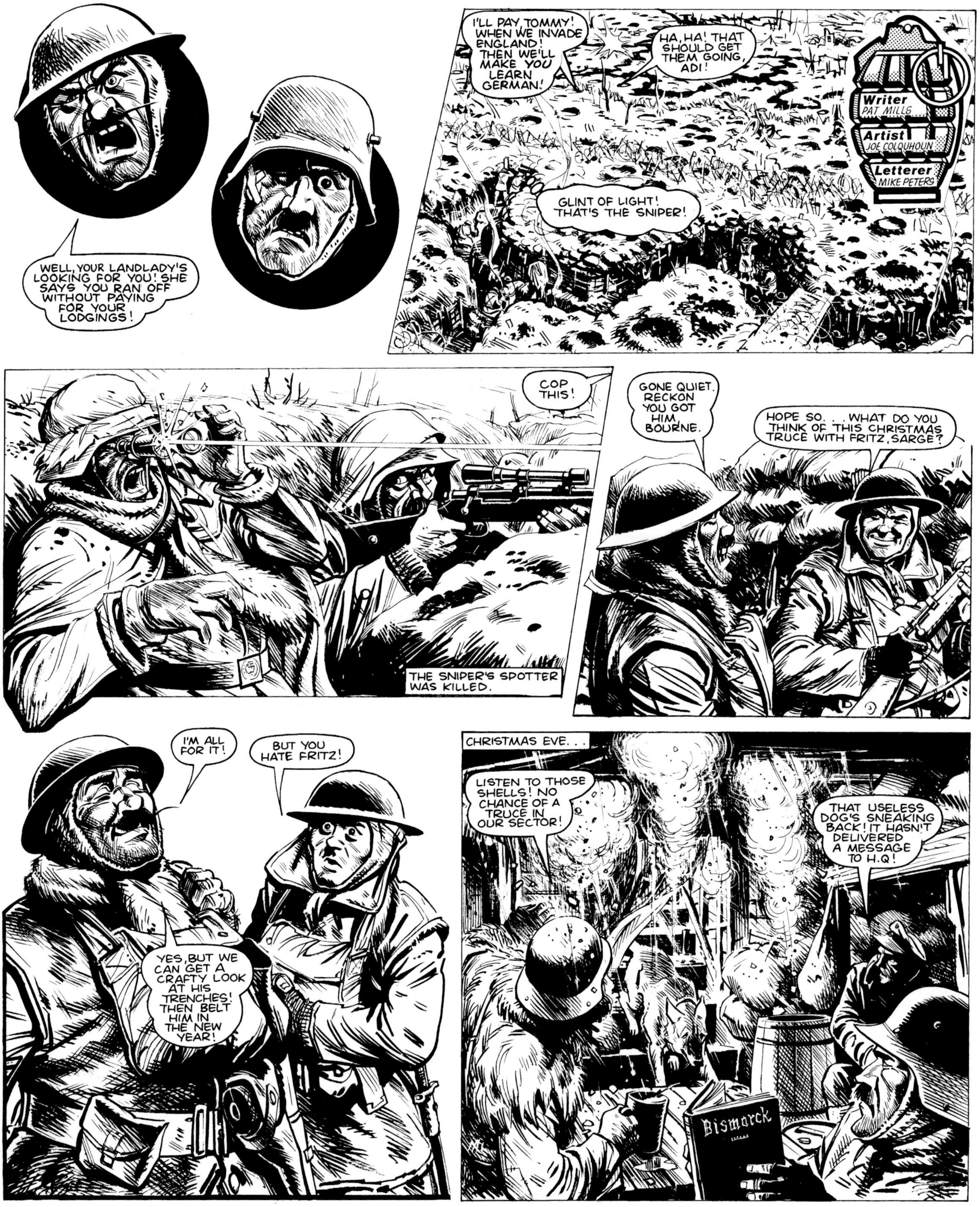
WELL, YOUR LANDLADY'S LOOKING FOR YOU! SHE SAYS YOU RAN OFF WITHOUT PAYING FOR YOUR LODGINGS!
I'LL PAY TOMMY! WHEN WE INVADE ENGLAND! THEN WE'LL MAKE YOU LEARN GERMAN!
HA, HA! THAT SHOULD GET THEM GOING, ADI!
Writer PAT MILLS
Artist JOE COLQUHOUN
Letterer MIKE PETERS
GLINT OF LIGHT! THAT'S THE SNIPER!
COP THIS!
THE SNIPER'S SPOTTER WAS KILLED.
GONE QUIET. RECKON YOU GOT HIM, BOURNE.
HOPE SO. . . WHAT DO YOU THINK OF THIS CHRISTMAS TRUCE WITH FRITZ, SARGE?
I'M ALL FOR IT!
BUT YOU HATE FRITZ!
YES, BUT WE CAN GET A CRAFTY LOOK AT HIS TRENCHES! THEN BELT HIM IN THE NEW YEAR!
CHRISTMAS EVE. . .
LISTEN TO THOSE SHELLS! NO CHANCE OF A TRUCE IN OUR SECTOR!
THAT USELESS DOG'S SNEAKING BACK! IT HASN'T DELIVERED A MESSAGE TO H.Q!
Bismarck

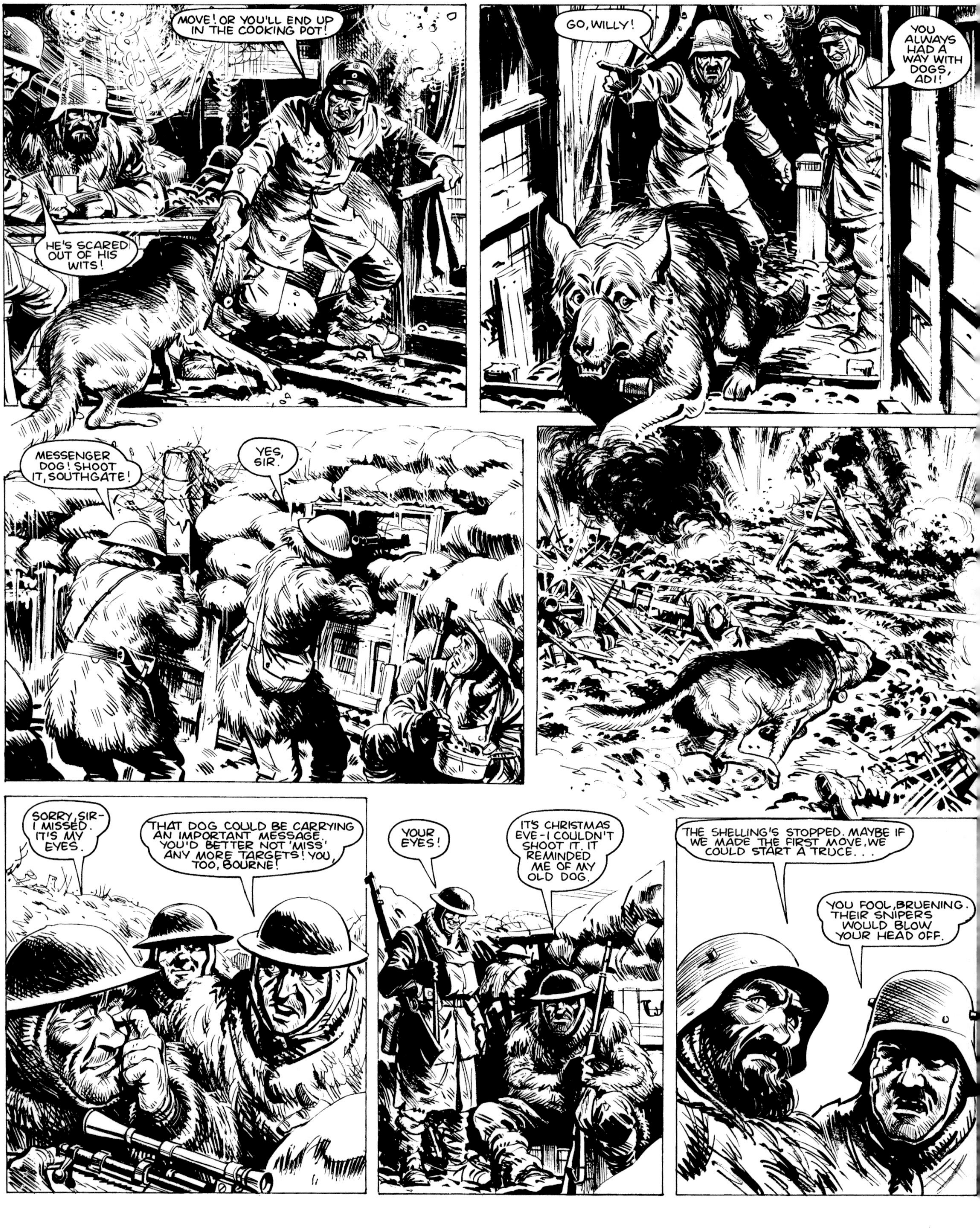
MOVE! OR YOU'LL END UP IN THE COOKING POT!
HE'S SCARED OUT OF HIS WITS!
GO, WILLY!
YOU ALWAYS HAD A WAY WITH DOGS, ADI!
MESSENGER DOG! SHOOT IT, SOUTHGATE!
YES, SIR.
SORRY, SIR- I MISSED. IT'S MY EYES.
THAT DOG COULD BE CARRYING AN IMPORTANT MESSAGE. YOU'D BETTER NOT 'MISS' ANY MORE TARGETS! YOU, TOO, BOURNE!
YOUR EYES!
IT'S CHRISTMAS EVE - I COULDN'T SHOOT IT. IT REMINDED ME OF MY OLD DOG.
THE SHELLING'S STOPPED. MAYBE IF WE MADE THE FIRST MOVE, WE COULD START A TRUCE...
YOU FOOL, BRUENING. THEIR SNIPERS WOULD BLOW YOUR HEAD OFF.

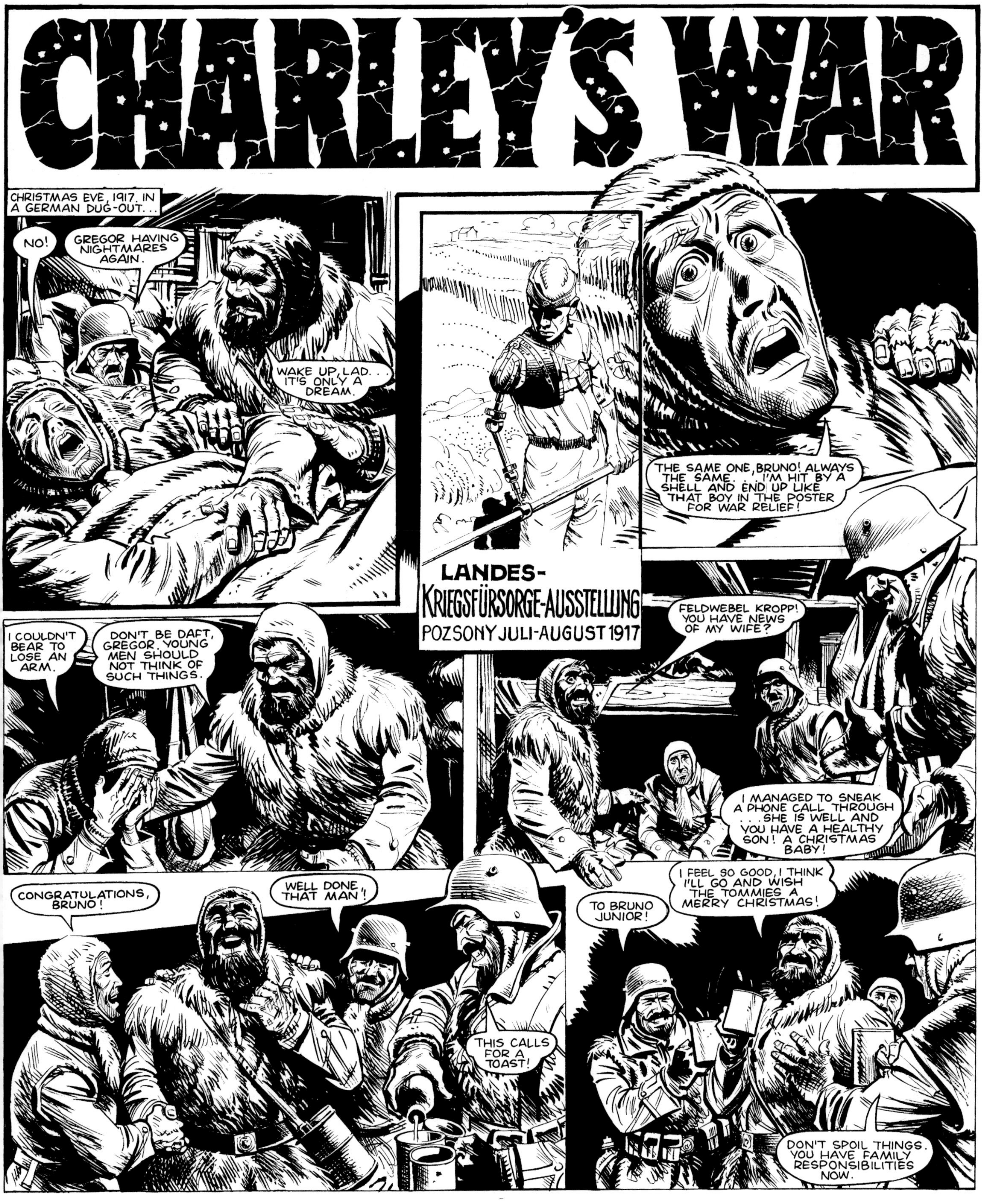
CHARLEY'S WAR
CHRISTMAS EVE, 1917. IN A GERMAN DUG-OUT...
NO!
GREGOR HAVING NIGHTMARES AGAIN.
WAKE UP, LAD... IT'S ONLY A DREAM.
LANDES-
KRIEGSFÜRSORGE-AUSSTELLUNG
POZSONY JULI-AUGUST 1917
THE SAME ONE, BRUNO! ALWAYS THE SAME... I'M HIT BY A SHELL AND END UP LIKE THAT BOY IN THE POSTER FOR WAR RELIEF!
I COULDN'T BEAR TO LOSE AN ARM.
DON'T BE DAFT, GREGOR. YOUNG MEN SHOULD NOT THINK OF SUCH THINGS.
FELDWEBEL KROPP! YOU HAVE NEWS OF MY WIFE?
I MANAGED TO SNEAK A PHONE CALL THROUGH... SHE IS WELL AND YOU HAVE A HEALTHY SON! A CHRISTMAS BABY!
CONGRATULATIONS, BRUNO!
WELL DONE, THAT MAN!
THIS CALLS FOR A TOAST!
TO BRUNO JUNIOR!
I FEEL SO GOOD, I THINK I'LL GO AND WISH THE TOMMIES A MERRY CHRISTMAS!
DON'T SPOIL THINGS. YOU HAVE FAMILY RESPONSIBILITIES NOW.

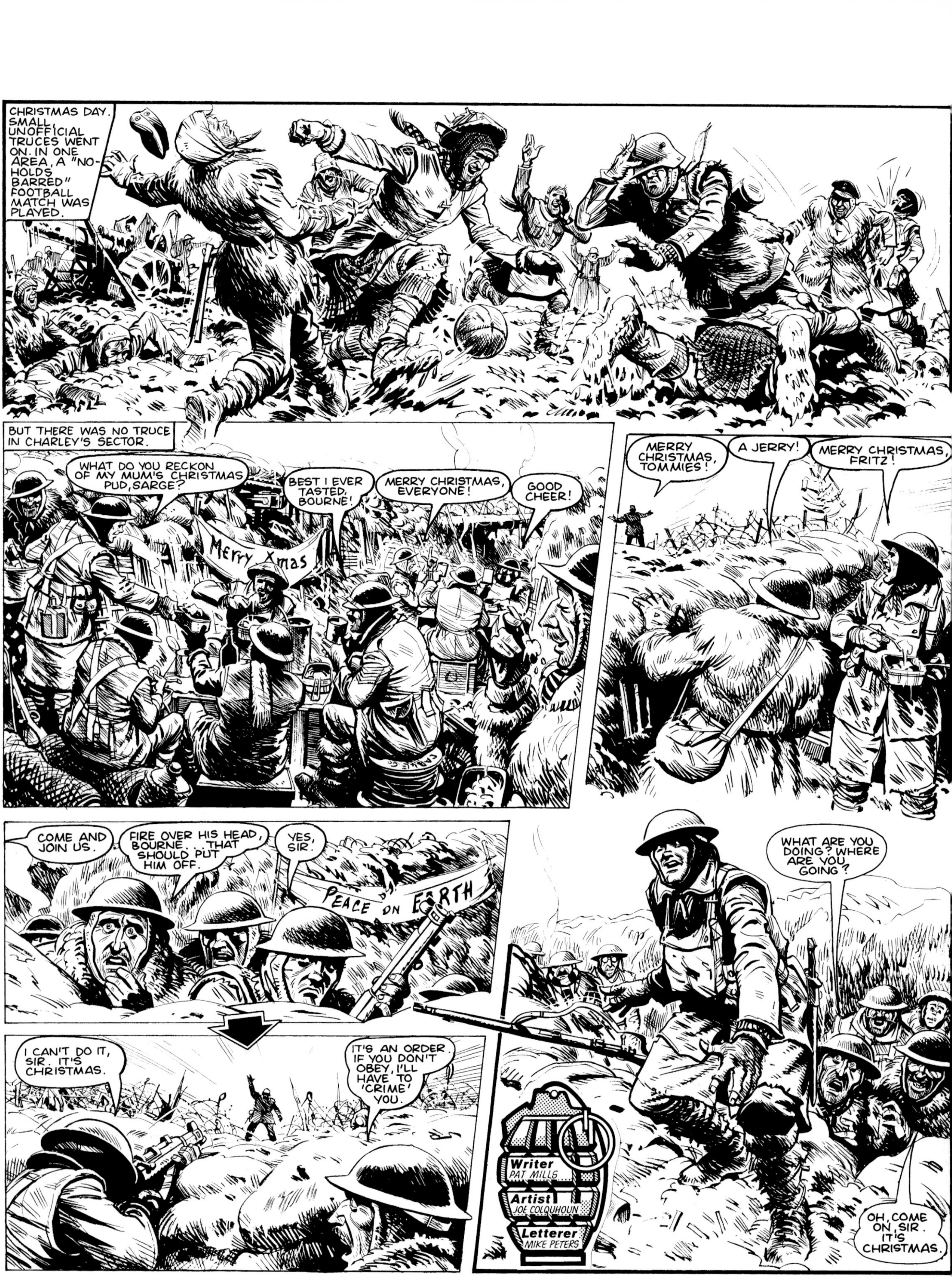

CHRISTMAS DAY. SMALL, UNOFFICIAL TRUCES WENT ON. IN ONE AREA, A "NO-HOLDS BARRED" FOOTBALL MATCH WAS PLAYED.
BUT THERE WAS NO TRUCE IN CHARLEY'S SECTOR.
WHAT DO YOU RECKON OF MY MUM'S CHRISTMAS PUD, SARGE?
BEST I EVER TASTED, BOURNE!
MERRY CHRISTMAS, EVERYONE!
GOOD CHEER!
Merry Xmas
MERRY CHRISTMAS, TOMMIES!
A JERRY!
MERRY CHRISTMAS, FRITZ!
COME AND JOIN US.
FIRE OVER HIS HEAD, BOURNE... THAT SHOULD PUT HIM OFF.
YES, SIR.
PEACE ON EARTH
I CAN'T DO IT, SIR. IT'S CHRISTMAS.
IT'S AN ORDER. IF YOU DON'T OBEY, I'LL HAVE TO 'CRIME' YOU.
WHAT ARE YOU DOING? WHERE ARE YOU GOING?
Writer PAT MILLS
Artist JOE COLQUHOUN
Letterer MIKE PETERS
OH, COME ON, SIR. IT'S CHRISTMAS.

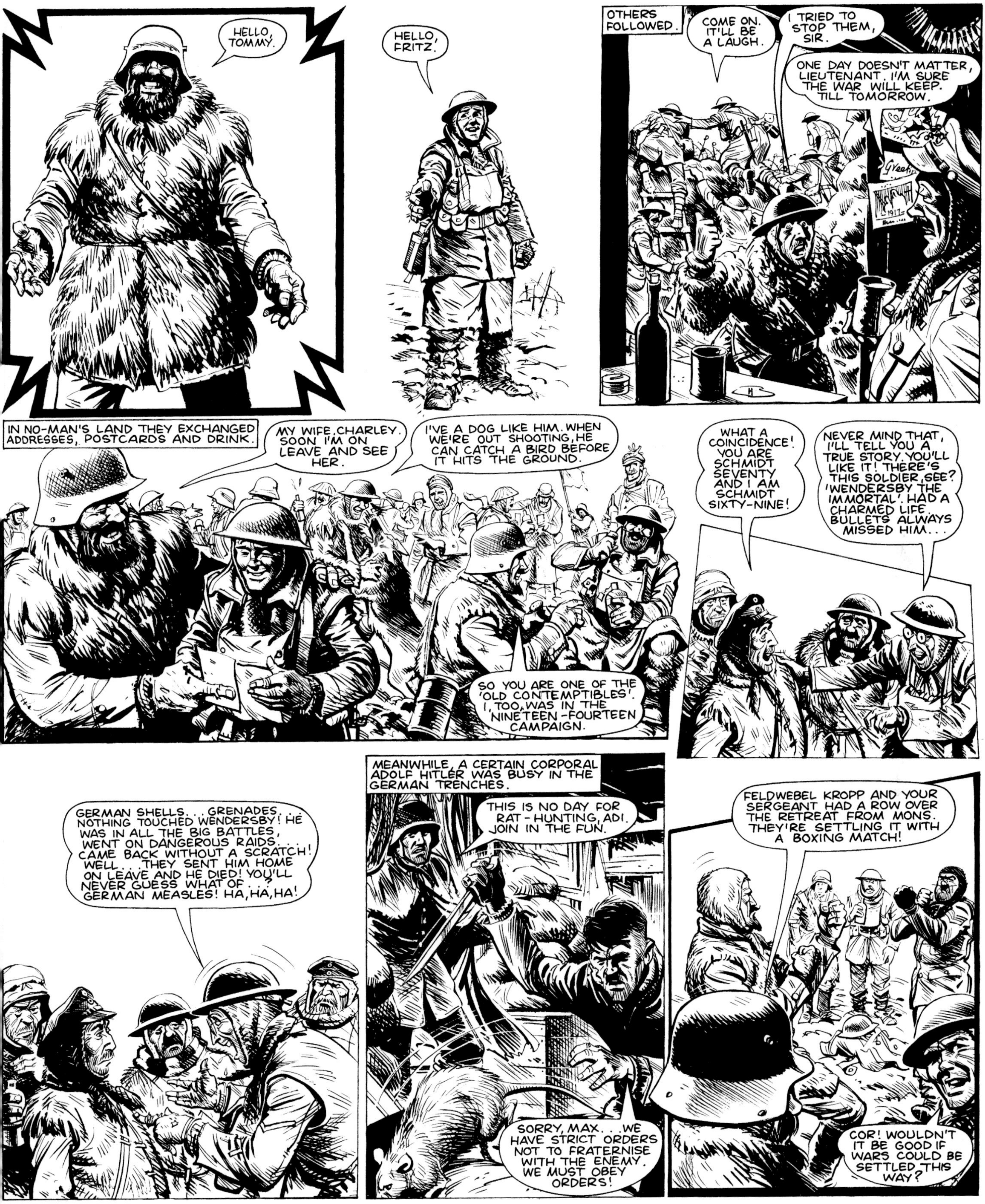
HELLO, TOMMY.
HELLO, FRITZ.
OTHERS FOLLOWED.
COME ON. IT'LL BE A LAUGH.
I TRIED TO STOP THEM, SIR.
ONE DAY DOESN'T MATTER, LIEUTENANT. I'M SURE THE WAR WILL KEEP. TILL TOMORROW.
IN NO-MAN'S LAND THEY EXCHANGED ADDRESSES, POSTCARDS AND DRINK.
MY WIFE, CHARLEY. SOON I'M ON LEAVE AND SEE HER.
I'VE A DOG LIKE HIM. WHEN WE'RE OUT SHOOTING, HE CAN CATCH A BIRD BEFORE IT HITS THE GROUND.
SO YOU ARE ONE OF THE 'OLD CONTEMPTIBLES'. I, TOO, WAS IN THE NINETEEN-FOURTEEN CAMPAIGN.
WHAT A COINCIDENCE! YOU ARE SCHMIDT SEVENTY AND I AM SCHMIDT SIXTY-NINE!
NEVER MIND THAT, I'LL TELL YOU A TRUE STORY. YOU'LL LIKE IT! THERE'S THIS SOLDIER, SEE? 'WENDERSBY THE IMMORTAL'. HAD A CHARMED LIFE. BULLETS ALWAYS MISSED HIM...
GERMAN SHELLS... GRENADES. NOTHING TOUCHED WENDERSBY! HE WAS IN ALL THE BIG BATTLES, WENT ON DANGEROUS RAIDS... CAME BACK WITHOUT A SCRATCH! WELL... THEY SENT HIM HOME ON LEAVE AND HE DIED! YOU'LL NEVER GUESS WHAT OF...? GERMAN MEASLES! HA, HA, HA!
MEANWHILE, A CERTAIN CORPORAL ADOLF HITLER WAS BUSY IN THE GERMAN TRENCHES.
THIS IS NO DAY FOR RAT-HUNTING, ADI. JOIN IN THE FUN.
SORRY, MAX... WE HAVE STRICT ORDERS NOT TO FRATERNISE WITH THE ENEMY. WE MUST OBEY ORDERS!
FELDWEBEL KROPP AND YOUR SERGEANT HAD A ROW OVER THE RETREAT FROM MONS. THEY'RE SETTLING IT WITH A BOXING MATCH!
COR! WOULDN'T IT BE GOOD IF WARS COULD BE SETTLED THIS WAY?

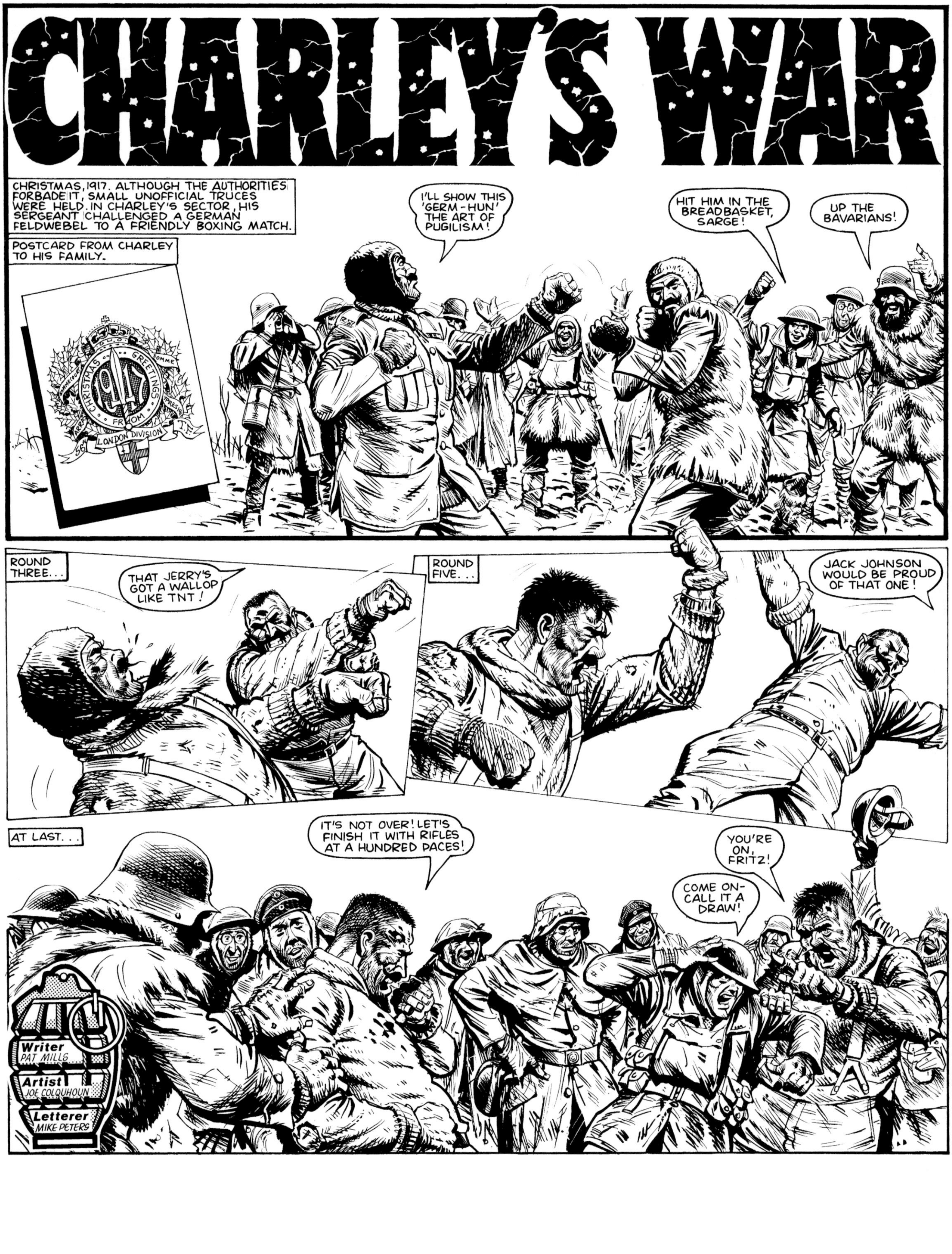
CHARLEY'S WAR
CHRISTMAS, 1917. ALTHOUGH THE AUTHORITIES FORBADE IT, SMALL UNOFFICIAL TRUCES WERE HELD. IN CHARLEY'S SECTOR, HIS SERGEANT CHALLENGED A GERMAN FELDWEBEL TO A FRIENDLY BOXING MATCH.
POSTCARD FROM CHARLEY TO HIS FAMILY.
I'LL SHOW THIS 'GERM-HUN' THE ART OF PUGILISM!
HIT HIM IN THE BREADBASKET, SARGE!
UP THE BAVARIANS!
ROUND THREE...
THAT JERRY'S GOT A WALLOP LIKE TNT!
ROUND FIVE...
JACK JOHNSON WOULD BE PROUD OF THAT ONE!
AT LAST...
IT'S NOT OVER! LET'S FINISH IT WITH RIFLES AT A HUNDRED PACES!
YOU'RE ON, FRITZ!
COME ON- CALL IT A DRAW!
Writer PAT MILLS
Artist JOE COLQUHOUN
Letterer MIKE PETERS

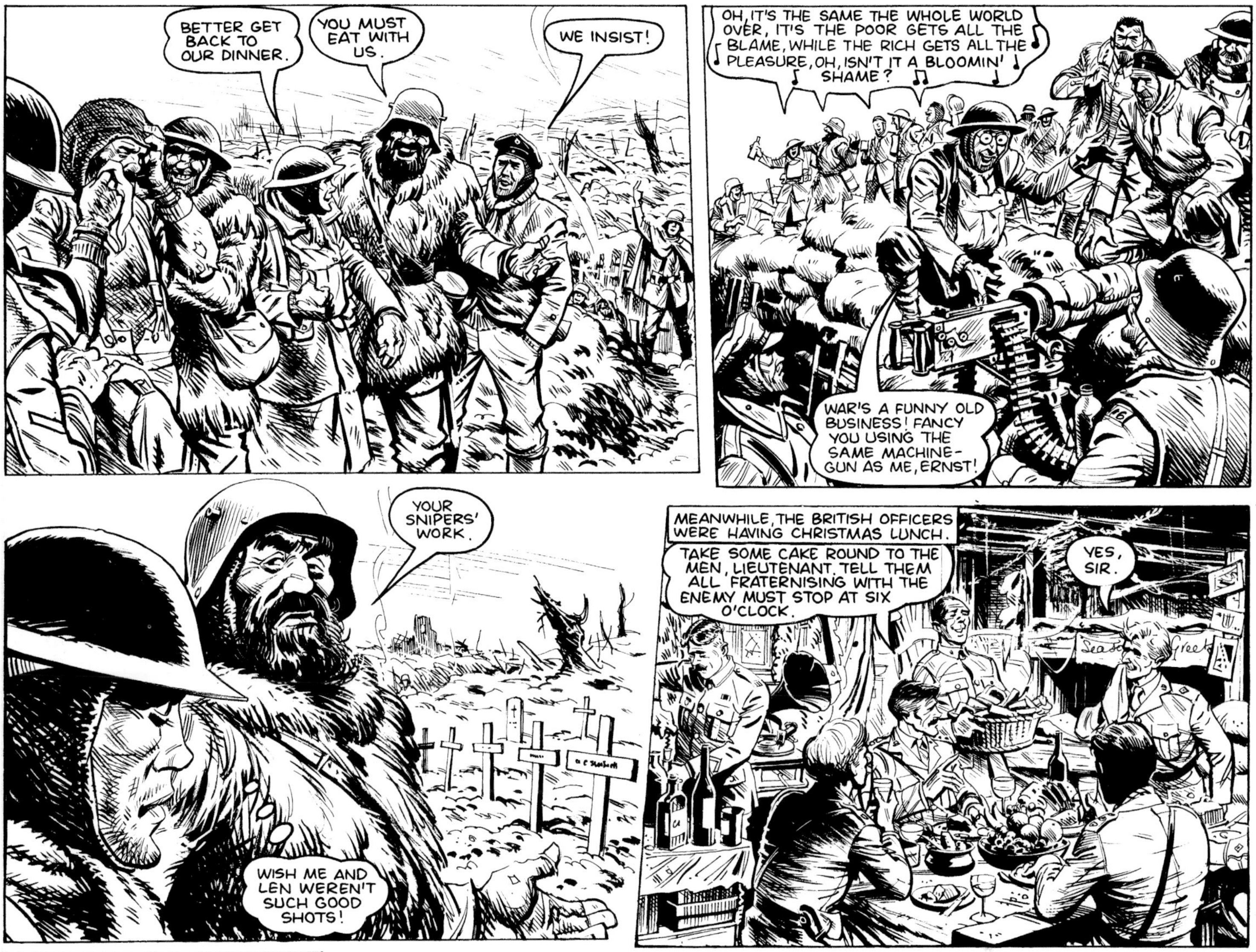
BETTER GET BACK TO OUR DINNER.
YOU MUST EAT WITH US.
WE INSIST!
OH, IT'S THE SAME THE WHOLE WORLD OVER, IT'S THE POOR GETS ALL THE BLAME, WHILE THE RICH GETS ALL THE PLEASURE, OH, ISN'T IT A BLOOMIN' SHAME?
WAR'S A FUNNY OLD BUSINESS! FANCY YOU USING THE SAME MACHINE-GUN AS ME, ERNST!
YOUR SNIPERS' WORK.
WISH ME AND LEN WEREN'T SUCH GOOD SHOTS!
MEANWHILE, THE BRITISH OFFICERS WERE HAVING CHRISTMAS LUNCH.
TAKE SOME CAKE ROUND TO THE MEN, LIEUTENANT. TELL THEM ALL FRATERNISING WITH THE ENEMY MUST STOP AT SIX O'CLOCK.
YES, SIR.

SERVANTS WERE EXPECTED TO COOK FIVE COURSE MEALS. THIS WAS A TYPICAL CHRISTMAS MENU...

Turtle Soup
Smoked Salmon

Turkey, Sausages
Roast Potatoes, Cranberry Sauce

Christmas Pudding, Minced Pies
Custard, Rum Butter

Wood Pigeon

Cheese, Caviare

Apples, Oranges, Dates, Figs, Nuts
Turkish Delight, Chocolate

Coffee

Champagne, Wine
Whiskey, Cognac
Port
Liqueurs
Rum Punch

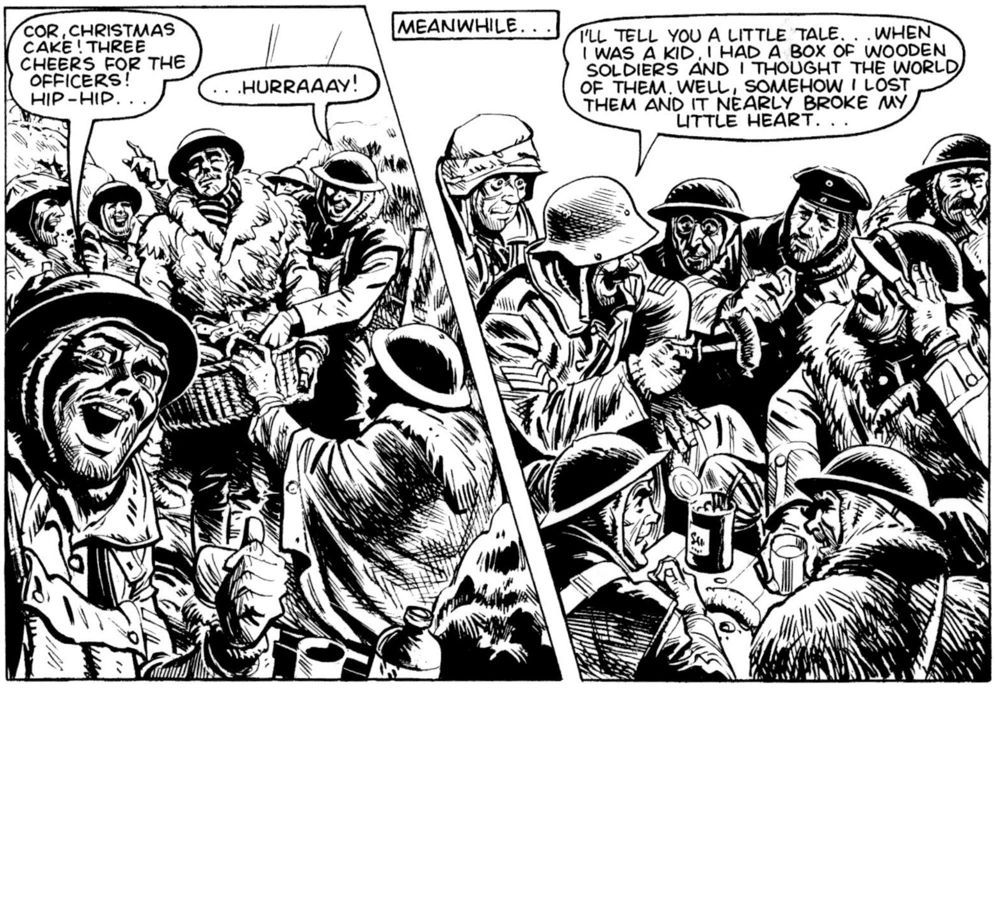
COR, CHRISTMAS CAKE! THREE CHEERS FOR THE OFFICERS! HIP-HIP...
...HURRAAAY!
MEANWHILE...
I'LL TELL YOU A LITTLE TALE... WHEN I WAS A KID, I HAD A BOX OF WOODEN SOLDIERS AND I THOUGHT THE WORLD OF THEM. WELL, SOMEHOW I LOST THEM AND IT NEARLY BROKE MY LITTLE HEART...

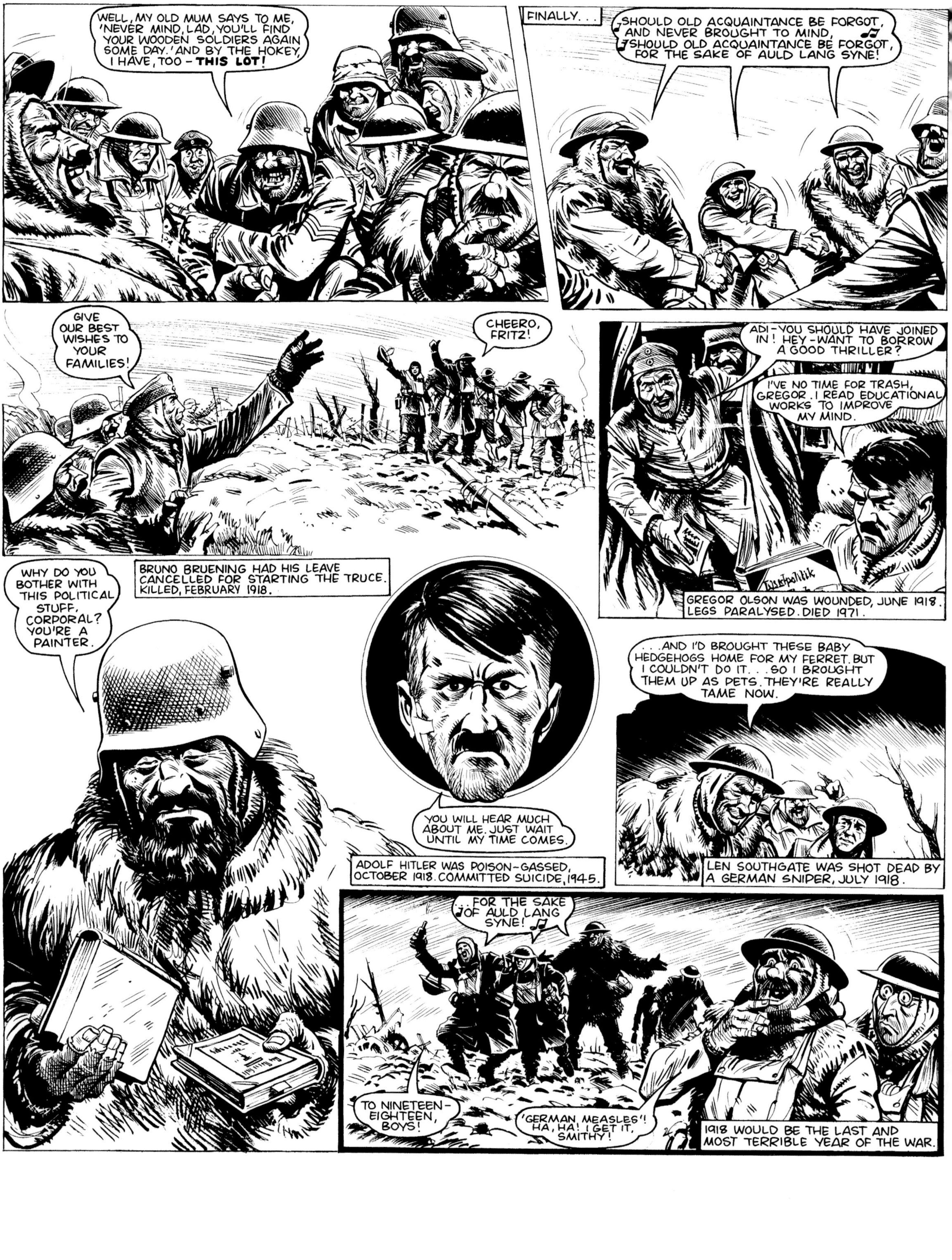

WELL, MY OLD MUM SAYS TO ME, 'NEVER MIND, LAD, YOU'LL FIND YOUR WOODEN SOLDIERS AGAIN SOME DAY.' AND BY THE HOKEY, I HAVE, TOO - **THIS LOT!**
FINALLY...
SHOULD OLD ACQUAINTANCE BE FORGOT, AND NEVER BROUGHT TO MIND, SHOULD OLD ACQUAINTANCE BE FORGOT, FOR THE SAKE OF AULD LANG SYNE!
GIVE OUR BEST WISHES TO YOUR FAMILIES!
CHEERO, FRITZ!
ADI - YOU SHOULD HAVE JOINED IN! HEY - WANT TO BORROW A GOOD THRILLER?
I'VE NO TIME FOR TRASH, GREGOR. I READ EDUCATIONAL WORKS TO IMPROVE MY MIND.
GREGOR OLSON WAS WOUNDED, JUNE 1918. LEGS PARALYSED. DIED 1971.
WHY DO YOU BOTHER WITH THIS POLITICAL STUFF, CORPORAL? YOU'RE A PAINTER.
BRUNO BRUENING HAD HIS LEAVE CANCELLED FOR STARTING THE TRUCE. KILLED, FEBRUARY 1918.
YOU WILL HEAR MUCH ABOUT ME. JUST WAIT UNTIL MY TIME COMES.
ADOLF HITLER WAS POISON-GASSED, OCTOBER 1918. COMMITTED SUICIDE, 1945.
...AND I'D BROUGHT THESE BABY HEDGEHOGS HOME FOR MY FERRET. BUT I COULDN'T DO IT...SO I BROUGHT THEM UP AS PETS. THEY'RE REALLY TAME NOW.
LEN SOUTHGATE WAS SHOT DEAD BY A GERMAN SNIPER, JULY 1918.
...FOR THE SAKE OF AULD LANG SYNE!
TO NINETEEN-EIGHTEEN, BOYS!
'GERMAN MEASLES'! HA, HA! I GET IT, SMITHY!
1918 WOULD BE THE LAST AND MOST TERRIBLE YEAR OF THE WAR.

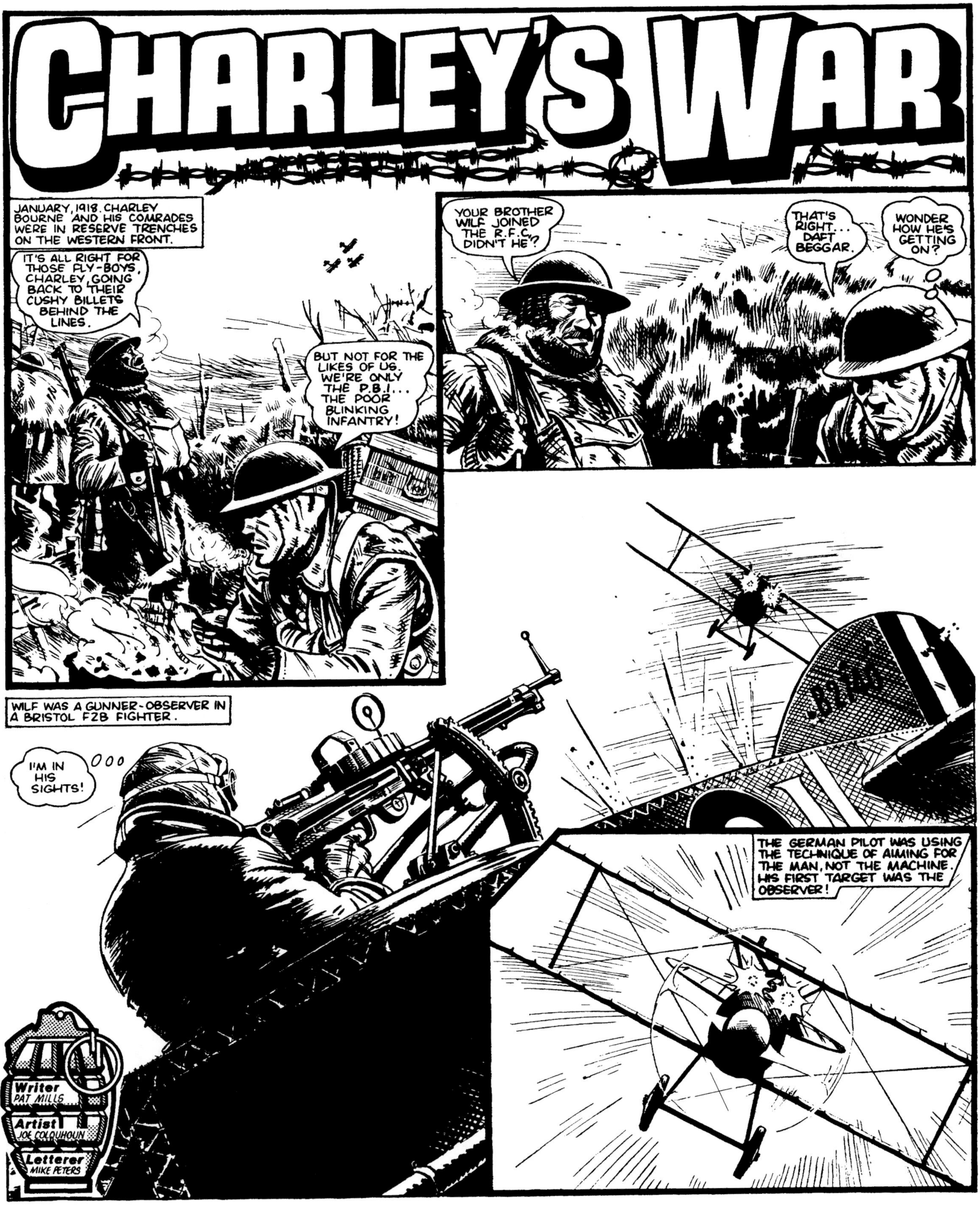
CHARLEY'S WAR
JANUARY, 1918. CHARLEY BOURNE AND HIS COMRADES WERE IN RESERVE TRENCHES ON THE WESTERN FRONT.
IT'S ALL RIGHT FOR THOSE FLY-BOYS, CHARLEY, GOING BACK TO THEIR CUSHY BILLETS BEHIND THE LINES.
BUT NOT FOR THE LIKES OF US. WE'RE ONLY THE P.B.I... THE POOR BLINKING INFANTRY!
YOUR BROTHER WILF JOINED THE R.F.C., DIDN'T HE?
THAT'S RIGHT... DAFT BEGGAR.
WONDER HOW HE'S GETTING ON?
WILF WAS A GUNNER-OBSERVER IN A BRISTOL F2B FIGHTER.
I'M IN HIS SIGHTS!
THE GERMAN PILOT WAS USING THE TECHNIQUE OF AIMING FOR THE MAN, NOT THE MACHINE. HIS FIRST TARGET WAS THE OBSERVER!
Writer PAT MILLS
Artist JOE COLQUHOUN
Letterer MIKE PETERS

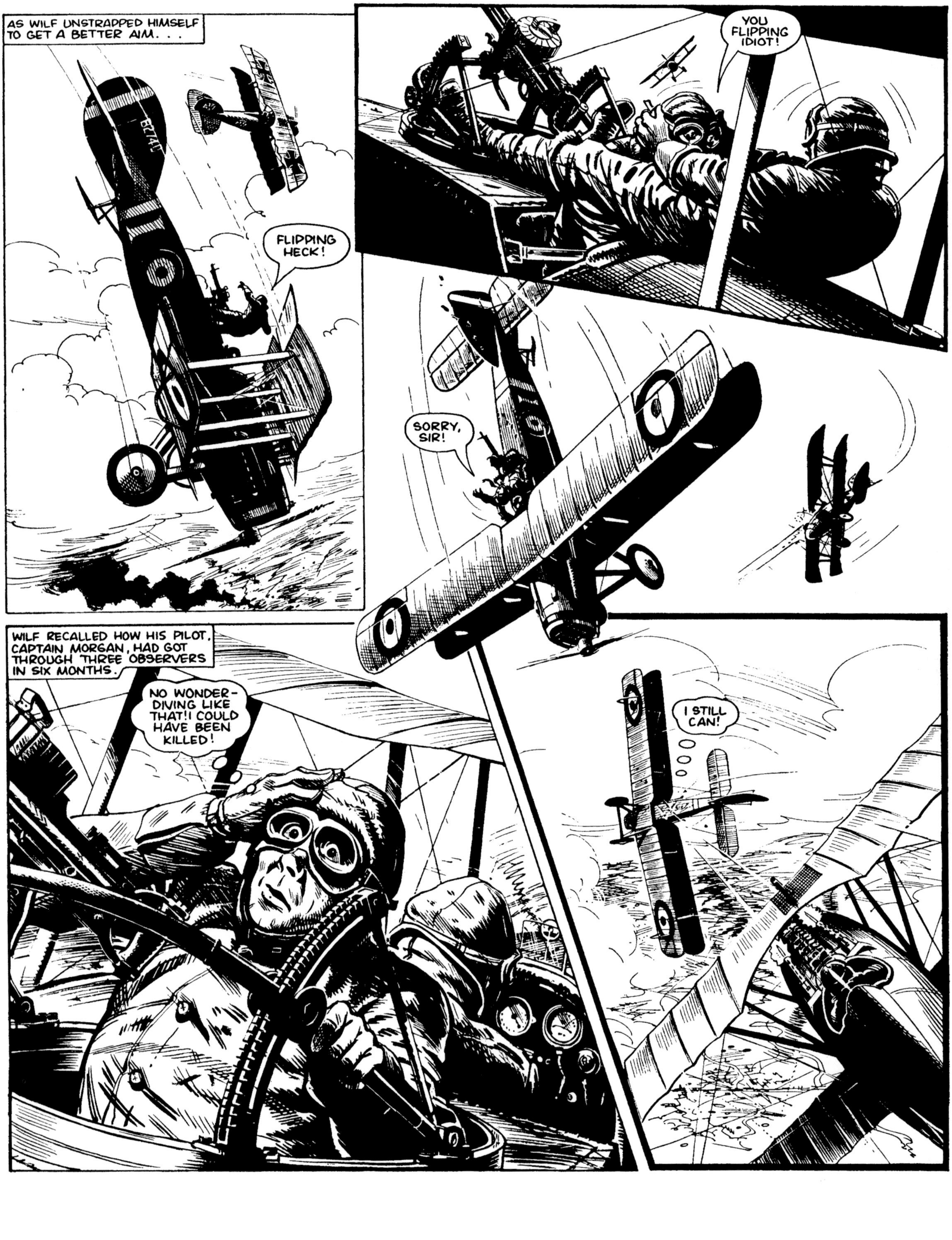
AS WILF UNSTRAPPED HIMSELF TO GET A BETTER AIM. . .
FLIPPING HECK!
YOU FLIPPING IDIOT!
SORRY, SIR!
WILF RECALLED HOW HIS PILOT, CAPTAIN MORGAN, HAD GOT THROUGH THREE OBSERVERS IN SIX MONTHS.
NO WONDER- DIVING LIKE THAT!! COULD HAVE BEEN KILLED!
I STILL CAN!

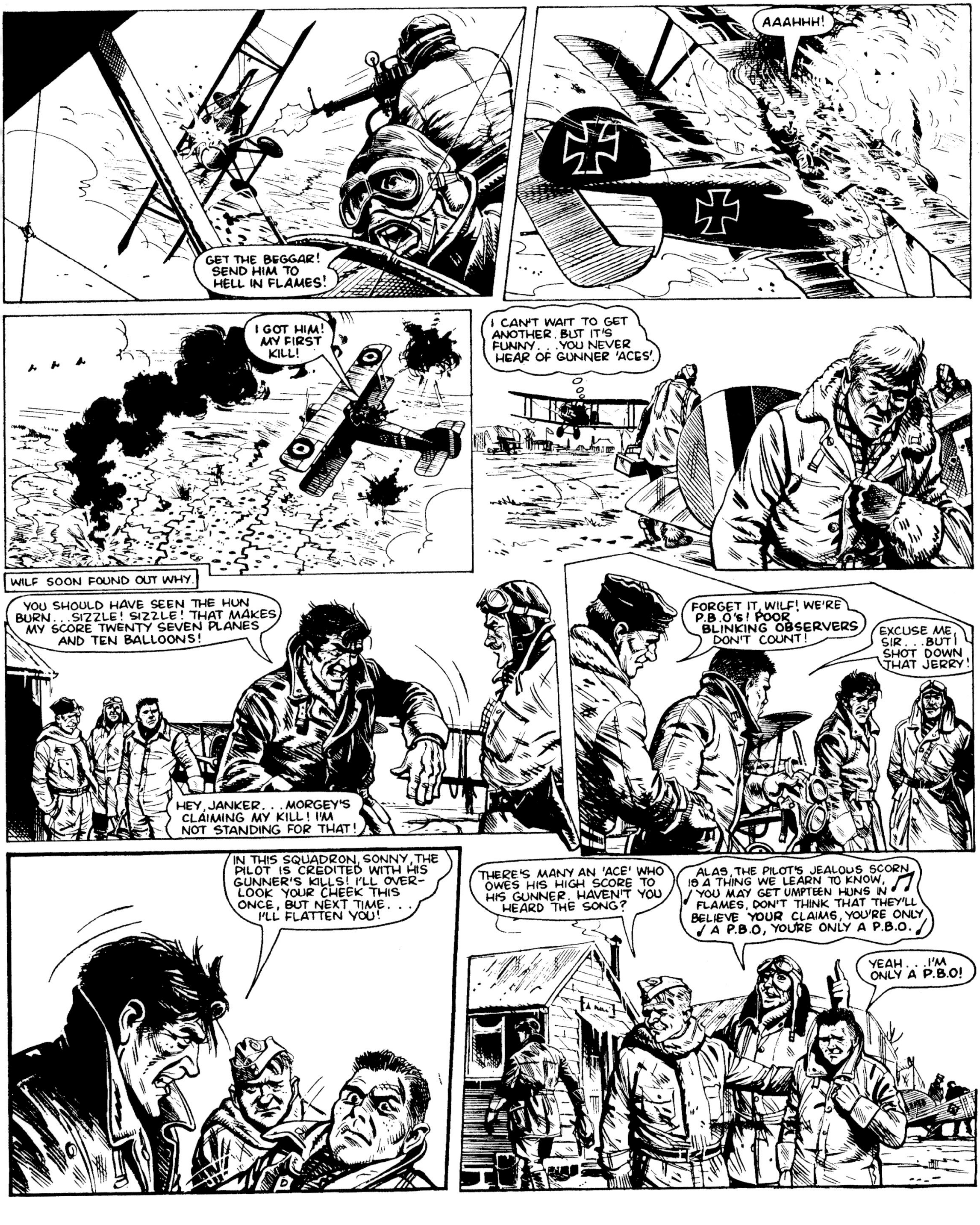
GET THE BEGGAR! SEND HIM TO HELL IN FLAMES!
AAAHHH!
I GOT HIM! MY FIRST KILL!
I CAN'T WAIT TO GET ANOTHER. BUT IT'S FUNNY. . . YOU NEVER HEAR OF GUNNER 'ACES'.
WILF SOON FOUND OUT WHY.
YOU SHOULD HAVE SEEN THE HUN BURN. . . SIZZLE! SIZZLE! THAT MAKES MY SCORE TWENTY SEVEN PLANES AND TEN BALLOONS!
HEY, JANKER. . . MORGEY'S CLAIMING MY KILL! I'M NOT STANDING FOR THAT!
FORGET IT, WILF! WE'RE P.B.O's! POOR BLINKING OBSERVERS DON'T COUNT!
EXCUSE ME, SIR. . . BUT I SHOT DOWN THAT JERRY!
IN THIS SQUADRON, SONNY, THE PILOT IS CREDITED WITH HIS GUNNER'S KILLS! I'LL OVER-LOOK YOUR CHEEK THIS ONCE, BUT NEXT TIME. . . I'LL FLATTEN YOU!
THERE'S MANY AN 'ACE' WHO OWES HIS HIGH SCORE TO HIS GUNNER. HAVEN'T YOU HEARD THE SONG?
ALAS, THE PILOT'S JEALOUS SCORN IS A THING WE LEARN TO KNOW, YOU MAY GET UMPTEEN HUNS IN FLAMES, DON'T THINK THAT THEY'LL BELIEVE YOUR CLAIMS, YOU'RE ONLY A P.B.O, YOU'RE ONLY A P.B.O.
YEAH. . . I'M ONLY A P.B.O!

# CHARLEY'S WAR

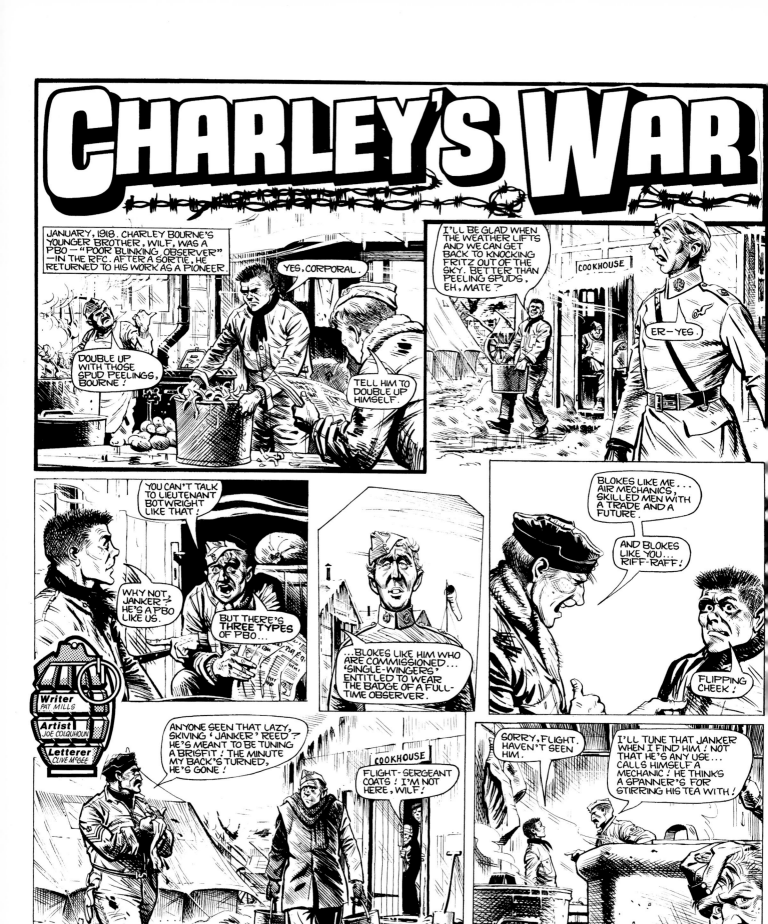

JANUARY, 1918. CHARLEY BOURNE'S YOUNGER BROTHER, WILF, WAS A PBO — "POOR BLINKING OBSERVER" — IN THE RFC. AFTER A SORTIE, HE RETURNED TO HIS WORK AS A PIONEER.

YES, CORPORAL.

DOUBLE UP WITH THOSE SPUD PEELINGS, BOURNE!

TELL HIM TO DOUBLE UP HIMSELF.

I'LL BE GLAD WHEN THE WEATHER LIFTS AND WE CAN GET BACK TO KNOCKING FRITZ OUT OF THE SKY. BETTER THAN PEELING SPUDS, EH, MATE?

COOKHOUSE

ER—YES.

YOU CAN'T TALK TO LIEUTENANT BOTWRIGHT LIKE THAT!

WHY NOT, JANKER? HE'S A PBO LIKE US.

BUT THERE'S THREE TYPES OF PBO...

...BLOKES LIKE HIM WHO ARE COMMISSIONED... 'SINGLE-WINGERS' ENTITLED TO WEAR THE BADGE OF A FULL-TIME OBSERVER.

BLOKES LIKE ME,... AIR MECHANICS, SKILLED MEN WITH A TRADE AND A FUTURE.

AND BLOKES LIKE YOU... RIFF-RAFF!

FLIPPING CHEEK!

**Writer** PAT MILLS

**Artist** JOE COLQUHOUN

**Letterer** CLIVE McGEE

ANYONE SEEN THAT LAZY, SKIVING 'JANKER' REED? HE'S MEANT TO BE TUNING A BRISFIT! THE MINUTE MY BACK'S TURNED, HE'S GONE!

FLIGHT-SERGEANT COATS! I'M NOT HERE, WILF!

COOKHOUSE

SORRY, FLIGHT. HAVEN'T SEEN HIM.

I'LL TUNE THAT JANKER WHEN I FIND HIM! NOT THAT HE'S ANY USE... CALLS HIMSELF A MECHANIC! HE THINKS A SPANNER'S FOR STIRRING HIS TEA WITH!

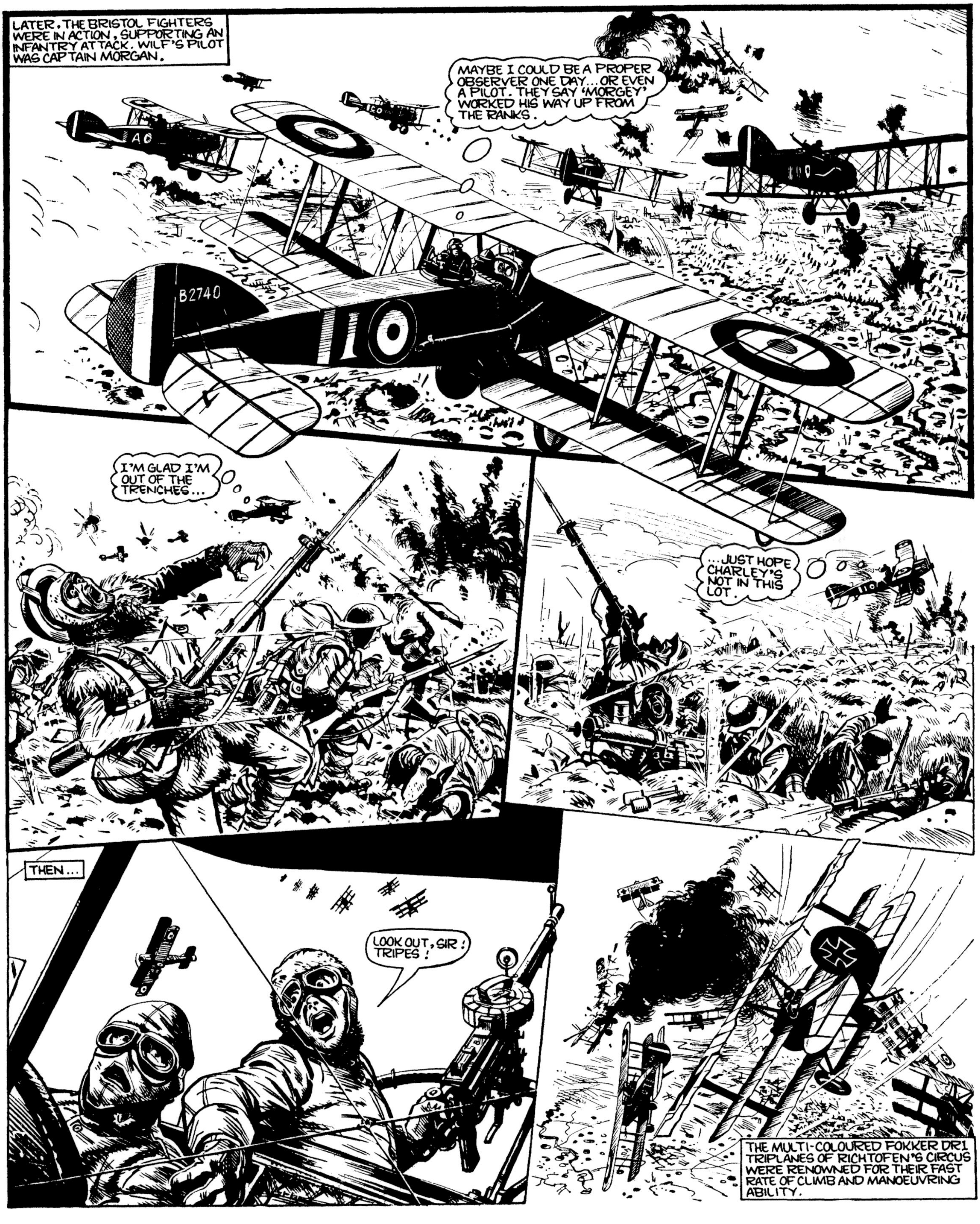
LATER, THE BRISTOL FIGHTERS WERE IN ACTION, SUPPORTING AN INFANTRY ATTACK. WILF'S PILOT WAS CAPTAIN MORGAN.
MAYBE I COULD BE A PROPER OBSERVER ONE DAY... OR EVEN A PILOT. THEY SAY 'MORGEY' WORKED HIS WAY UP FROM THE RANKS.
B2740
I'M GLAD I'M OUT OF THE TRENCHES...
...JUST HOPE CHARLEY'S NOT IN THIS LOT.
THEN...
LOOK OUT, SIR! TRIPES!
THE MULTI-COLOURED FOKKER DR1 TRIPLANES OF RICHTOFEN'S CIRCUS WERE RENOWNED FOR THEIR FAST RATE OF CLIMB AND MANOEUVRING ABILITY.

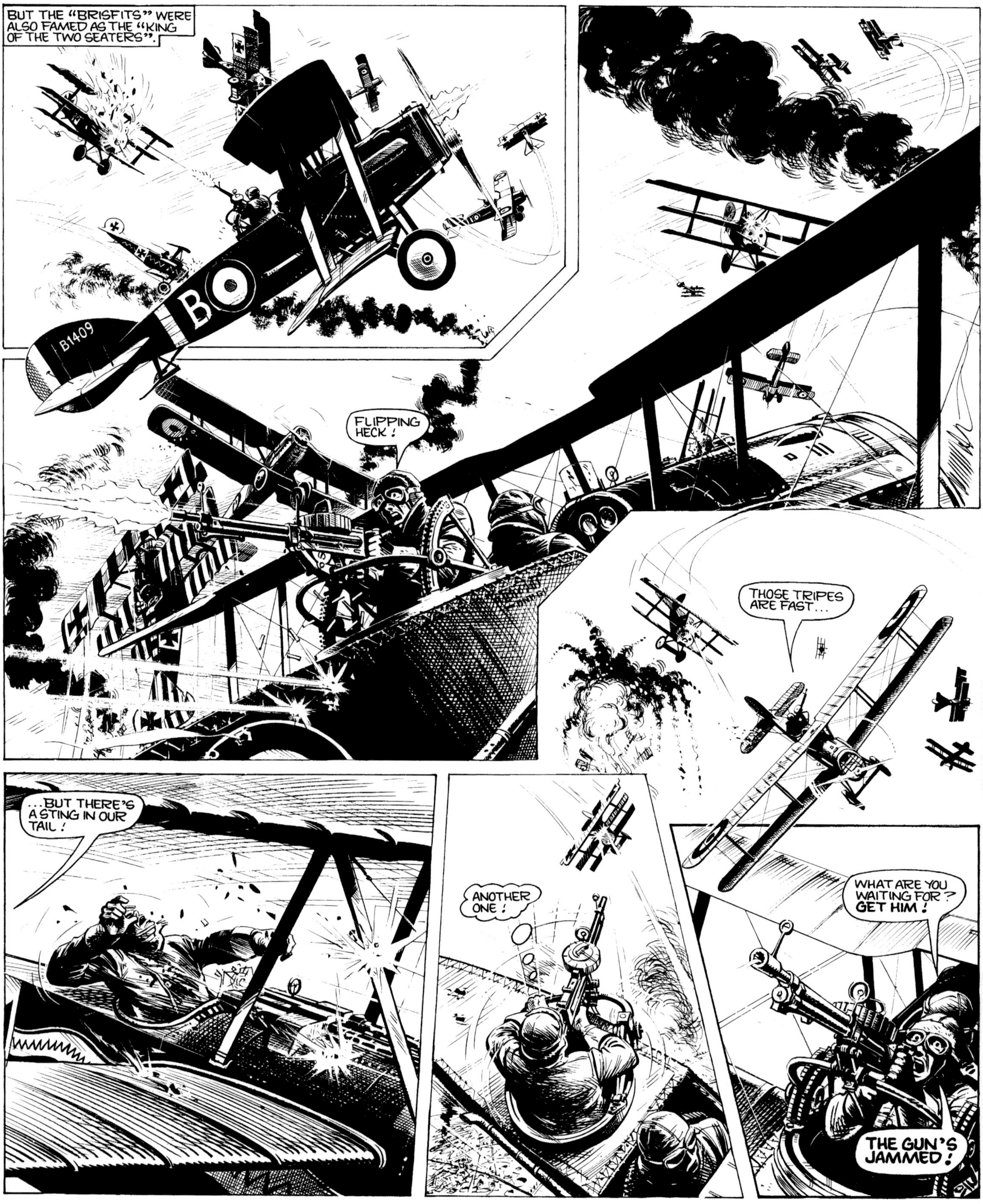
BUT THE "BRISFITS" WERE ALSO FAMED AS THE "KING OF THE TWO SEATERS".
B1409
FLIPPING HECK!
THOSE TRIPES ARE FAST...
...BUT THERE'S A STING IN OUR TAIL!
ANOTHER ONE!
WHAT ARE YOU WAITING FOR? GET HIM!
THE GUN'S JAMMED!

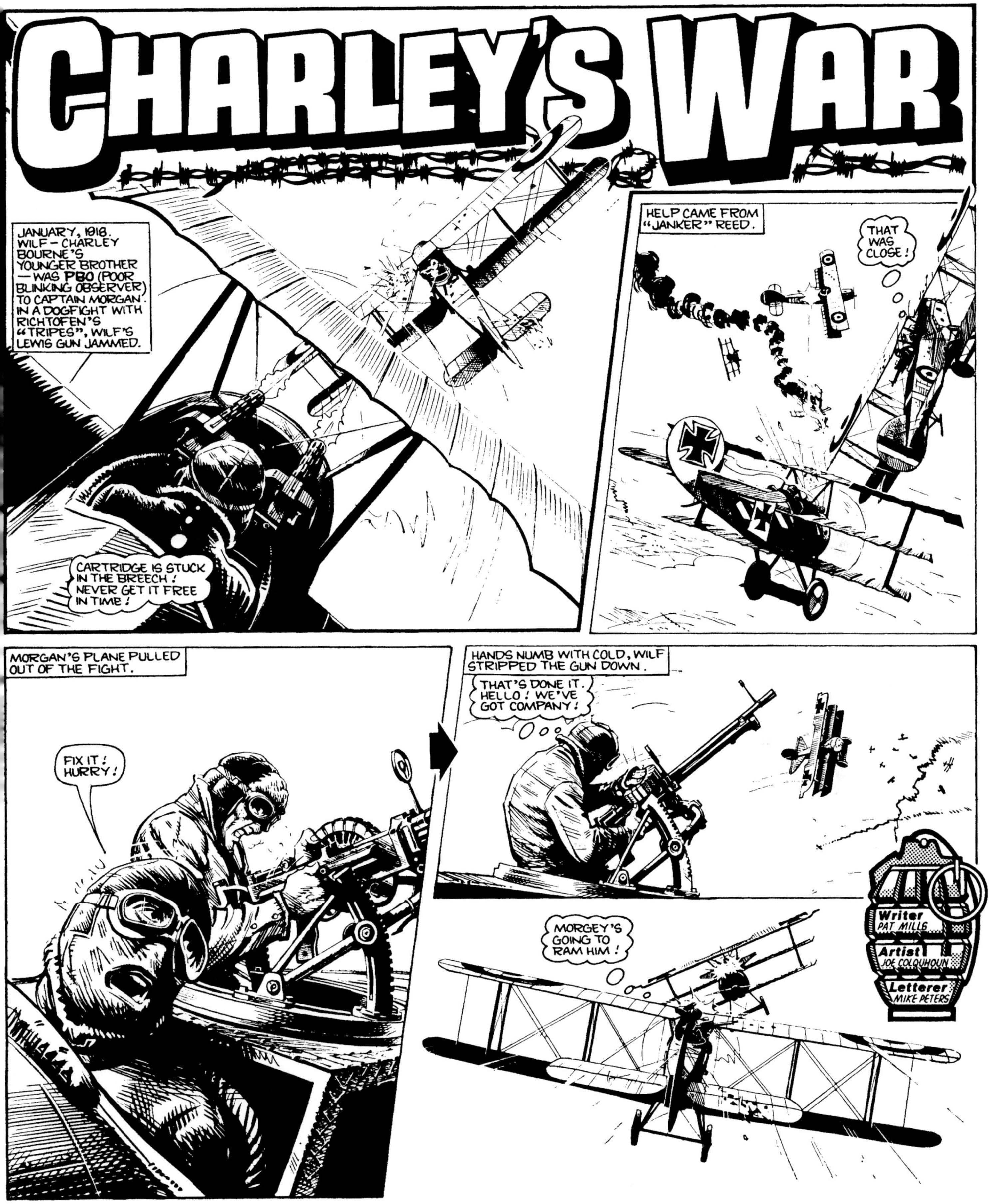

CHARLEY'S WAR
JANUARY, 1918. WILF – CHARLEY BOURNE'S YOUNGER BROTHER — WAS PBO (POOR BLINKING OBSERVER) TO CAPTAIN MORGAN. IN A DOGFIGHT WITH RICHTOFEN'S "TRIPES", WILF'S LEWIS GUN JAMMED.
CARTRIDGE IS STUCK IN THE BREECH! NEVER GET IT FREE IN TIME!
HELP CAME FROM "JANKER" REED.
THAT WAS CLOSE!
MORGAN'S PLANE PULLED OUT OF THE FIGHT.
FIX IT! HURRY!
HANDS NUMB WITH COLD, WILF STRIPPED THE GUN DOWN.
THAT'S DONE IT. HELLO! WE'VE GOT COMPANY!
MORGEY'S GOING TO RAM HIM!
Writer PAT MILLS
Artist JOE COLQUHOUN
Letterer MIKE PETERS

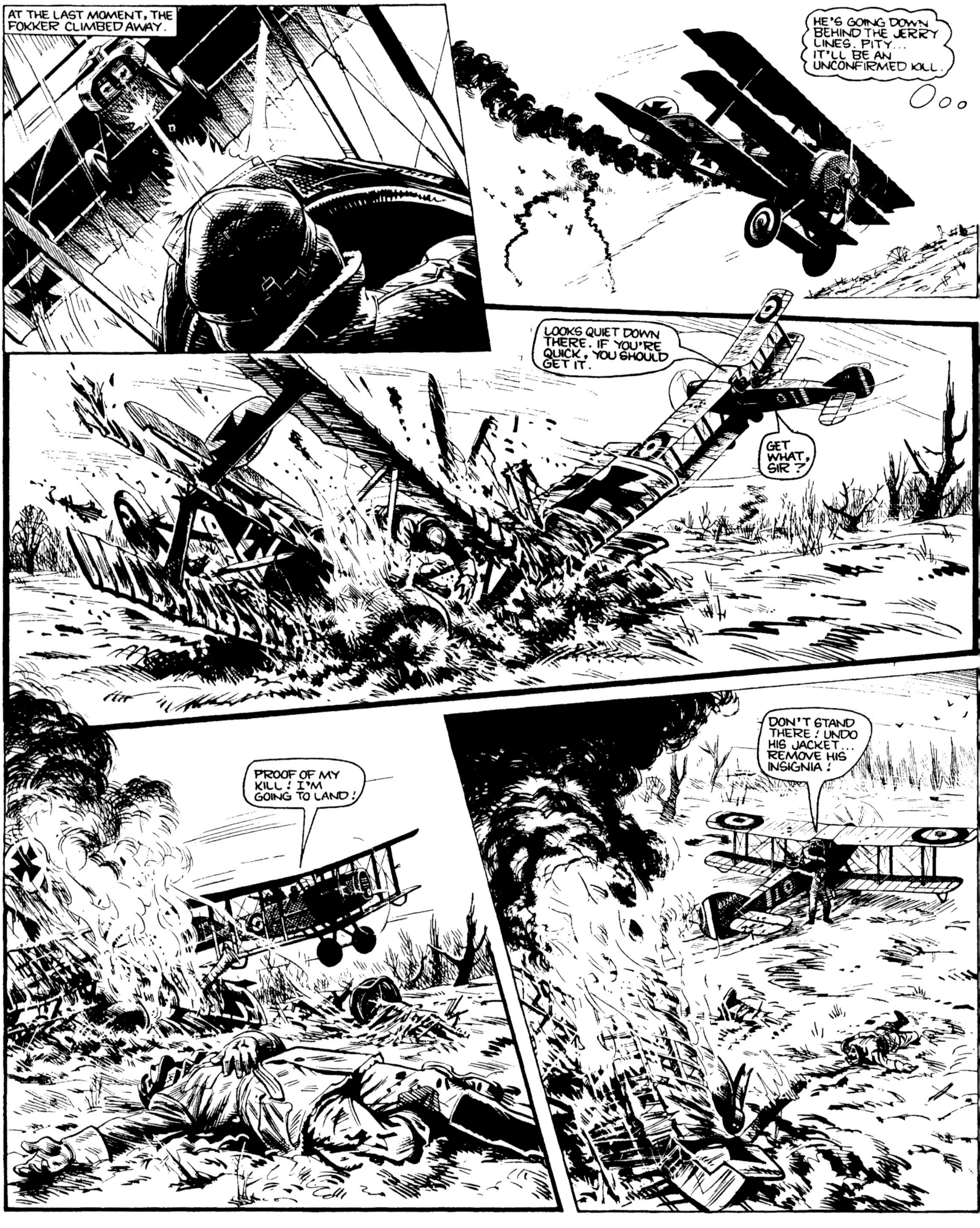
AT THE LAST MOMENT, THE FOKKER CLIMBED AWAY.
HE'S GOING DOWN BEHIND THE JERRY LINES. PITY... IT'LL BE AN UNCONFIRMED KILL.
LOOKS QUIET DOWN THERE. IF YOU'RE QUICK, YOU SHOULD GET IT.
GET WHAT, SIR?
PROOF OF MY KILL! I'M GOING TO LAND!
DON'T STAND THERE! UNDO HIS JACKET... REMOVE HIS INSIGNIA!

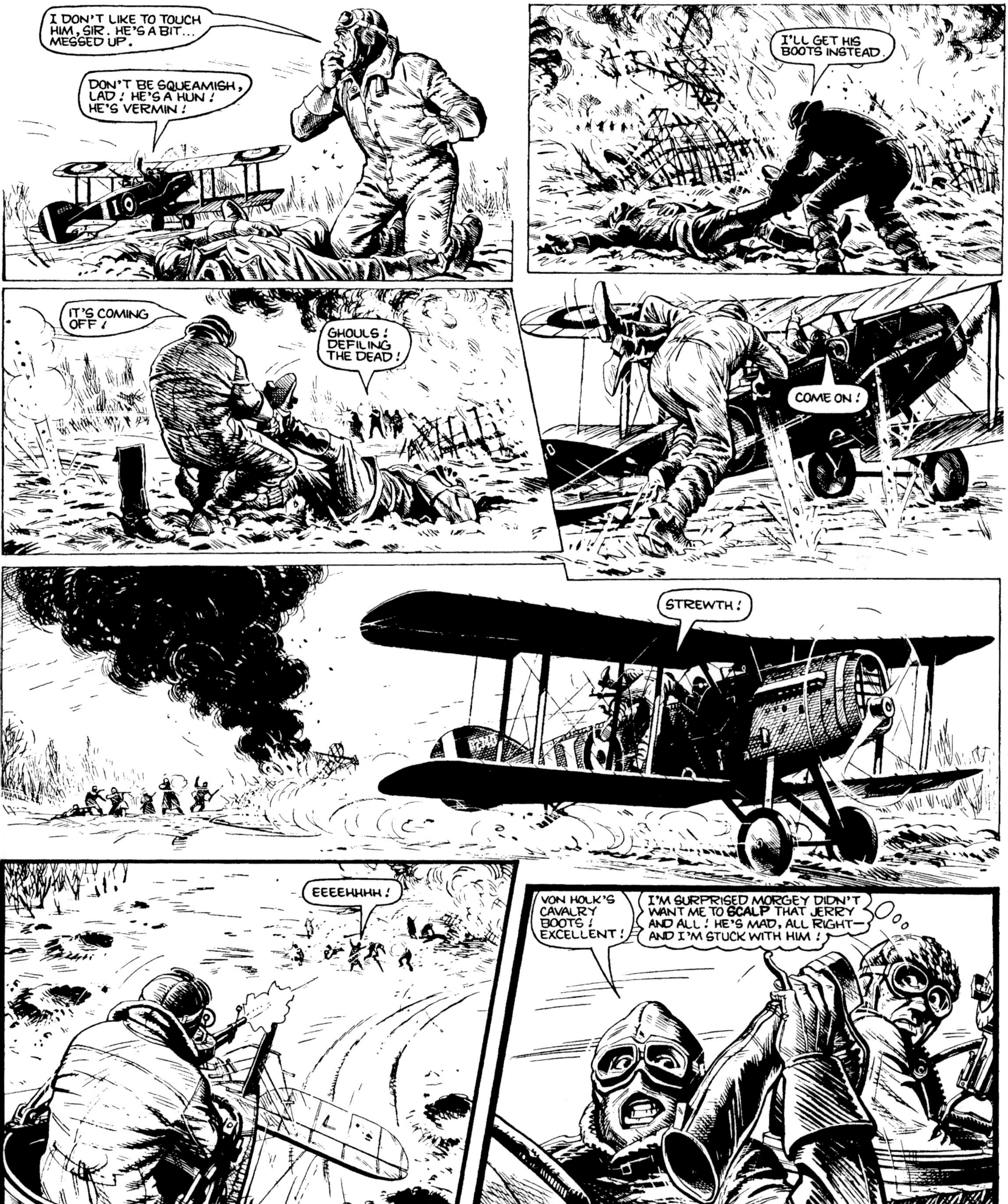

I DON'T LIKE TO TOUCH HIM, SIR. HE'S A BIT... MESSED UP.
DON'T BE SQUEAMISH, LAD! HE'S A HUN! HE'S VERMIN!
I'LL GET HIS BOOTS INSTEAD.
IT'S COMING OFF!
GHOULS! DEFILING THE DEAD!
COME ON!
STREWTH!
EEEEHHHH!
VON HOLK'S CAVALRY BOOTS! EXCELLENT!
I'M SURPRISED MORGEY DIDN'T WANT ME TO SCALP THAT JERRY AND ALL! HE'S MAD, ALL RIGHT— AND I'M STUCK WITH HIM!

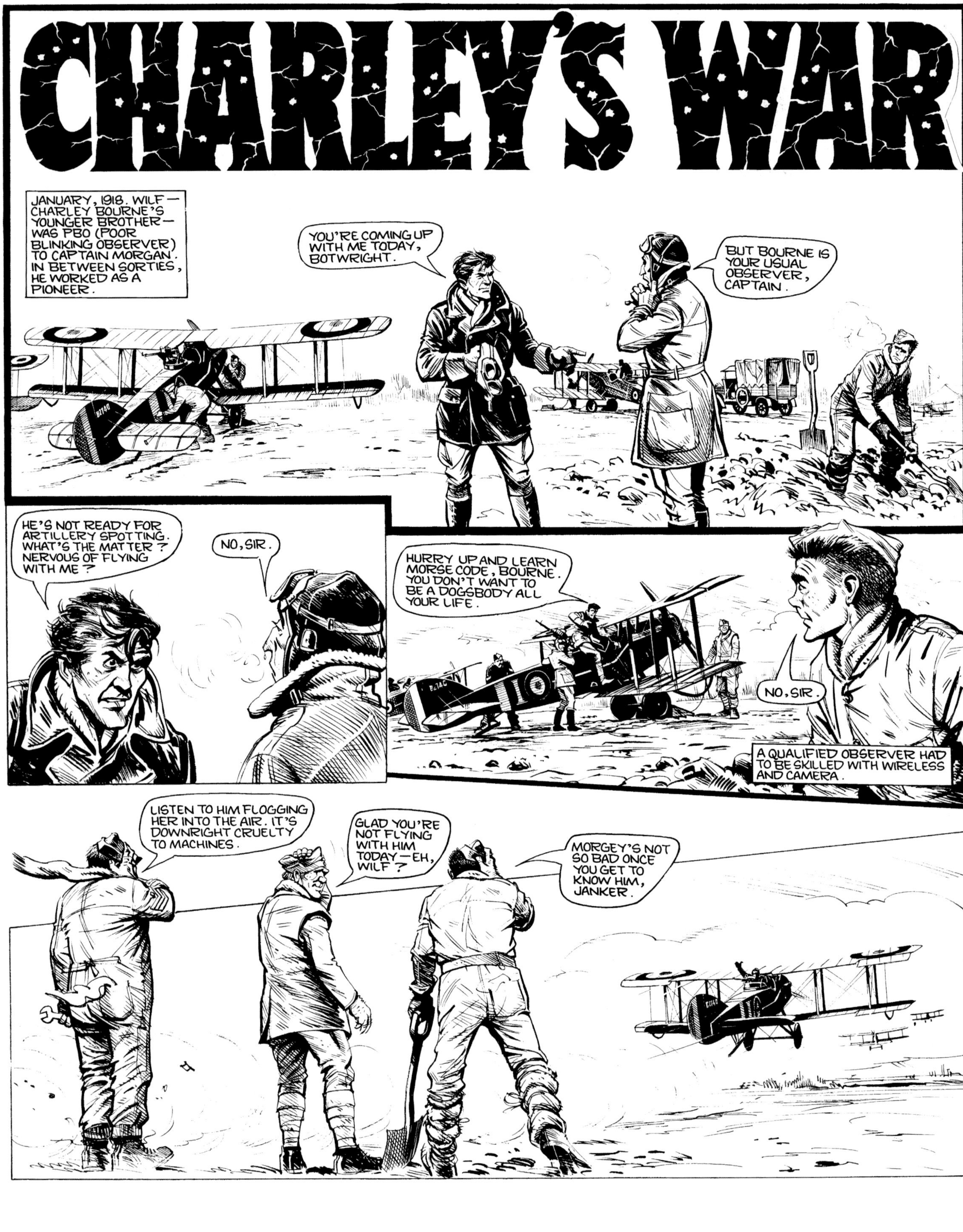
CHARLEY'S WAR
JANUARY, 1918. WILF — CHARLEY BOURNE'S YOUNGER BROTHER — WAS PBO (POOR BLINKING OBSERVER) TO CAPTAIN MORGAN. IN BETWEEN SORTIES, HE WORKED AS A PIONEER.
YOU'RE COMING UP WITH ME TODAY, BOTWRIGHT.
BUT BOURNE IS YOUR USUAL OBSERVER, CAPTAIN.
HE'S NOT READY FOR ARTILLERY SPOTTING. WHAT'S THE MATTER? NERVOUS OF FLYING WITH ME?
NO, SIR.
HURRY UP AND LEARN MORSE CODE, BOURNE. YOU DON'T WANT TO BE A DOGSBODY ALL YOUR LIFE.
NO, SIR.
A QUALIFIED OBSERVER HAD TO BE SKILLED WITH WIRELESS AND CAMERA.
LISTEN TO HIM FLOGGING HER INTO THE AIR. IT'S DOWNRIGHT CRUELTY TO MACHINES.
GLAD YOU'RE NOT FLYING WITH HIM TODAY — EH, WILF?
MORGEY'S NOT SO BAD ONCE YOU GET TO KNOW HIM, JANKER.

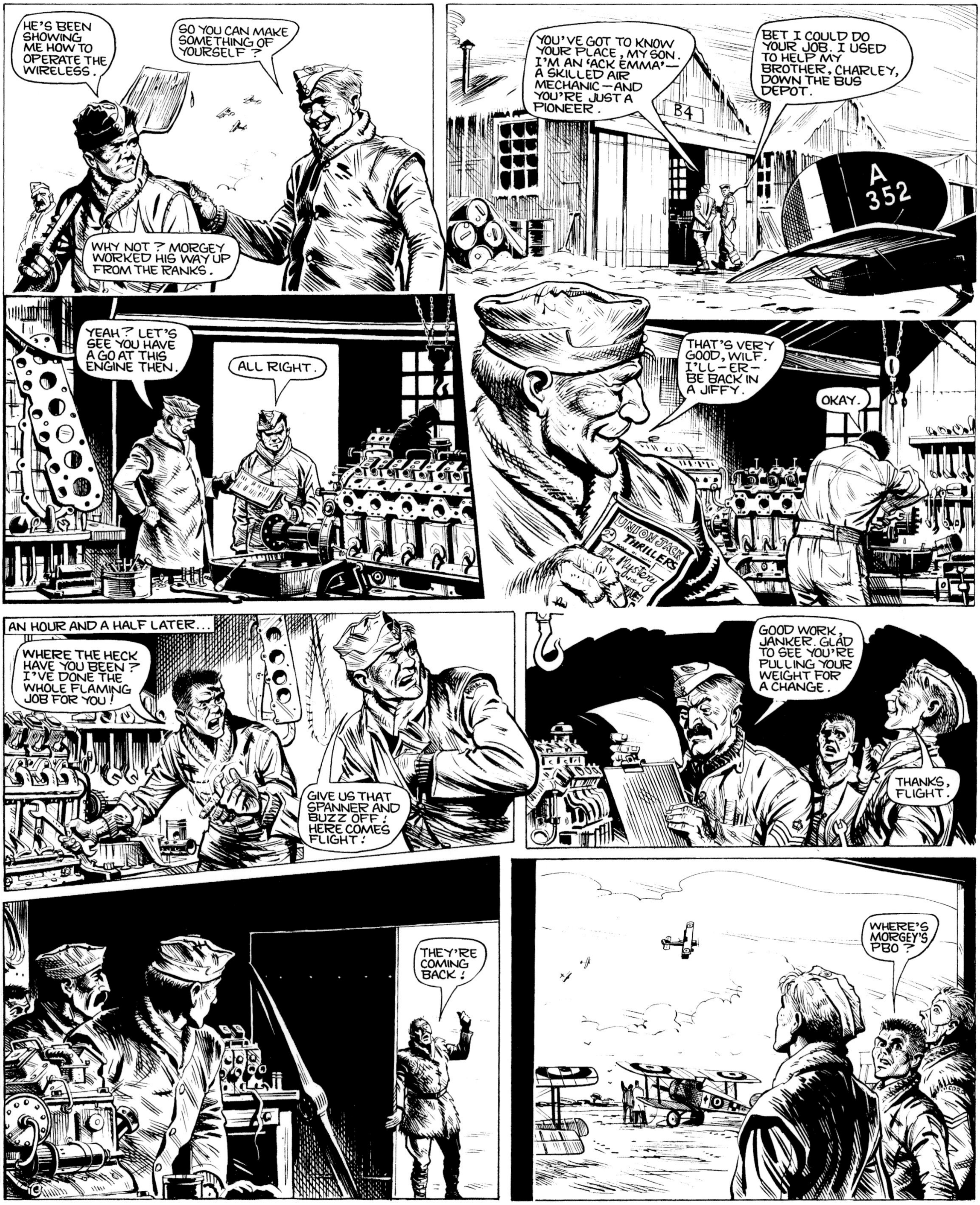

HE'S BEEN SHOWING ME HOW TO OPERATE THE WIRELESS.
SO YOU CAN MAKE SOMETHING OF YOURSELF?
WHY NOT? MORGEY WORKED HIS WAY UP FROM THE RANKS.
YOU'VE GOT TO KNOW YOUR PLACE, MY SON. I'M AN 'ACK EMMA' — A SKILLED AIR MECHANIC — AND YOU'RE JUST A PIONEER.
B4
BET I COULD DO YOUR JOB. I USED TO HELP MY BROTHER, CHARLEY, DOWN THE BUS DEPOT.
A 352
YEAH? LET'S SEE YOU HAVE A GO AT THIS ENGINE THEN.
ALL RIGHT.
THAT'S VERY GOOD, WILF. I'LL—ER—BE BACK IN A JIFFY.
OKAY.
UNION JACK THRILLERS
AN HOUR AND A HALF LATER...
WHERE THE HECK HAVE YOU BEEN? I'VE DONE THE WHOLE FLAMING JOB FOR YOU!
GIVE US THAT SPANNER AND BUZZ OFF! HERE COMES FLIGHT!
GOOD WORK, JANKER. GLAD TO SEE YOU'RE PULLING YOUR WEIGHT FOR A CHANGE.
THANKS, FLIGHT.
THEY'RE COMING BACK!
WHERE'S MORGEY'S PBO?

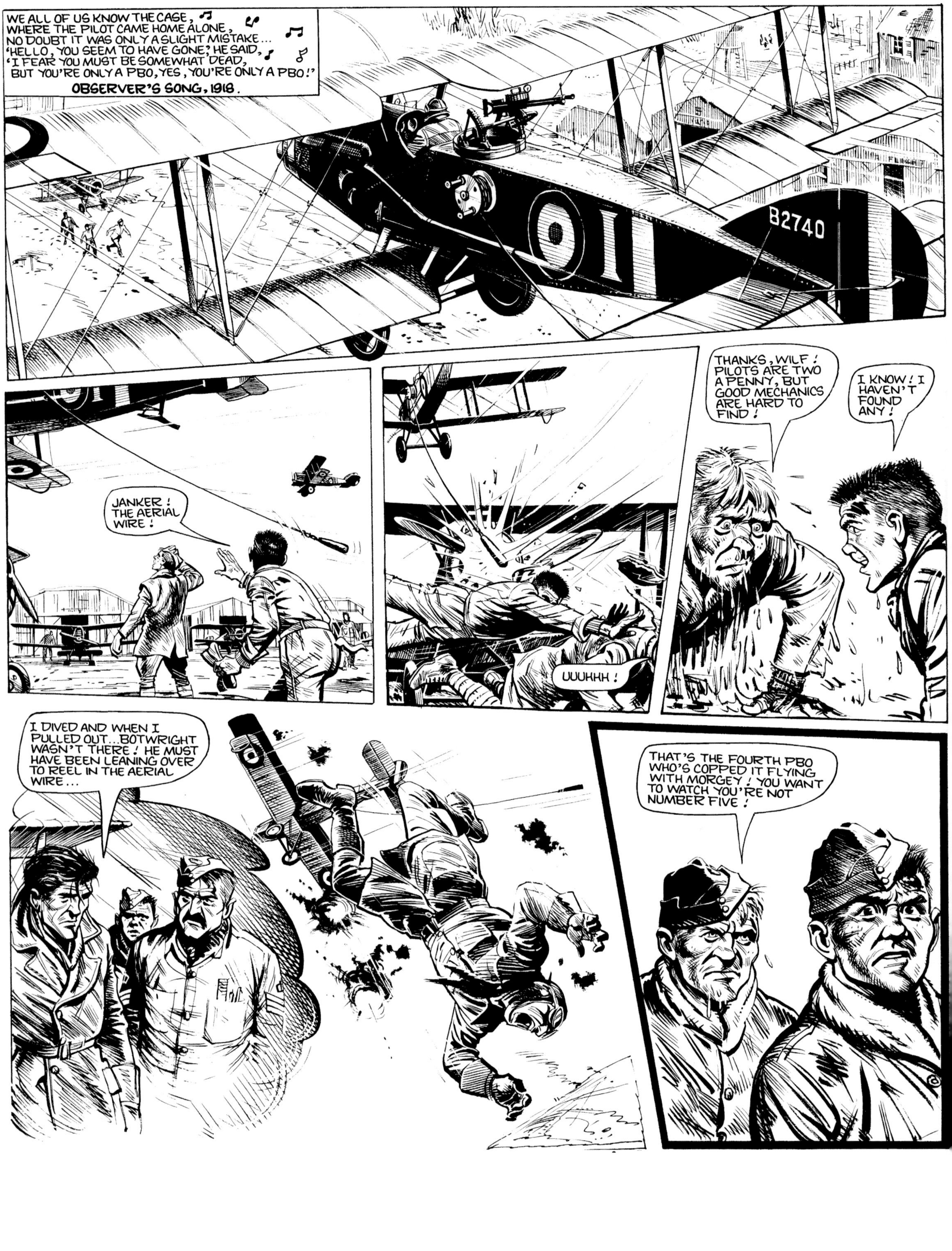
WE ALL OF US KNOW THE CASE,
WHERE THE PILOT CAME HOME ALONE,
NO DOUBT IT WAS ONLY A SLIGHT MISTAKE...
'HELLO, YOU SEEM TO HAVE GONE,' HE SAID,
'I FEAR YOU MUST BE SOMEWHAT DEAD,
BUT YOU'RE ONLY A PBO, YES, YOU'RE ONLY A PBO!'
OBSERVER'S SONG, 1918.
B2740
JANKER! THE AERIAL WIRE!
UUUHHH!
THANKS, WILF! PILOTS ARE TWO A PENNY, BUT GOOD MECHANICS ARE HARD TO FIND!
I KNOW! I HAVEN'T FOUND ANY!
I DIVED AND WHEN I PULLED OUT... BOTWRIGHT WASN'T THERE! HE MUST HAVE BEEN LEANING OVER TO REEL IN THE AERIAL WIRE...
THAT'S THE FOURTH PBO WHO'S COPPED IT FLYING WITH MORGEY! YOU WANT TO WATCH YOU'RE NOT NUMBER FIVE!

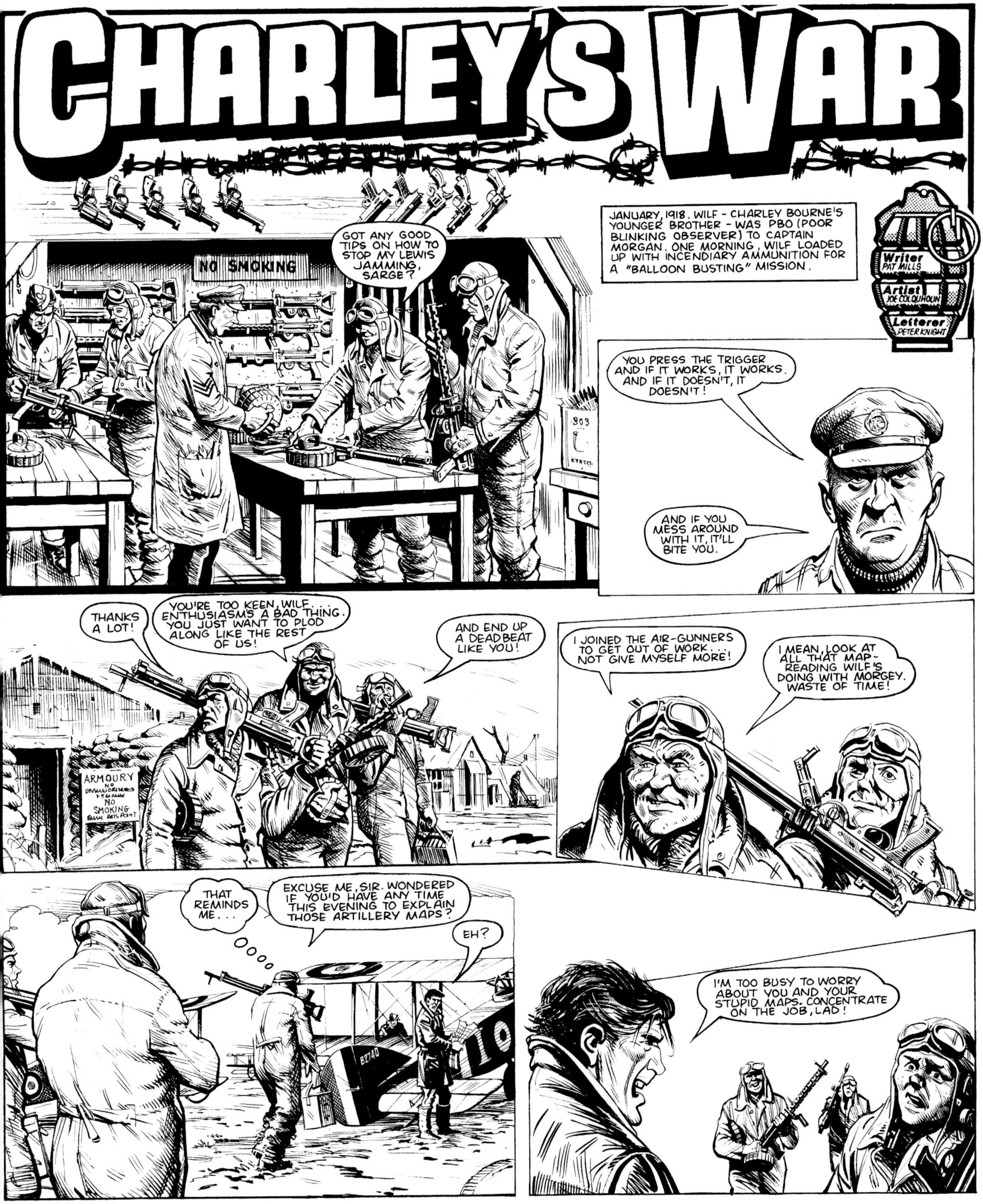
CHARLEY'S WAR
JANUARY, 1918. WILF - CHARLEY BOURNE'S YOUNGER BROTHER - WAS PBO (POOR BLINKING OBSERVER) TO CAPTAIN MORGAN. ONE MORNING, WILF LOADED UP WITH INCENDIARY AMMUNITION FOR A "BALLOON BUSTING" MISSION.
Writer PAT MILLS
Artist JOE COLQUHOUN
Letterer PETER KNIGHT
NO SMOKING
GOT ANY GOOD TIPS ON HOW TO STOP MY LEWIS JAMMING, SARGE?
YOU PRESS THE TRIGGER AND IF IT WORKS, IT WORKS. AND IF IT DOESN'T, IT DOESN'T!
AND IF YOU MESS AROUND WITH IT, IT'LL BITE YOU.
THANKS A LOT!
YOU'RE TOO KEEN, WILF. ENTHUSIASM'S A BAD THING. YOU JUST WANT TO PLOD ALONG LIKE THE REST OF US!
AND END UP A DEADBEAT LIKE YOU!
ARMOURY
NO SMOKING
I JOINED THE AIR-GUNNERS TO GET OUT OF WORK... NOT GIVE MYSELF MORE!
I MEAN, LOOK AT ALL THAT MAP-READING WILF'S DOING WITH MORGEY. WASTE OF TIME!
THAT REMINDS ME...
EXCUSE ME, SIR. WONDERED IF YOU'D HAVE ANY TIME THIS EVENING TO EXPLAIN THOSE ARTILLERY MAPS?
EH?
OOOO
I'M TOO BUSY TO WORRY ABOUT YOU AND YOUR STUPID MAPS. CONCENTRATE ON THE JOB, LAD!

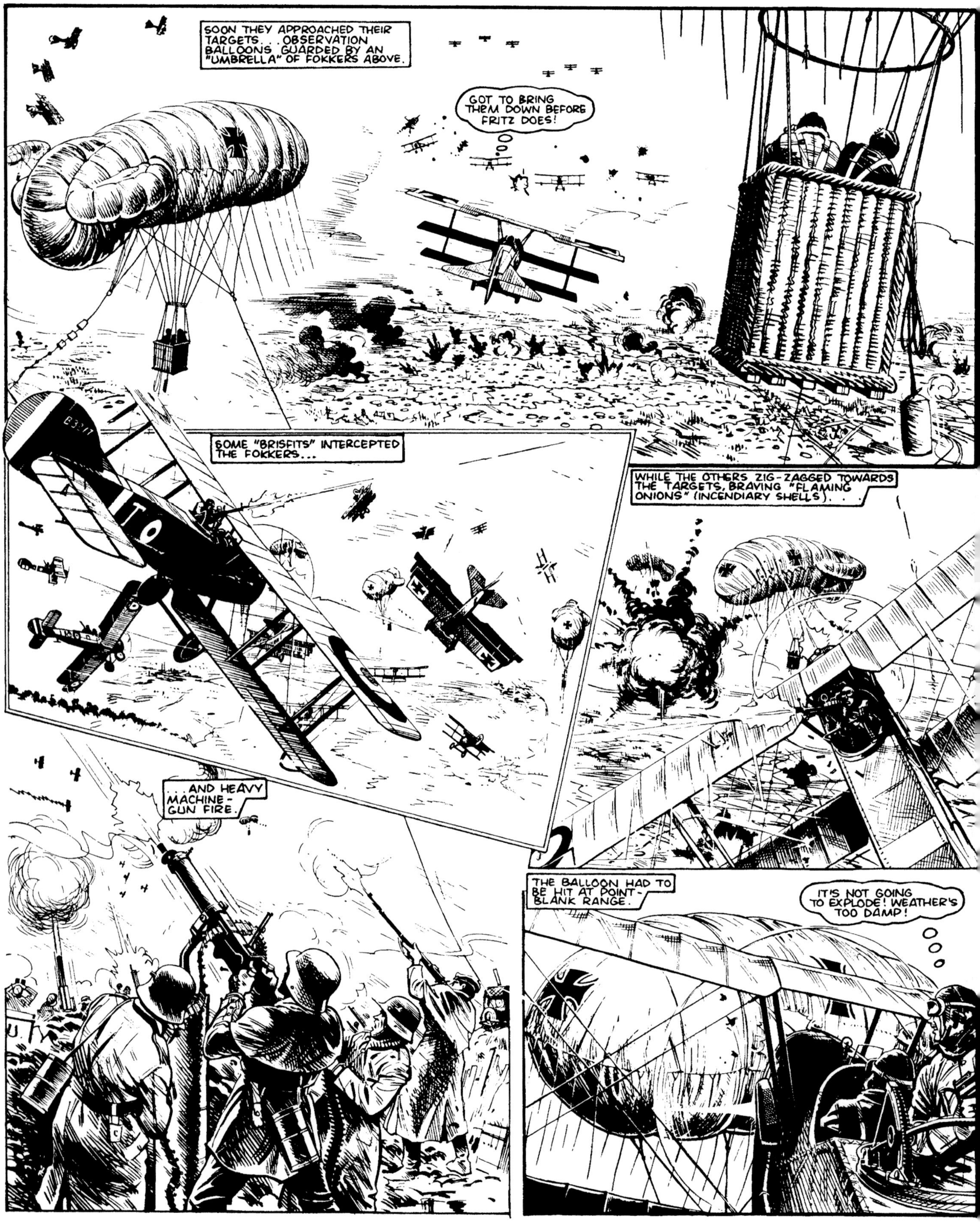
SOON THEY APPROACHED THEIR TARGETS. . .OBSERVATION BALLOONS GUARDED BY AN "UMBRELLA" OF FOKKERS ABOVE.
GOT TO BRING THEM DOWN BEFORE FRITZ DOES!
SOME "BRISFITS" INTERCEPTED THE FOKKERS...
WHILE THE OTHERS ZIG-ZAGGED TOWARDS THE TARGETS, BRAVING "FLAMING ONIONS" (INCENDIARY SHELLS). . .
. . AND HEAVY MACHINE-GUN FIRE.
THE BALLOON HAD TO BE HIT AT POINT-BLANK RANGE.
IT'S NOT GOING TO EXPLODE! WEATHER'S TOO DAMP!

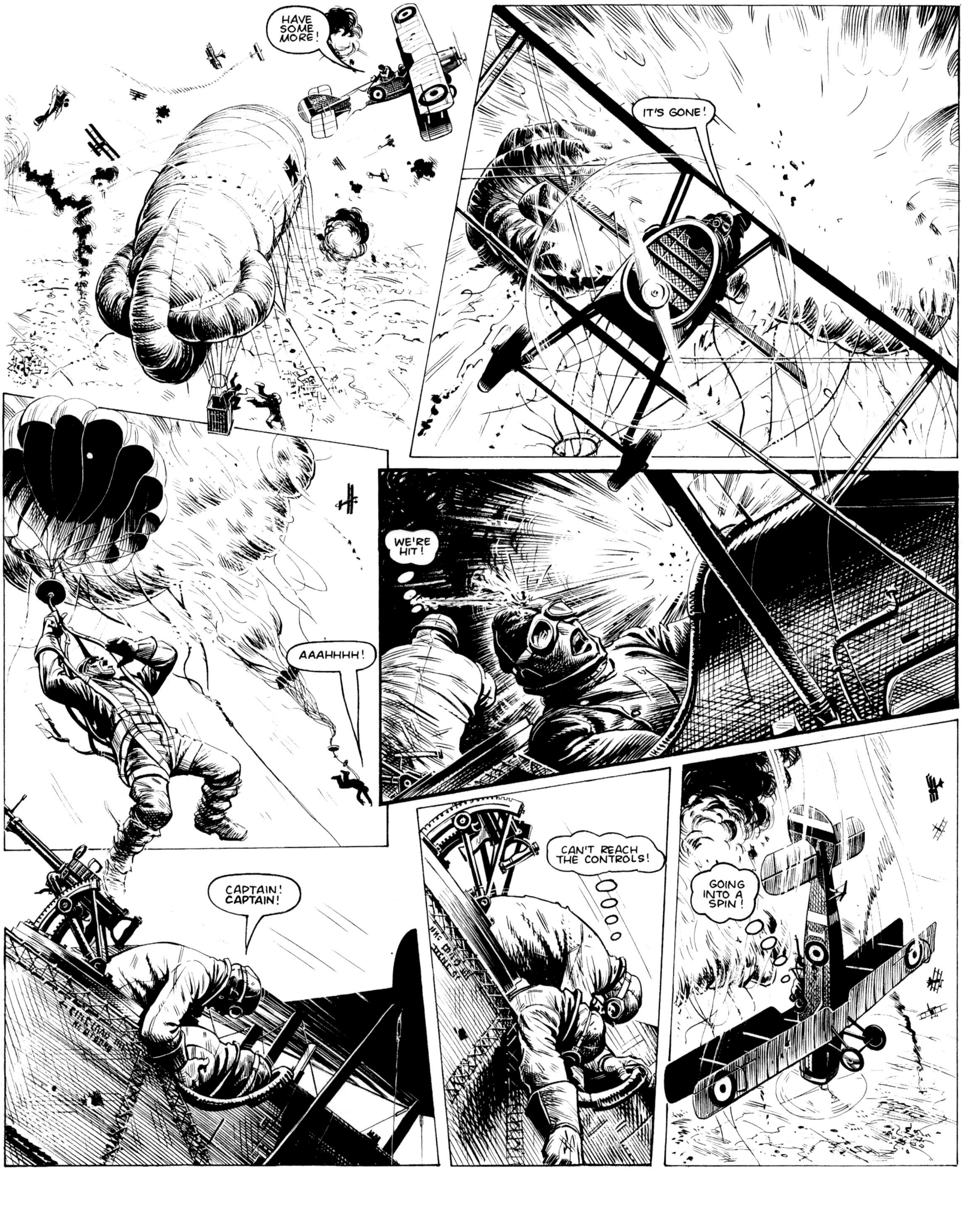
HAVE SOME MORE!
IT'S GONE!
AAAHHHH!
WE'RE HIT!
CAPTAIN! CAPTAIN!
CAN'T REACH THE CONTROLS!
GOING INTO A SPIN!

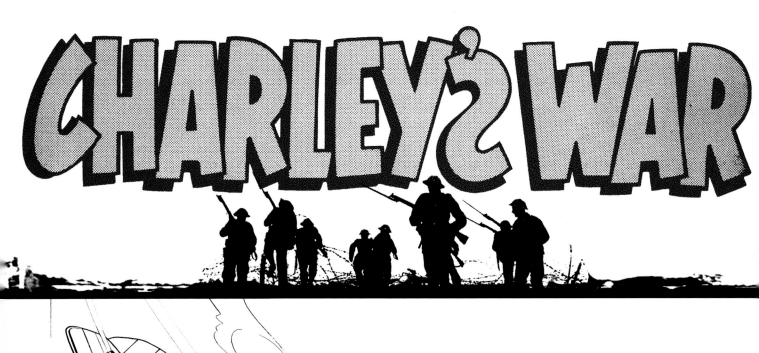

# CHARLEY'S WAR

CHARLEY'S WAR.
JANUARY, 1918. PIONEER
WILF BOURNE — CHARLEY'S
YOUNGER BROTHER — WAS
PBO (POOR BLINKING
OBSERVER) TO CAPTAIN
MORGAN. AFTER A BALLOON-
BUSTING MISSION, MORGAN
WAS HIT AND THEIR "BRISFIT"
WENT INTO A SPIN.

WE'RE
OUT OF
CONTROL!

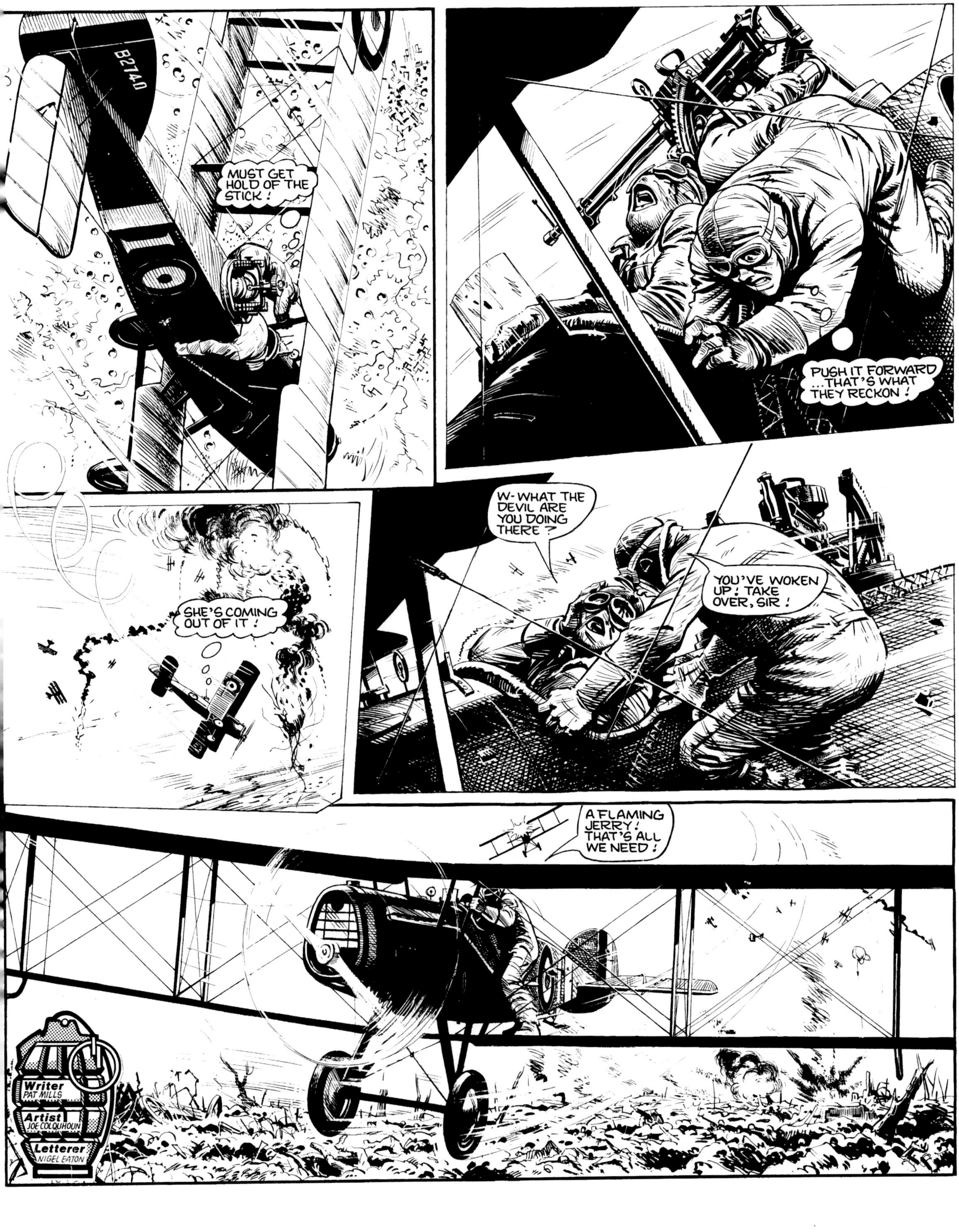
MUST GET HOLD OF THE STICK!
PUSH IT FORWARD ...THAT'S WHAT THEY RECKON!
SHE'S COMING OUT OF IT!
W-WHAT THE DEVIL ARE YOU DOING THERE?
YOU'VE WOKEN UP! TAKE OVER, SIR!
A FLAMING JERRY! THAT'S ALL WE NEED!
B2740
Writer PAT MILLS
Artist JOE COLQUHOUN
Letterer NIGEL EATON

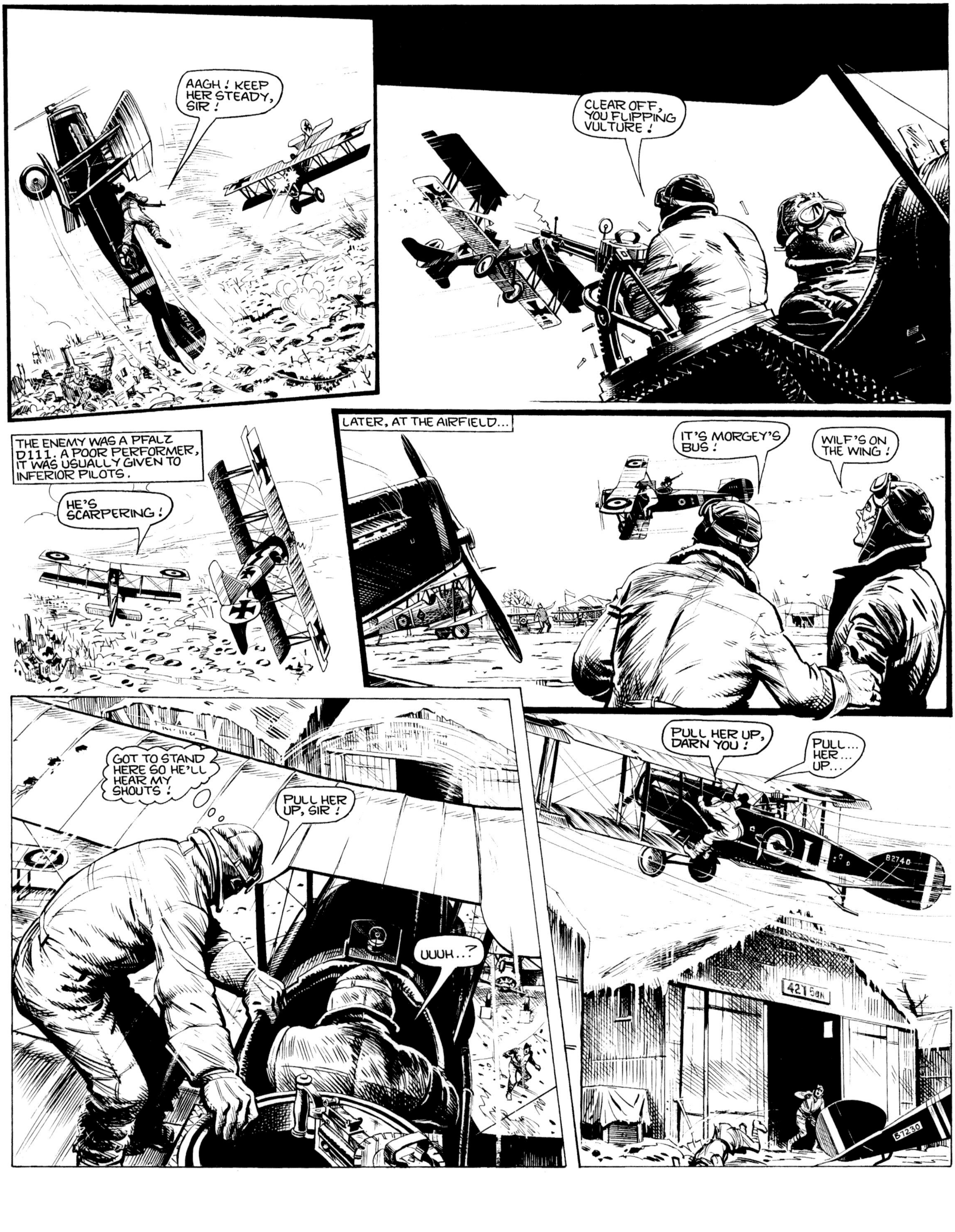
AAGH! KEEP HER STEADY, SIR!
CLEAR OFF, YOU FLIPPING VULTURE!
THE ENEMY WAS A PFALZ D111. A POOR PERFORMER, IT WAS USUALLY GIVEN TO INFERIOR PILOTS.
HE'S SCARPERING!
LATER, AT THE AIRFIELD...
IT'S MORGEY'S BUS!
WILF'S ON THE WING!
GOT TO STAND HERE SO HE'LL HEAR MY SHOUTS!
PULL HER UP, SIR!
UUUH...?
PULL HER UP, DARN YOU!
PULL... HER... UP...
B2740
42 SQN
B7230

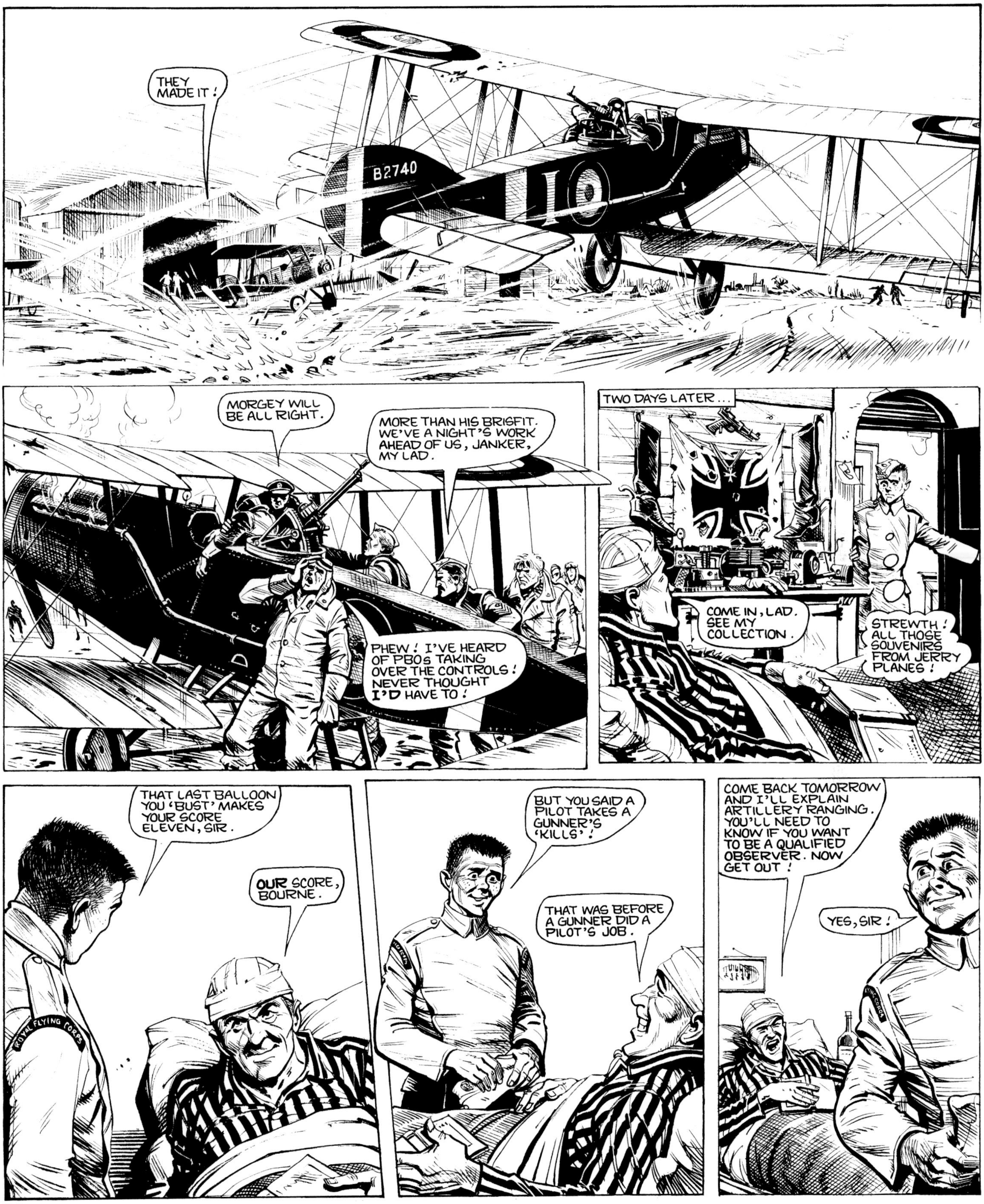
THEY MADE IT!
MORGEY WILL BE ALL RIGHT.
MORE THAN HIS BRISFIT. WE'VE A NIGHT'S WORK AHEAD OF US, JANKER, MY LAD.
PHEW! I'VE HEARD OF PBOs TAKING OVER THE CONTROLS! NEVER THOUGHT I'D HAVE TO!
TWO DAYS LATER...
COME IN, LAD. SEE MY COLLECTION.
STREWTH! ALL THOSE SOUVENIRS FROM JERRY PLANES!
THAT LAST BALLOON YOU 'BUST' MAKES YOUR SCORE ELEVEN, SIR.
OUR SCORE, BOURNE.
BUT YOU SAID A PILOT TAKES A GUNNER'S 'KILLS'!
THAT WAS BEFORE A GUNNER DID A PILOT'S JOB.
COME BACK TOMORROW AND I'LL EXPLAIN ARTILLERY RANGING. YOU'LL NEED TO KNOW IF YOU WANT TO BE A QUALIFIED OBSERVER. NOW GET OUT!
YES, SIR!

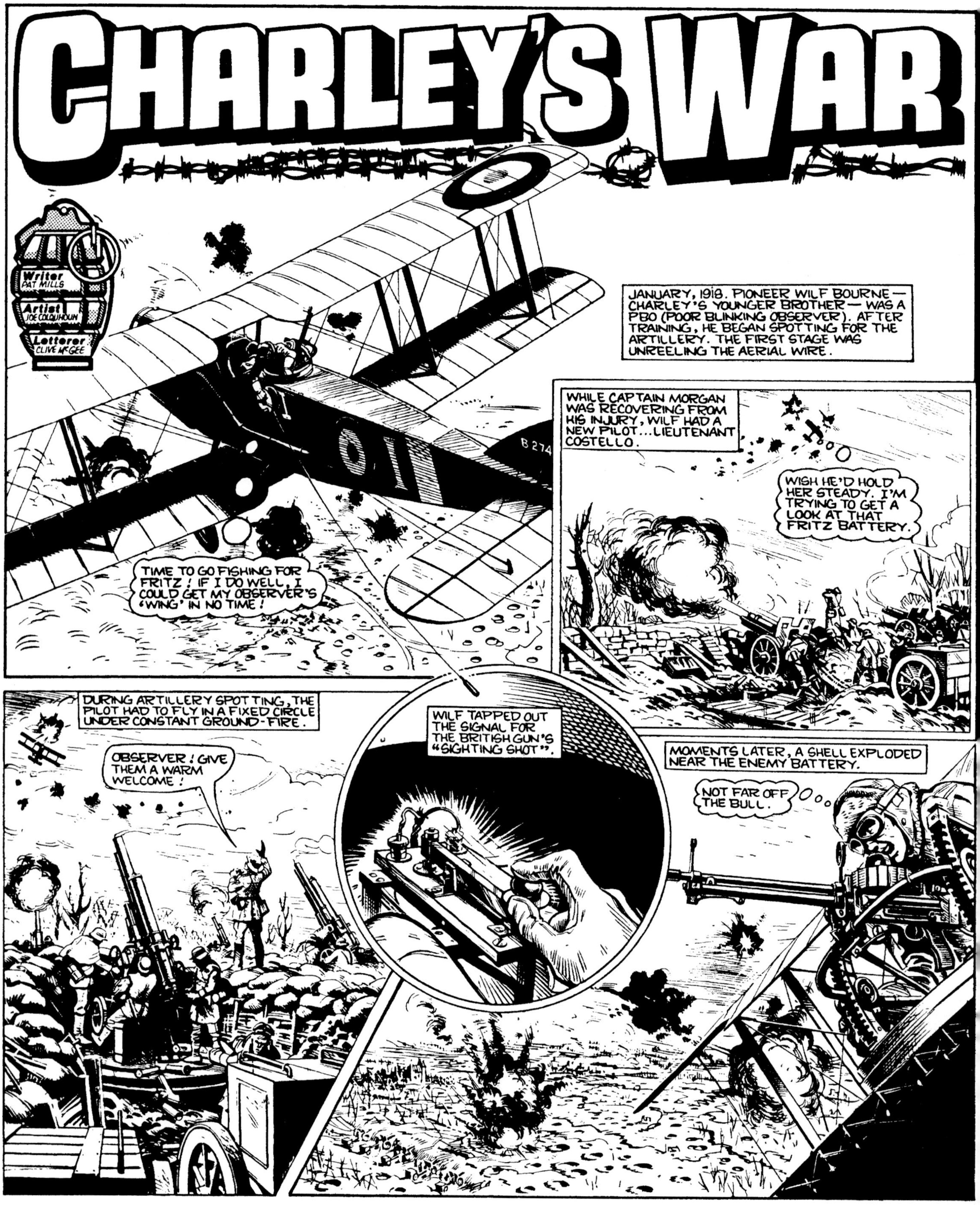

CHARLEY'S WAR
Writer PAT MILLS
Artist JOE COLQUHOUN
Letterer CLIVE McGEE
JANUARY, 1918. PIONEER WILF BOURNE — CHARLEY'S YOUNGER BROTHER — WAS A PBO (POOR BLINKING OBSERVER). AFTER TRAINING, HE BEGAN SPOTTING FOR THE ARTILLERY. THE FIRST STAGE WAS UNREELING THE AERIAL WIRE.
TIME TO GO FISHING FOR FRITZ! IF I DO WELL, I COULD GET MY OBSERVER'S 'WING' IN NO TIME!
WHILE CAPTAIN MORGAN WAS RECOVERING FROM HIS INJURY, WILF HAD A NEW PILOT... LIEUTENANT COSTELLO.
WISH HE'D HOLD HER STEADY. I'M TRYING TO GET A LOOK AT THAT FRITZ BATTERY.
DURING ARTILLERY SPOTTING, THE PILOT HAD TO FLY IN A FIXED CIRCLE UNDER CONSTANT GROUND-FIRE.
OBSERVER! GIVE THEM A WARM WELCOME!
WILF TAPPED OUT THE SIGNAL FOR THE BRITISH GUN'S "SIGHTING SHOT".
MOMENTS LATER, A SHELL EXPLODED NEAR THE ENEMY BATTERY.
NOT FAR OFF THE BULL.

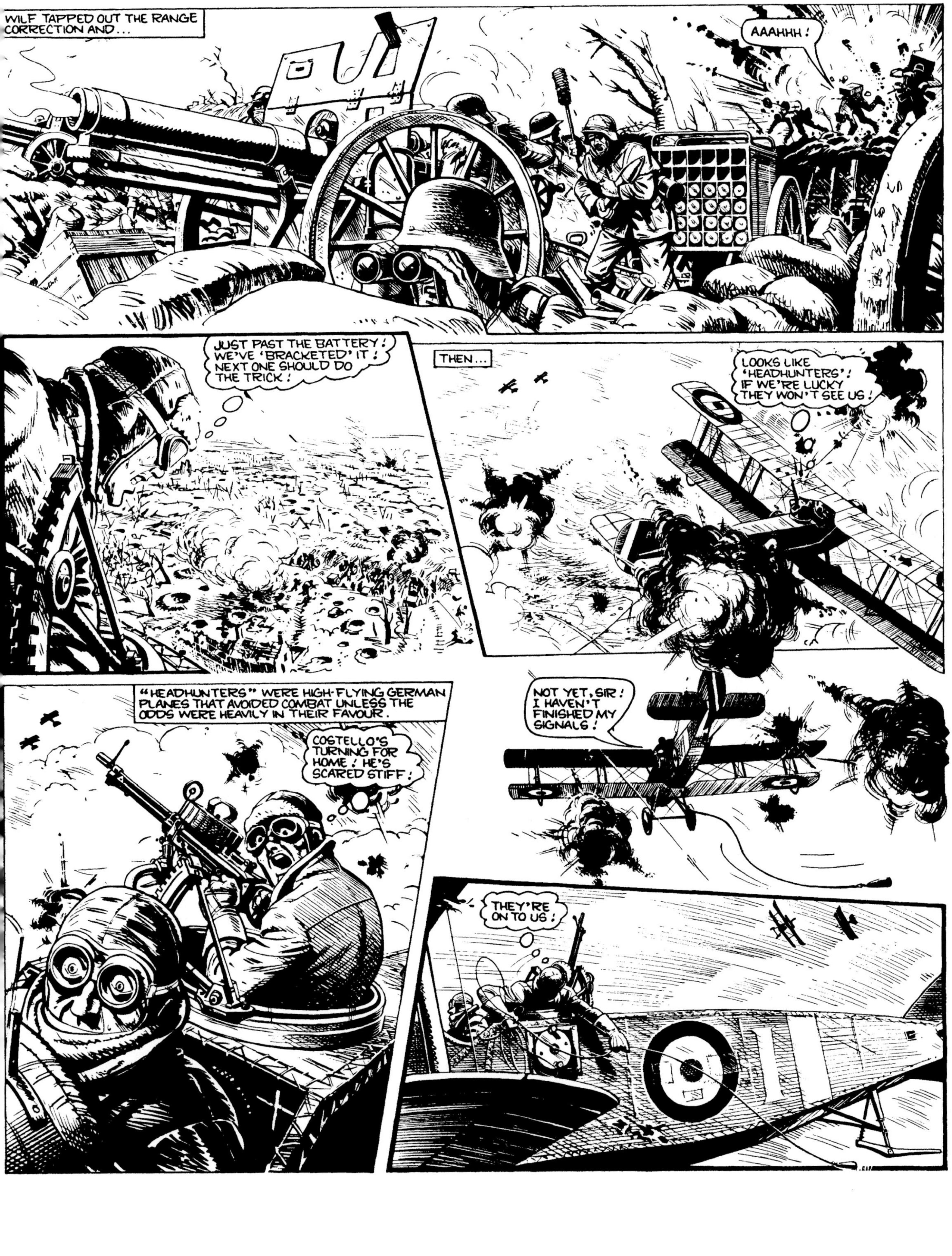
WILF TAPPED OUT THE RANGE CORRECTION AND...
AAAHHH!
JUST PAST THE BATTERY! WE'VE 'BRACKETED' IT! NEXT ONE SHOULD DO THE TRICK!
THEN...
LOOKS LIKE 'HEADHUNTERS'! IF WE'RE LUCKY THEY WON'T SEE US!
"HEADHUNTERS" WERE HIGH-FLYING GERMAN PLANES THAT AVOIDED COMBAT UNLESS THE ODDS WERE HEAVILY IN THEIR FAVOUR.
COSTELLO'S TURNING FOR HOME! HE'S SCARED STIFF!
NOT YET, SIR! I HAVEN'T FINISHED MY SIGNALS!
THEY'RE ON TO US!

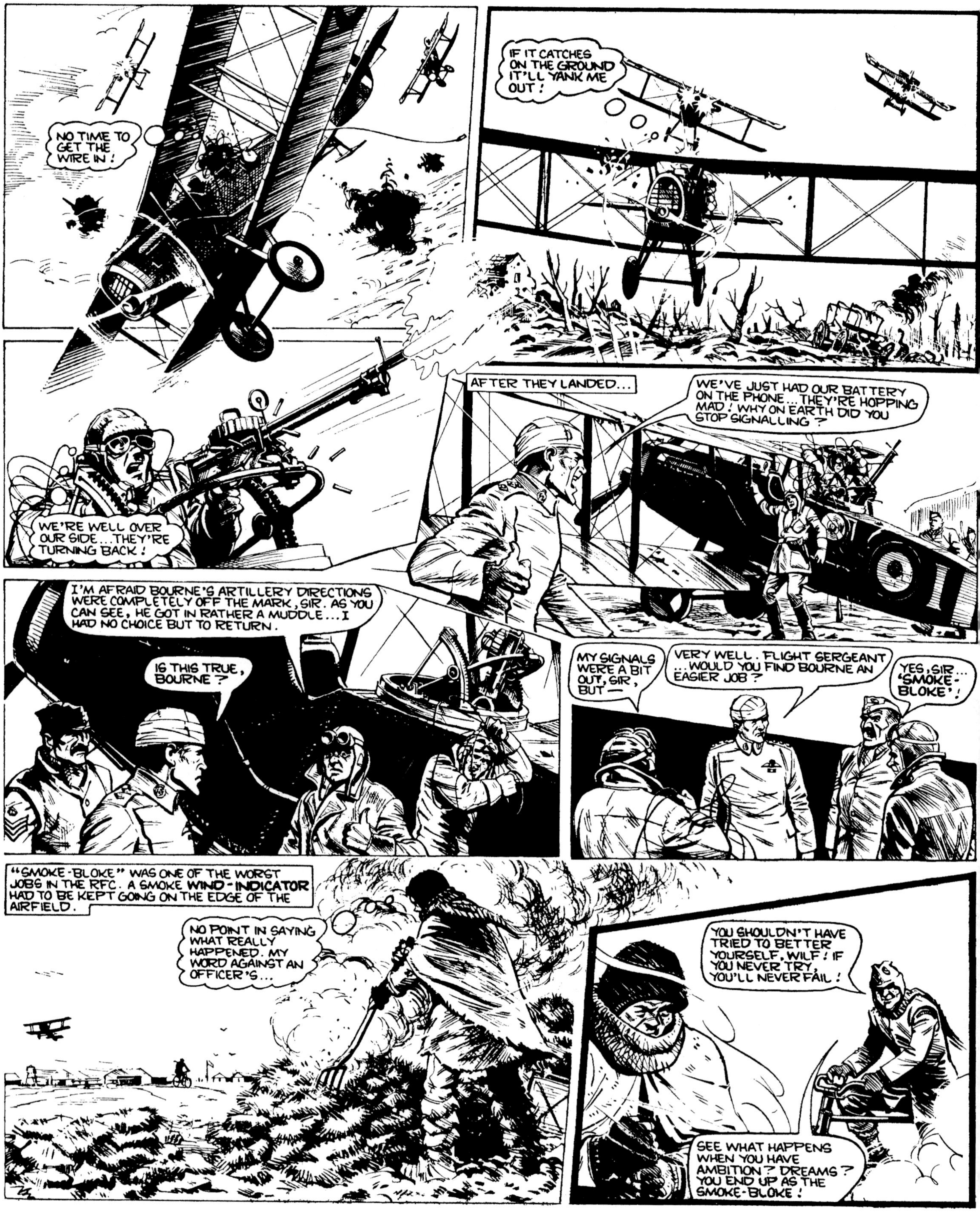
NO TIME TO GET THE WIRE IN!
IF IT CATCHES ON THE GROUND IT'LL YANK ME OUT!
WE'RE WELL OVER OUR SIDE... THEY'RE TURNING BACK!
AFTER THEY LANDED...
WE'VE JUST HAD OUR BATTERY ON THE PHONE... THEY'RE HOPPING MAD! WHY ON EARTH DID YOU STOP SIGNALLING?
I'M AFRAID BOURNE'S ARTILLERY DIRECTIONS WERE COMPLETELY OFF THE MARK, SIR. AS YOU CAN SEE, HE GOT IN RATHER A MUDDLE... I HAD NO CHOICE BUT TO RETURN.
IS THIS TRUE, BOURNE?
MY SIGNALS WERE A BIT OUT, SIR, BUT—
VERY WELL. FLIGHT SERGEANT... WOULD YOU FIND BOURNE AN EASIER JOB?
YES, SIR... 'SMOKE-BLOKE'!
"SMOKE-BLOKE" WAS ONE OF THE WORST JOBS IN THE RFC. A SMOKE WIND-INDICATOR HAD TO BE KEPT GOING ON THE EDGE OF THE AIRFIELD.
NO POINT IN SAYING WHAT REALLY HAPPENED. MY WORD AGAINST AN OFFICER'S...
YOU SHOULDN'T HAVE TRIED TO BETTER YOURSELF, WILF! IF YOU NEVER TRY, YOU'LL NEVER FAIL!
SEE WHAT HAPPENS WHEN YOU HAVE AMBITION? DREAMS? YOU END UP AS THE SMOKE-BLOKE!

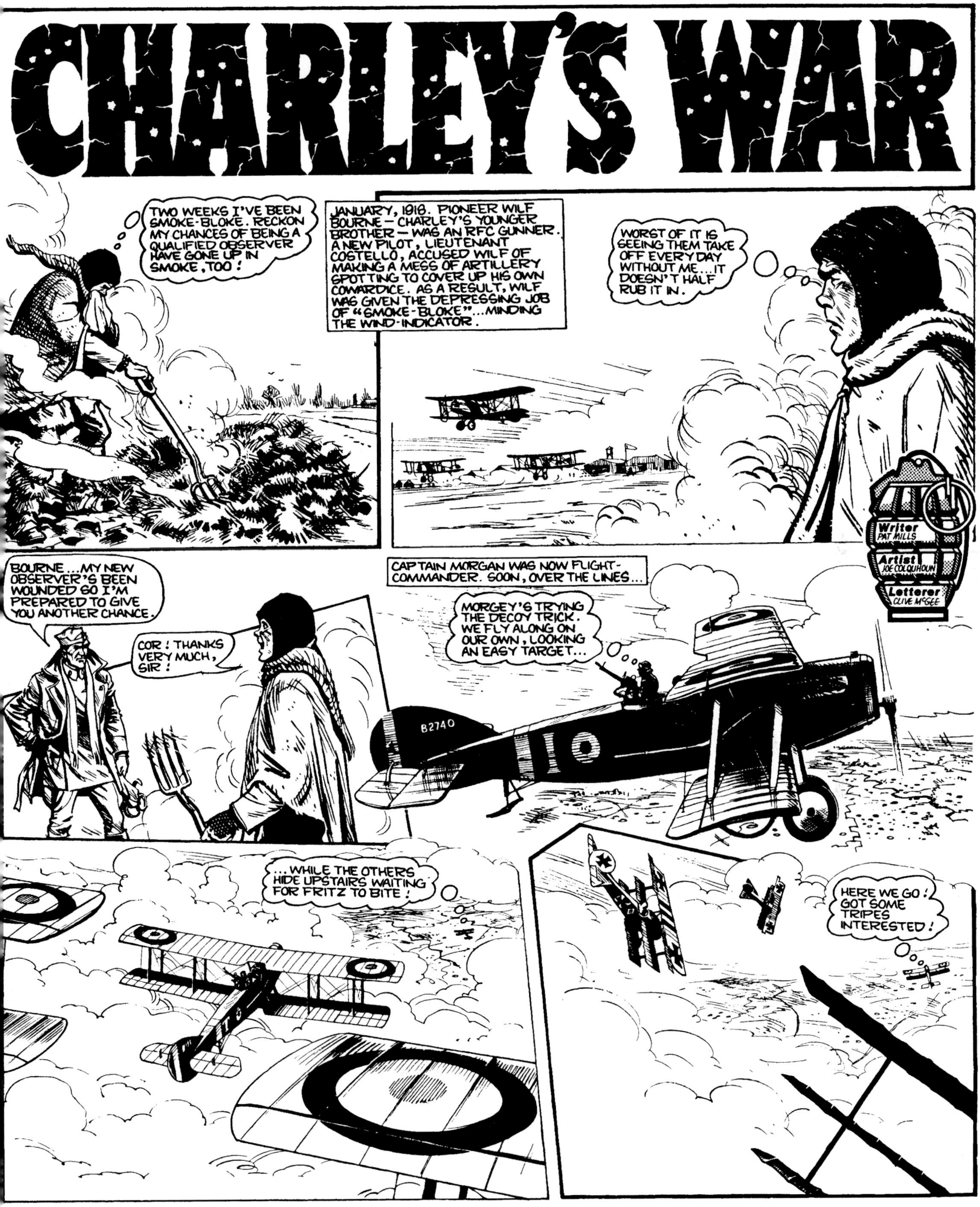
CHARLEY'S WAR
TWO WEEKS I'VE BEEN SMOKE-BLOKE. RECKON MY CHANCES OF BEING A QUALIFIED OBSERVER HAVE GONE UP IN SMOKE, TOO!
JANUARY, 1918. PIONEER WILF BOURNE — CHARLEY'S YOUNGER BROTHER — WAS AN RFC GUNNER. A NEW PILOT, LIEUTENANT COSTELLO, ACCUSED WILF OF MAKING A MESS OF ARTILLERY SPOTTING TO COVER UP HIS OWN COWARDICE. AS A RESULT, WILF WAS GIVEN THE DEPRESSING JOB OF "SMOKE-BLOKE"... MINDING THE WIND-INDICATOR.
WORST OF IT IS SEEING THEM TAKE OFF EVERY DAY WITHOUT ME... IT DOESN'T HALF RUB IT IN.
Writer PAT MILLS
Artist JOE COLQUHOUN
Letterer CLIVE McGEE
BOURNE... MY NEW OBSERVER'S BEEN WOUNDED SO I'M PREPARED TO GIVE YOU ANOTHER CHANCE.
COR! THANKS VERY MUCH, SIR!
CAPTAIN MORGAN WAS NOW FLIGHT-COMMANDER. SOON, OVER THE LINES...
MORGEY'S TRYING THE DECOY TRICK. WE FLY ALONG ON OUR OWN, LOOKING AN EASY TARGET...
B2740
...WHILE THE OTHERS HIDE UPSTAIRS WAITING FOR FRITZ TO BITE!
HERE WE GO! GOT SOME TRIPES INTERESTED!

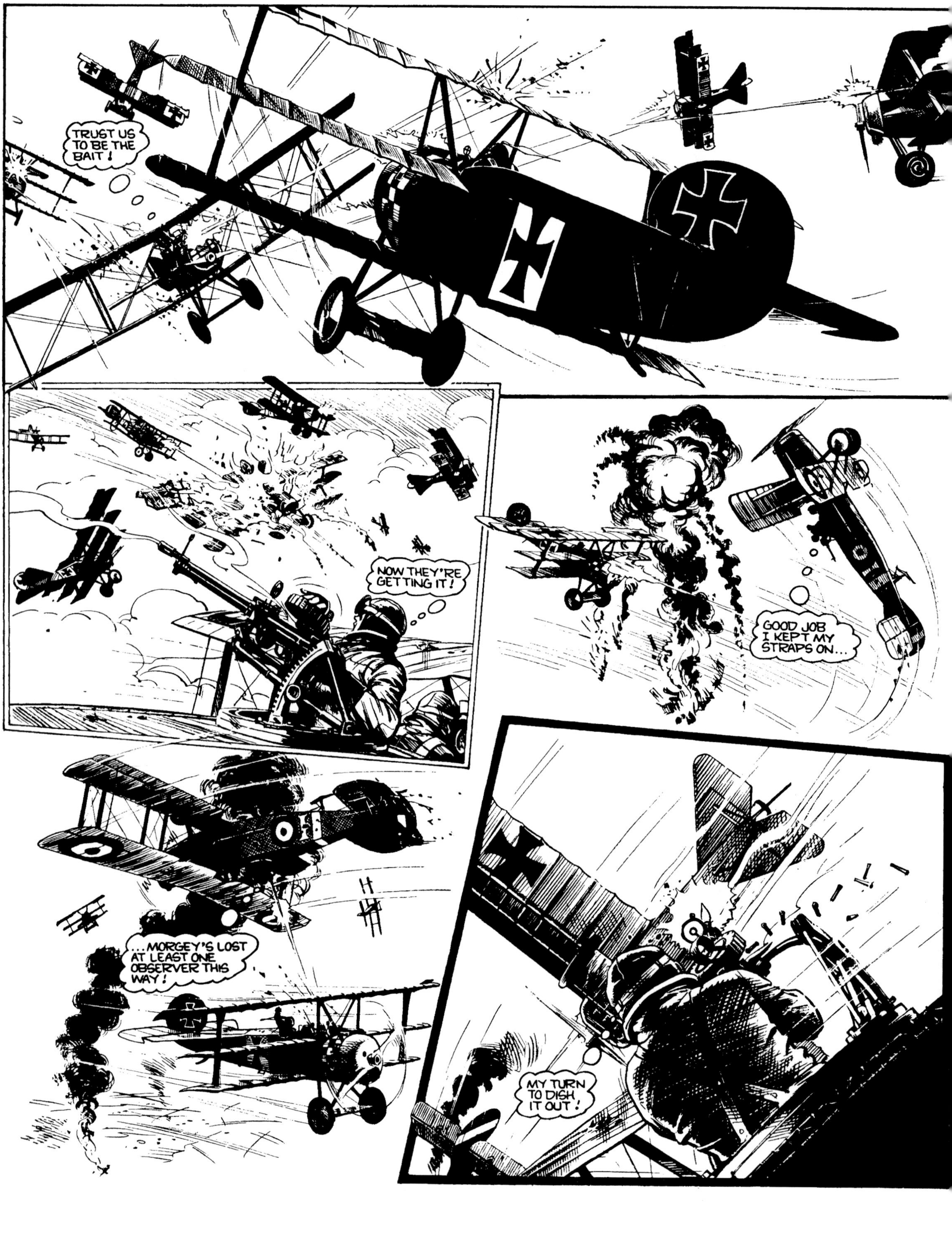
TRUST US TO BE THE BAIT!
NOW THEY'RE GETTING IT!
GOOD JOB I KEPT MY STRAPS ON...
...MORGEY'S LOST AT LEAST ONE OBSERVER THIS WAY!
MY TURN TO DISH IT OUT!

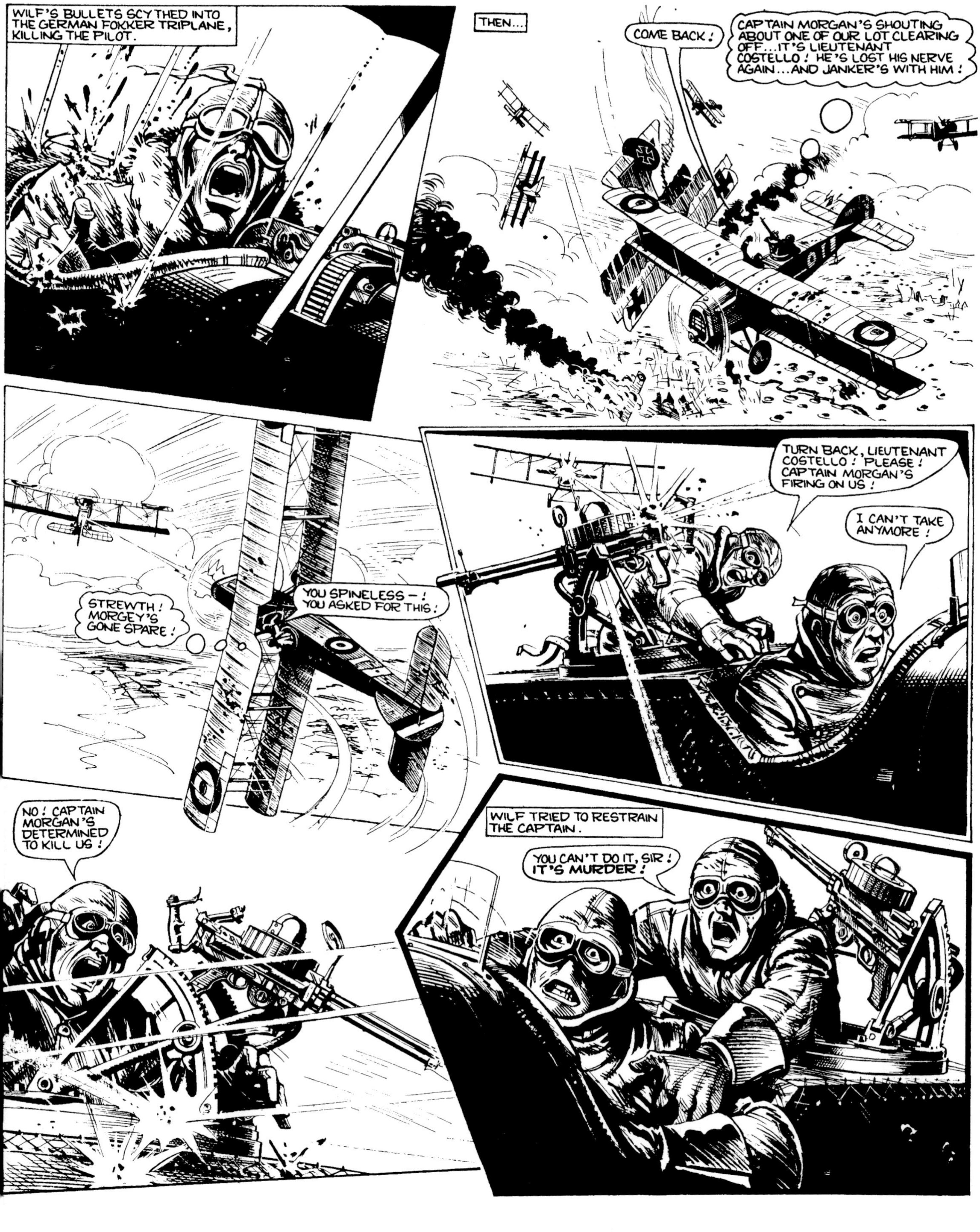

WILF'S BULLETS SCYTHED INTO THE GERMAN FOKKER TRIPLANE, KILLING THE PILOT.
THEN...
COME BACK!
CAPTAIN MORGAN'S SHOUTING ABOUT ONE OF OUR LOT CLEARING OFF... IT'S LIEUTENANT COSTELLO! HE'S LOST HIS NERVE AGAIN... AND JANKER'S WITH HIM!
STREWTH! MORGEY'S GONE SPARE!
YOU SPINELESS -! YOU ASKED FOR THIS!
TURN BACK, LIEUTENANT COSTELLO! PLEASE! CAPTAIN MORGAN'S FIRING ON US!
I CAN'T TAKE ANYMORE!
NO! CAPTAIN MORGAN'S DETERMINED TO KILL US!
WILF TRIED TO RESTRAIN THE CAPTAIN.
YOU CAN'T DO IT, SIR! IT'S MURDER!

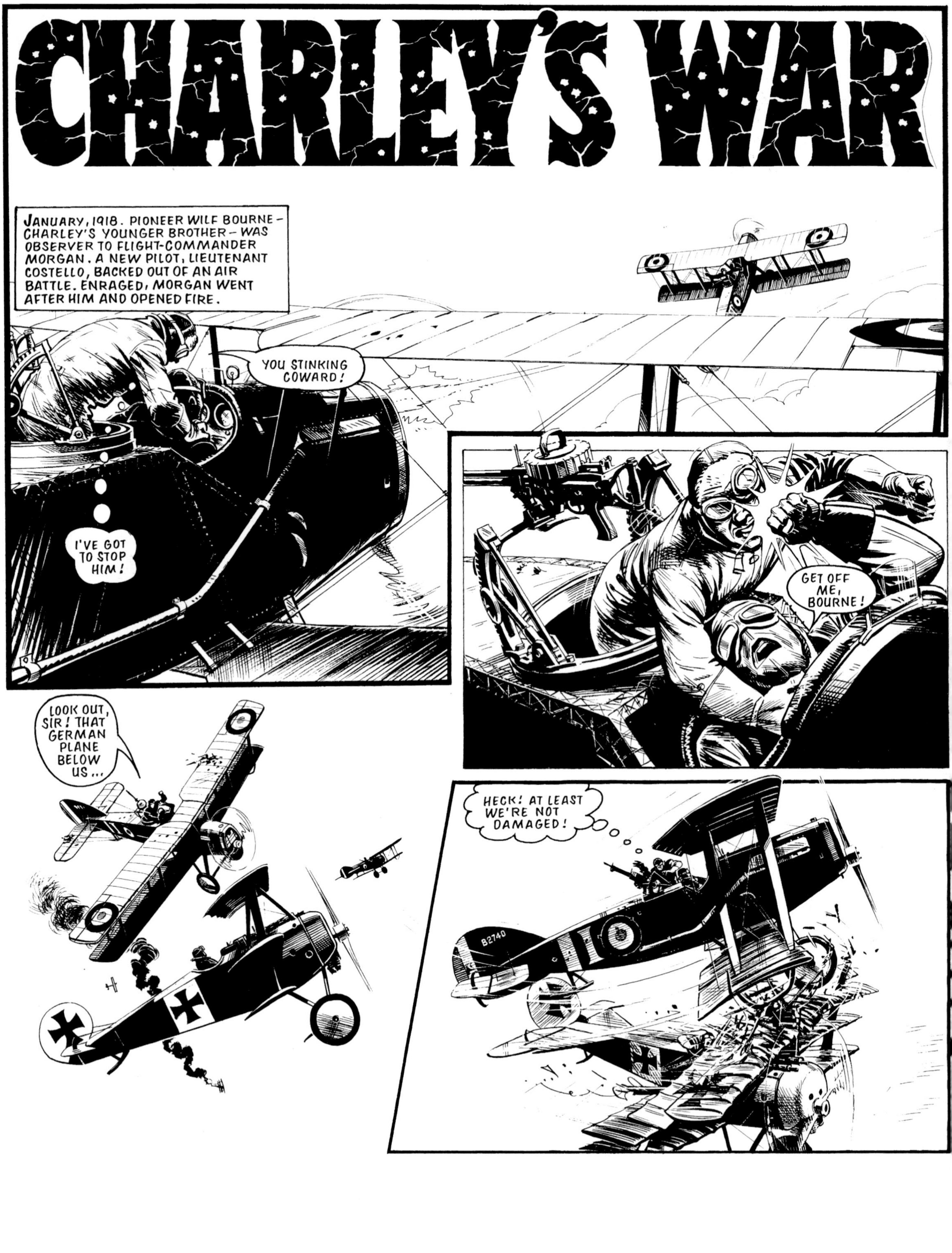
CHARLEY'S WAR
JANUARY, 1918. PIONEER WILF BOURNE - CHARLEY'S YOUNGER BROTHER - WAS OBSERVER TO FLIGHT-COMMANDER MORGAN. A NEW PILOT, LIEUTENANT COSTELLO, BACKED OUT OF AN AIR BATTLE. ENRAGED, MORGAN WENT AFTER HIM AND OPENED FIRE.
YOU STINKING COWARD!
I'VE GOT TO STOP HIM!
GET OFF ME, BOURNE!
LOOK OUT, SIR! THAT GERMAN PLANE BELOW US...
HECK! AT LEAST WE'RE NOT DAMAGED!
B2740

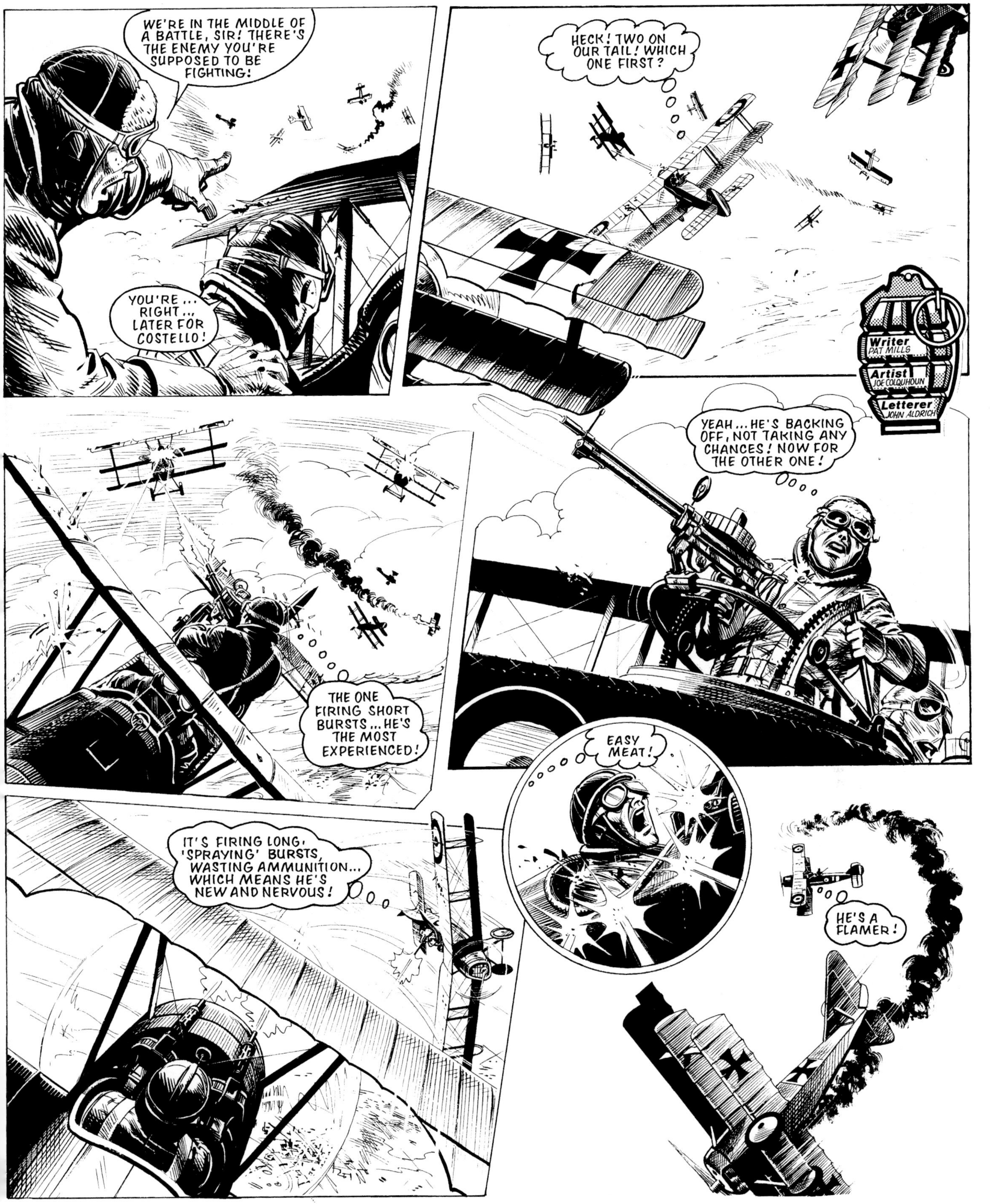
WE'RE IN THE MIDDLE OF A BATTLE, SIR! THERE'S THE ENEMY YOU'RE SUPPOSED TO BE FIGHTING!
YOU'RE ... RIGHT ... LATER FOR COSTELLO!
HECK! TWO ON OUR TAIL! WHICH ONE FIRST?
Writer PAT MILLS
Artist JOE COLQUHOUN
Letterer JOHN ALDRICH
THE ONE FIRING SHORT BURSTS ... HE'S THE MOST EXPERIENCED!
YEAH ... HE'S BACKING OFF, NOT TAKING ANY CHANCES! NOW FOR THE OTHER ONE!
IT'S FIRING LONG, 'SPRAYING' BURSTS, WASTING AMMUNITION ... WHICH MEANS HE'S NEW AND NERVOUS!
EASY MEAT!
HE'S A FLAMER!

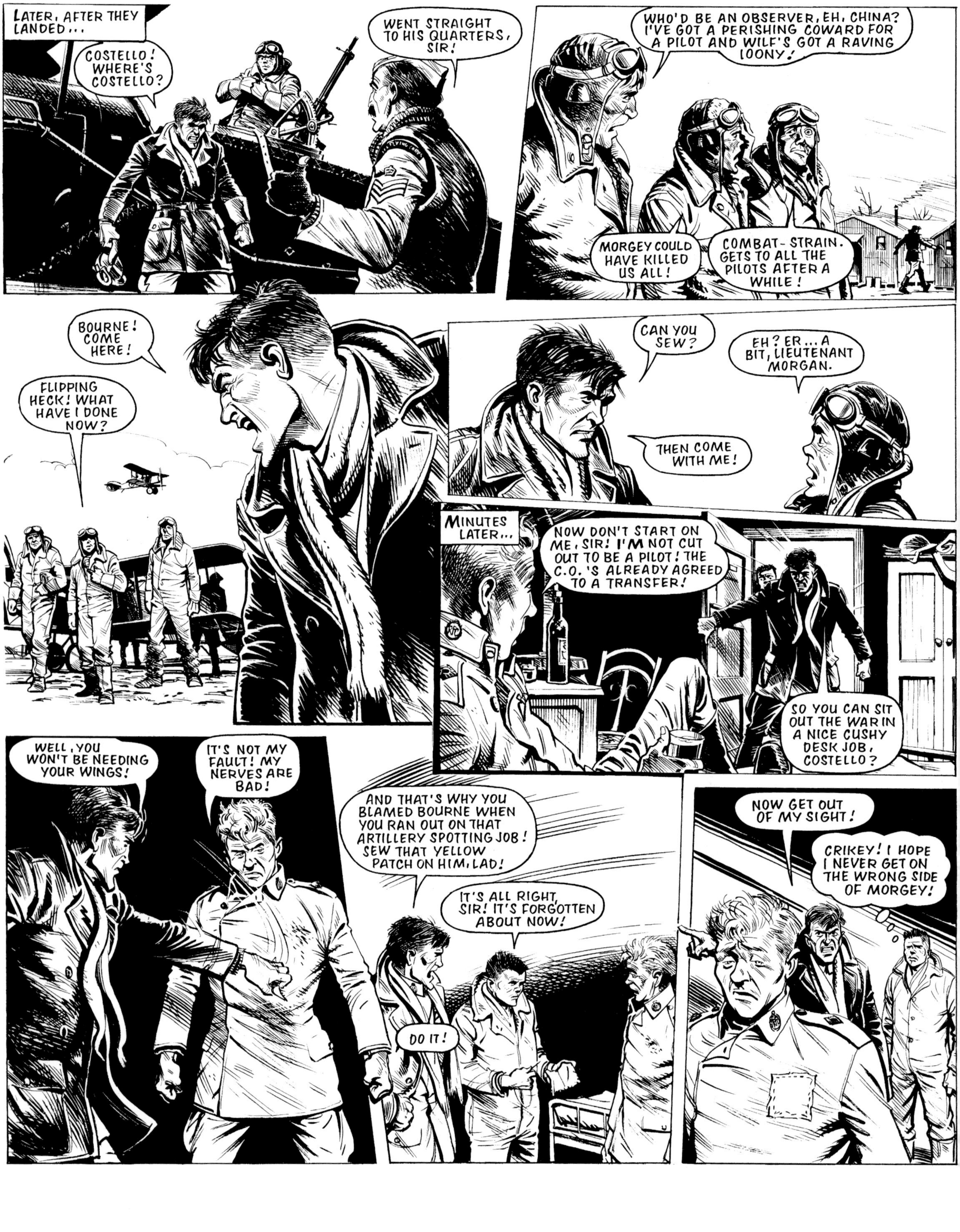

LATER, AFTER THEY LANDED...
COSTELLO! WHERE'S COSTELLO?
WENT STRAIGHT TO HIS QUARTERS, SIR!
WHO'D BE AN OBSERVER, EH, CHINA? I'VE GOT A PERISHING COWARD FOR A PILOT AND WILF'S GOT A RAVING LOONY!
MORGEY COULD HAVE KILLED US ALL!
COMBAT-STRAIN. GETS TO ALL THE PILOTS AFTER A WHILE!
BOURNE! COME HERE!
FLIPPING HECK! WHAT HAVE I DONE NOW?
CAN YOU SEW?
EH? ER... A BIT, LIEUTENANT MORGAN.
THEN COME WITH ME!
MINUTES LATER...
NOW DON'T START ON ME, SIR! I'M NOT CUT OUT TO BE A PILOT! THE C.O.'S ALREADY AGREED TO A TRANSFER!
SO YOU CAN SIT OUT THE WAR IN A NICE CUSHY DESK JOB, COSTELLO?
WELL, YOU WON'T BE NEEDING YOUR WINGS!
IT'S NOT MY FAULT! MY NERVES ARE BAD!
AND THAT'S WHY YOU BLAMED BOURNE WHEN YOU RAN OUT ON THAT ARTILLERY SPOTTING JOB! SEW THAT YELLOW PATCH ON HIM, LAD!
IT'S ALL RIGHT, SIR! IT'S FORGOTTEN ABOUT NOW!
DO IT!
NOW GET OUT OF MY SIGHT!
CRIKEY! I HOPE I NEVER GET ON THE WRONG SIDE OF MORGEY!

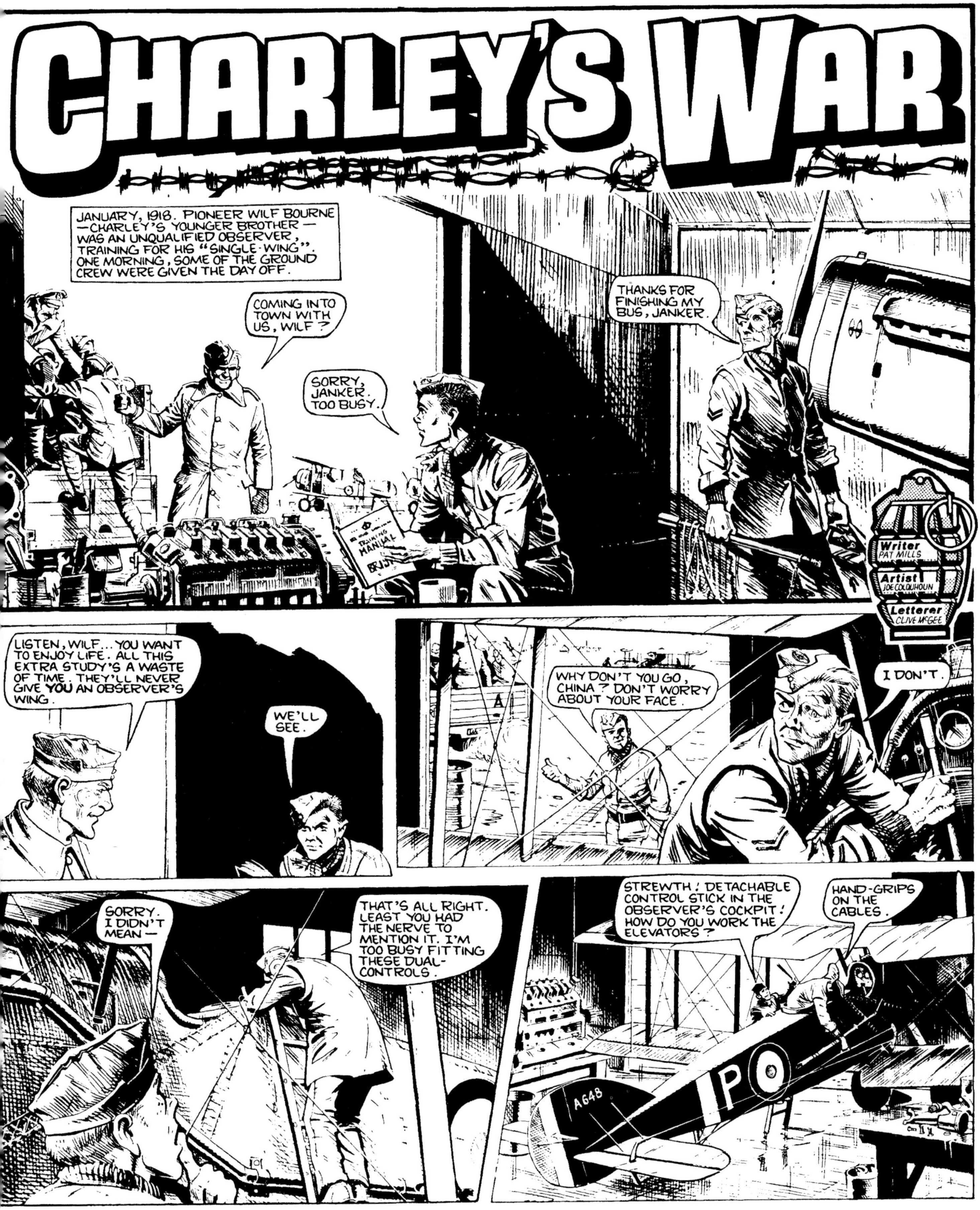
CHARLEY'S WAR
JANUARY, 1918. PIONEER WILF BOURNE —CHARLEY'S YOUNGER BROTHER — WAS AN UNQUALIFIED OBSERVER, TRAINING FOR HIS "SINGLE-WING". ONE MORNING, SOME OF THE GROUND CREW WERE GIVEN THE DAY OFF.
COMING INTO TOWN WITH US, WILF?
SORRY, JANKER. TOO BUSY.
THANKS FOR FINISHING MY BUS, JANKER.
TRAINING MANUAL
Writer PAT MILLS
Artist JOE COLQUHOUN
Letterer CLIVE McGEE
LISTEN, WILF... YOU WANT TO ENJOY LIFE. ALL THIS EXTRA STUDY'S A WASTE OF TIME. THEY'LL NEVER GIVE **YOU** AN OBSERVER'S WING.
WE'LL SEE.
WHY DON'T YOU GO, CHINA? DON'T WORRY ABOUT YOUR FACE.
I DON'T.
SORRY. I DIDN'T MEAN —
THAT'S ALL RIGHT. LEAST YOU HAD THE NERVE TO MENTION IT. I'M TOO BUSY FITTING THESE DUAL-CONTROLS.
STREWTH! DETACHABLE CONTROL STICK IN THE OBSERVER'S COCKPIT! HOW DO YOU WORK THE ELEVATORS?
HAND-GRIPS ON THE CABLES.
A648
P

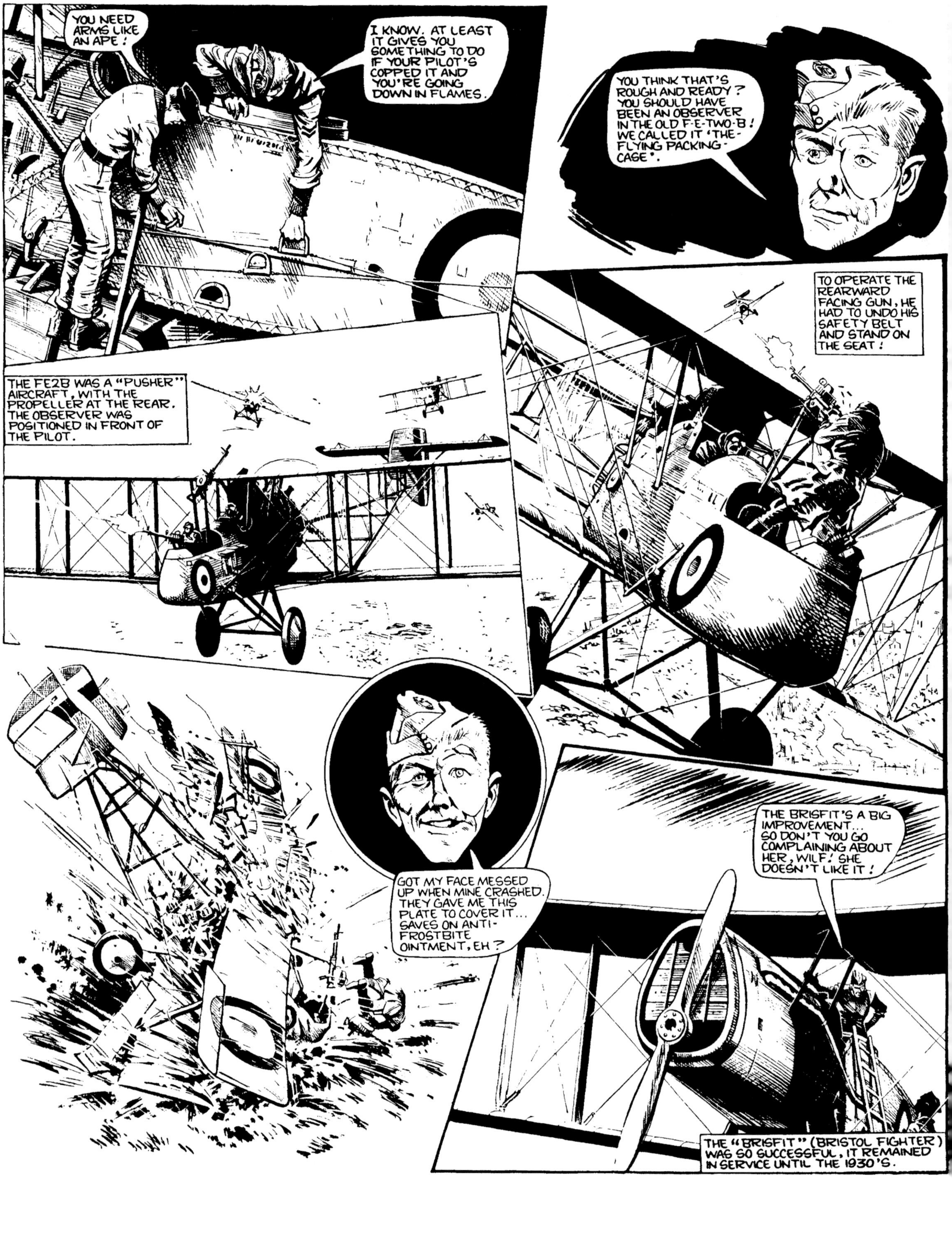
YOU NEED ARMS LIKE AN APE!
I KNOW. AT LEAST IT GIVES YOU SOMETHING TO DO IF YOUR PILOT'S COPPED IT AND YOU'RE GOING DOWN IN FLAMES.
YOU THINK THAT'S ROUGH AND READY? YOU SHOULD HAVE BEEN AN OBSERVER IN THE OLD F·E·TWO·B! WE CALLED IT 'THE FLYING PACKING-CASE'.
THE FE2B WAS A "PUSHER" AIRCRAFT, WITH THE PROPELLER AT THE REAR. THE OBSERVER WAS POSITIONED IN FRONT OF THE PILOT.
TO OPERATE THE REARWARD FACING GUN, HE HAD TO UNDO HIS SAFETY BELT AND STAND ON THE SEAT!
GOT MY FACE MESSED UP WHEN MINE CRASHED. THEY GAVE ME THIS PLATE TO COVER IT... SAVES ON ANTI-FROSTBITE OINTMENT, EH?
THE BRISFIT'S A BIG IMPROVEMENT... SO DON'T YOU GO COMPLAINING ABOUT HER, WILF! SHE DOESN'T LIKE IT!
THE "BRISFIT" (BRISTOL FIGHTER) WAS SO SUCCESSFUL, IT REMAINED IN SERVICE UNTIL THE 1930'S.

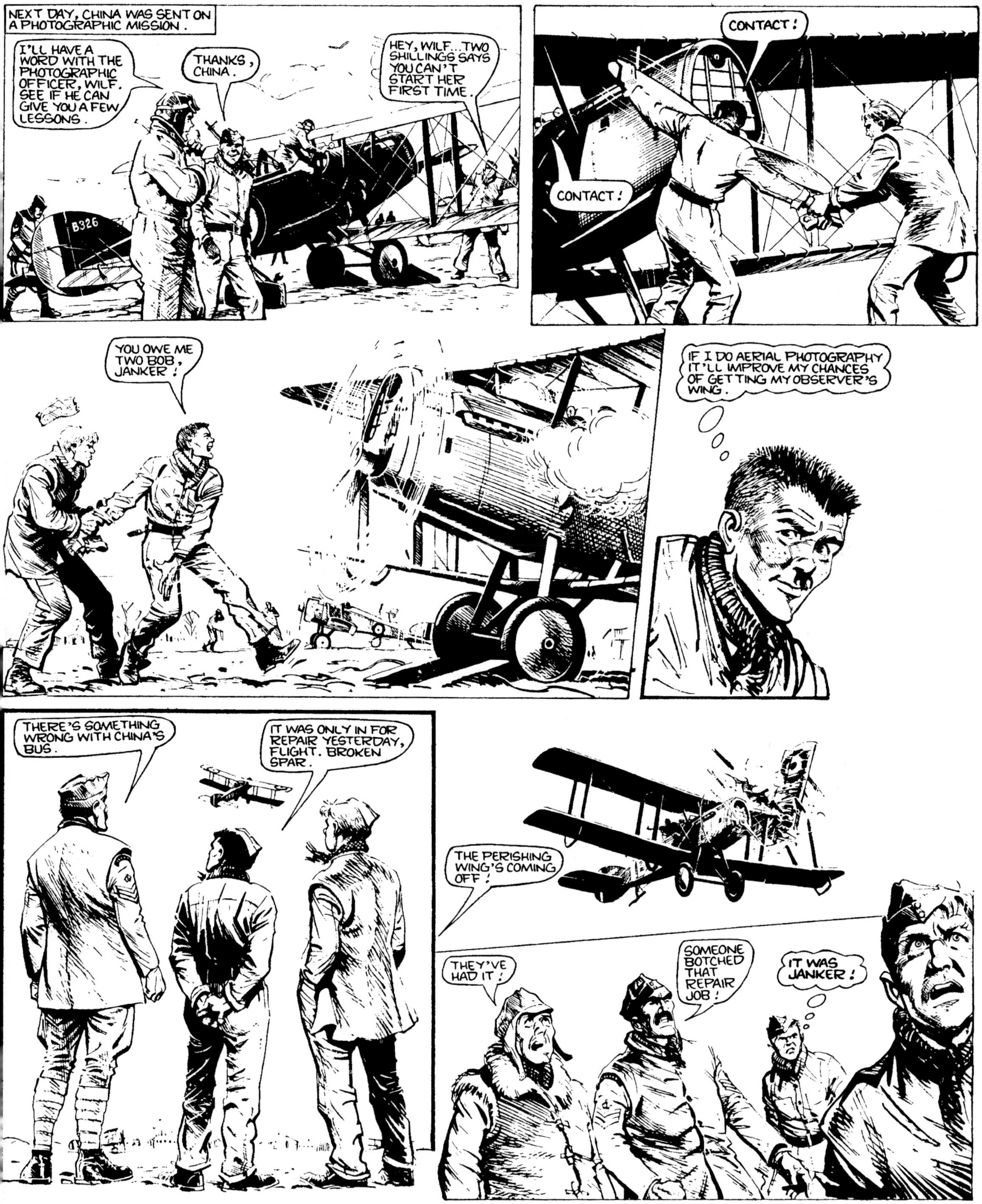
NEXT DAY, CHINA WAS SENT ON A PHOTOGRAPHIC MISSION.
I'LL HAVE A WORD WITH THE PHOTOGRAPHIC OFFICER, WILF. SEE IF HE CAN GIVE YOU A FEW LESSONS.
THANKS, CHINA.
HEY, WILF... TWO SHILLINGS SAYS YOU CAN'T START HER FIRST TIME.
B326
CONTACT!
CONTACT!
YOU OWE ME TWO BOB, JANKER!
IF I DO AERIAL PHOTOGRAPHY IT'LL IMPROVE MY CHANCES OF GETTING MY OBSERVER'S WING.
THERE'S SOMETHING WRONG WITH CHINA'S BUS.
IT WAS ONLY IN FOR REPAIR YESTERDAY, FLIGHT. BROKEN SPAR.
THE PERISHING WING'S COMING OFF!
THEY'VE HAD IT!
SOMEONE BOTCHED THAT REPAIR JOB!
IT WAS JANKER!

# CHARLEY'S WAR

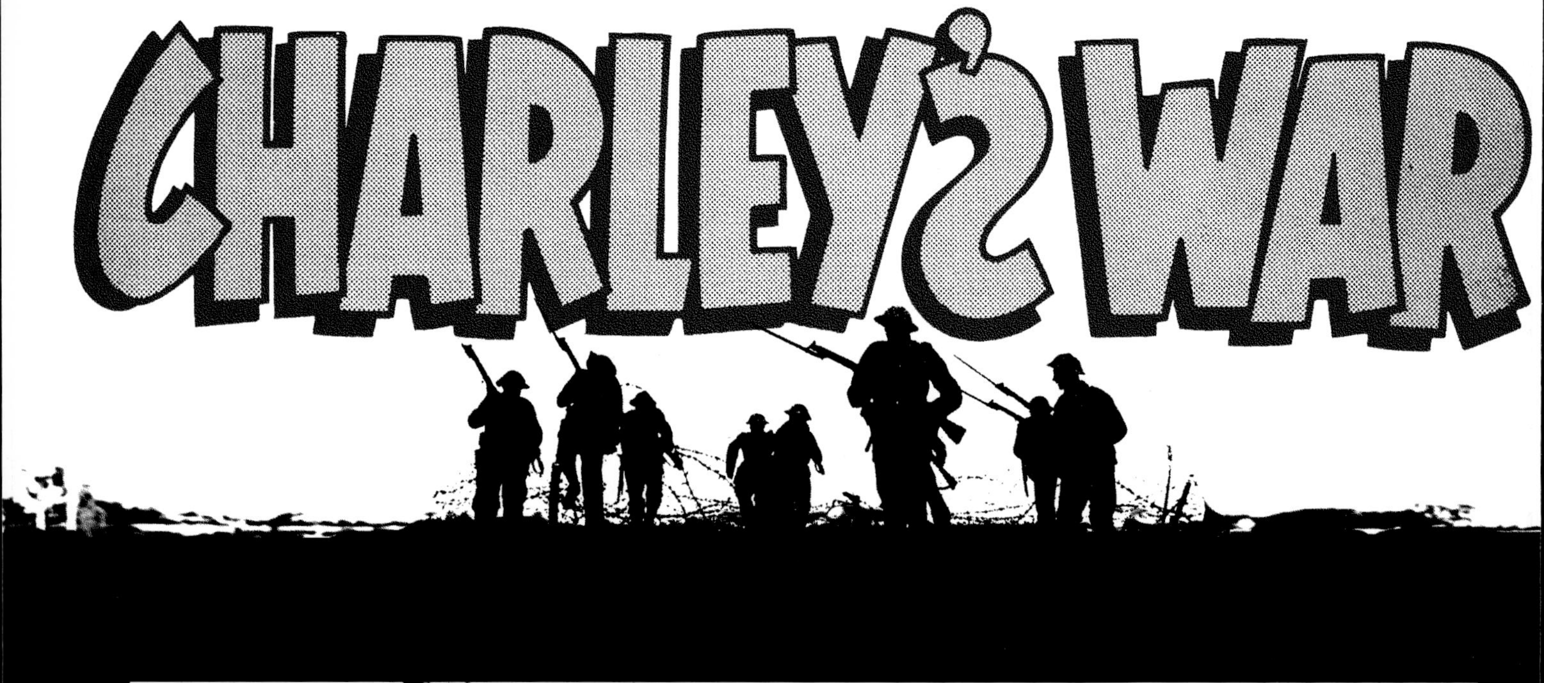

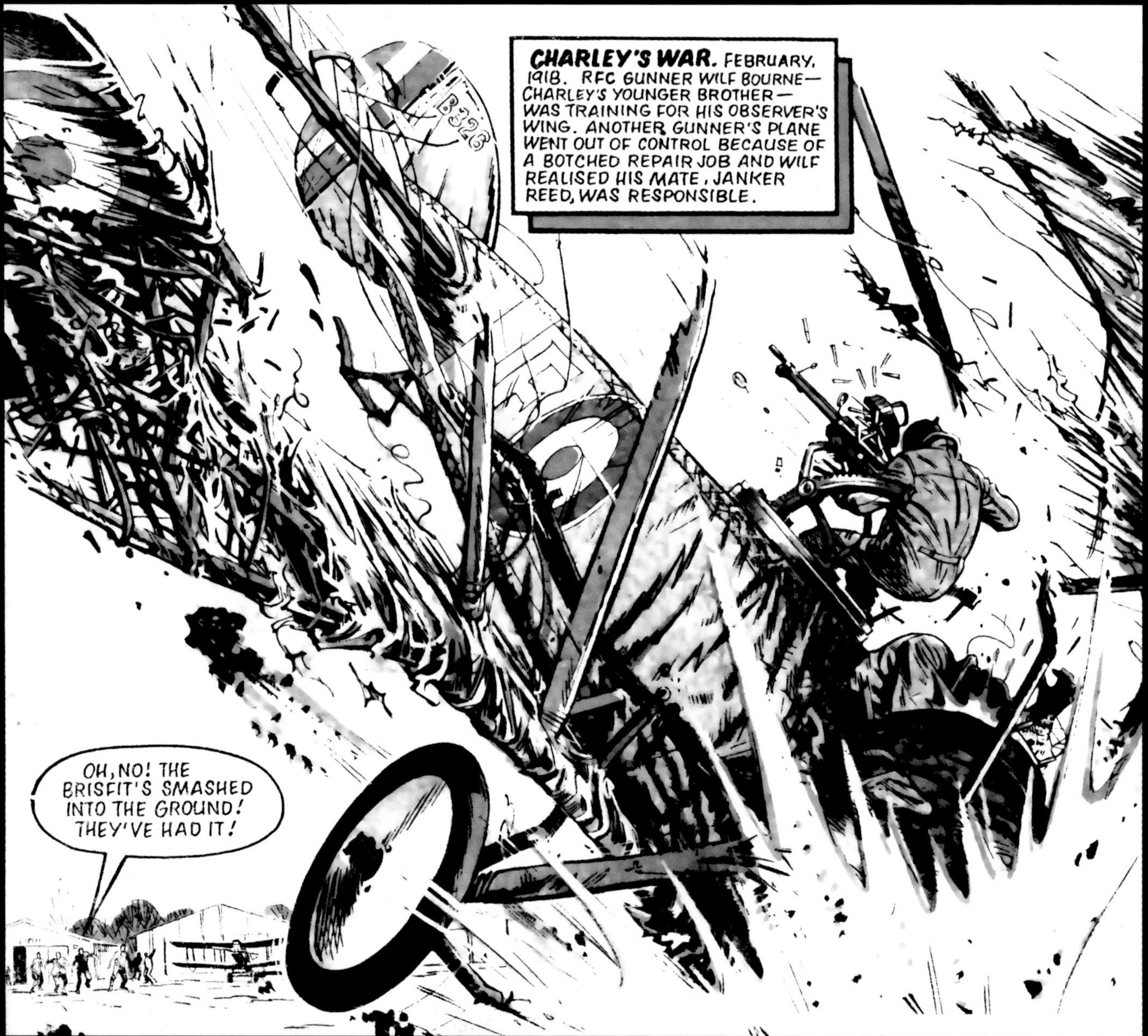

CHARLEY'S WAR. FEBRUARY, 1918. RFC GUNNER WILF BOURNE— CHARLEY'S YOUNGER BROTHER— WAS TRAINING FOR HIS OBSERVER'S WING. ANOTHER GUNNER'S PLANE WENT OUT OF CONTROL BECAUSE OF A BOTCHED REPAIR JOB AND WILF REALISED HIS MATE, JANKER REED, WAS RESPONSIBLE.
OH, NO! THE BRISFIT'S SMASHED INTO THE GROUND! THEY'VE HAD IT!

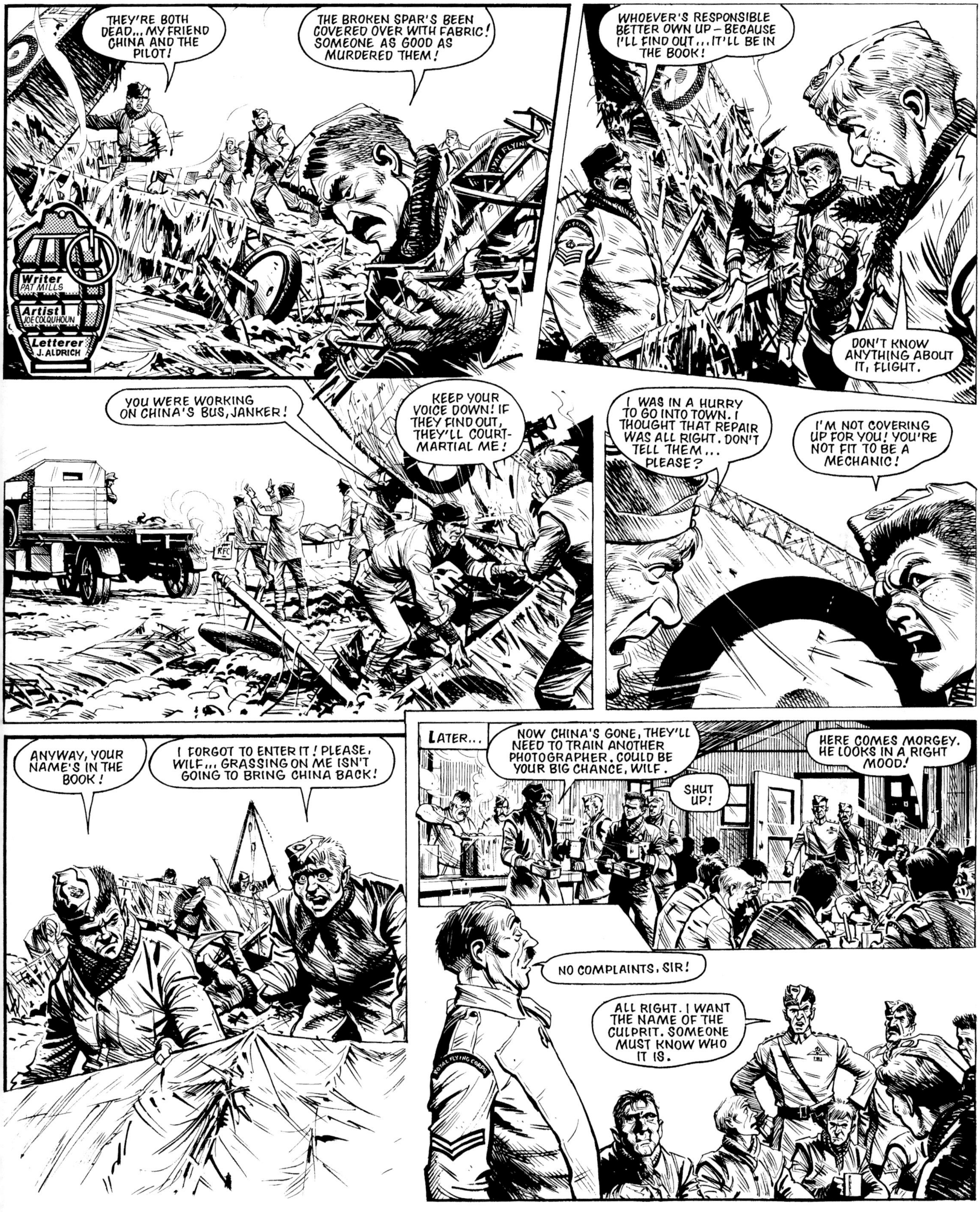

They're both dead... my friend China and the pilot!
The broken spar's been covered over with fabric! Someone as good as murdered them!
Writer PAT MILLS
Artist JOE COLQUHOUN
Letterer J. ALDRICH
Whoever's responsible better own up – because I'll find out... it'll be in the book!
Don't know anything about it, Flight.
You were working on China's bus, Janker!
Keep your voice down! If they find out, they'll court-martial me!
RFC
I was in a hurry to go into town. I thought that repair was all right. Don't tell them... please?
I'm not covering up for you! You're not fit to be a mechanic!
Anyway, your name's in the book!
I forgot to enter it! Please, Wilf... grassing on me isn't going to bring China back!
Later...
Now China's gone, they'll need to train another photographer. Could be your big chance, Wilf.
Shut up!
Here comes Morgey. He looks in a right mood!
No complaints, sir!
All right. I want the name of the culprit. Someone must know who it is.

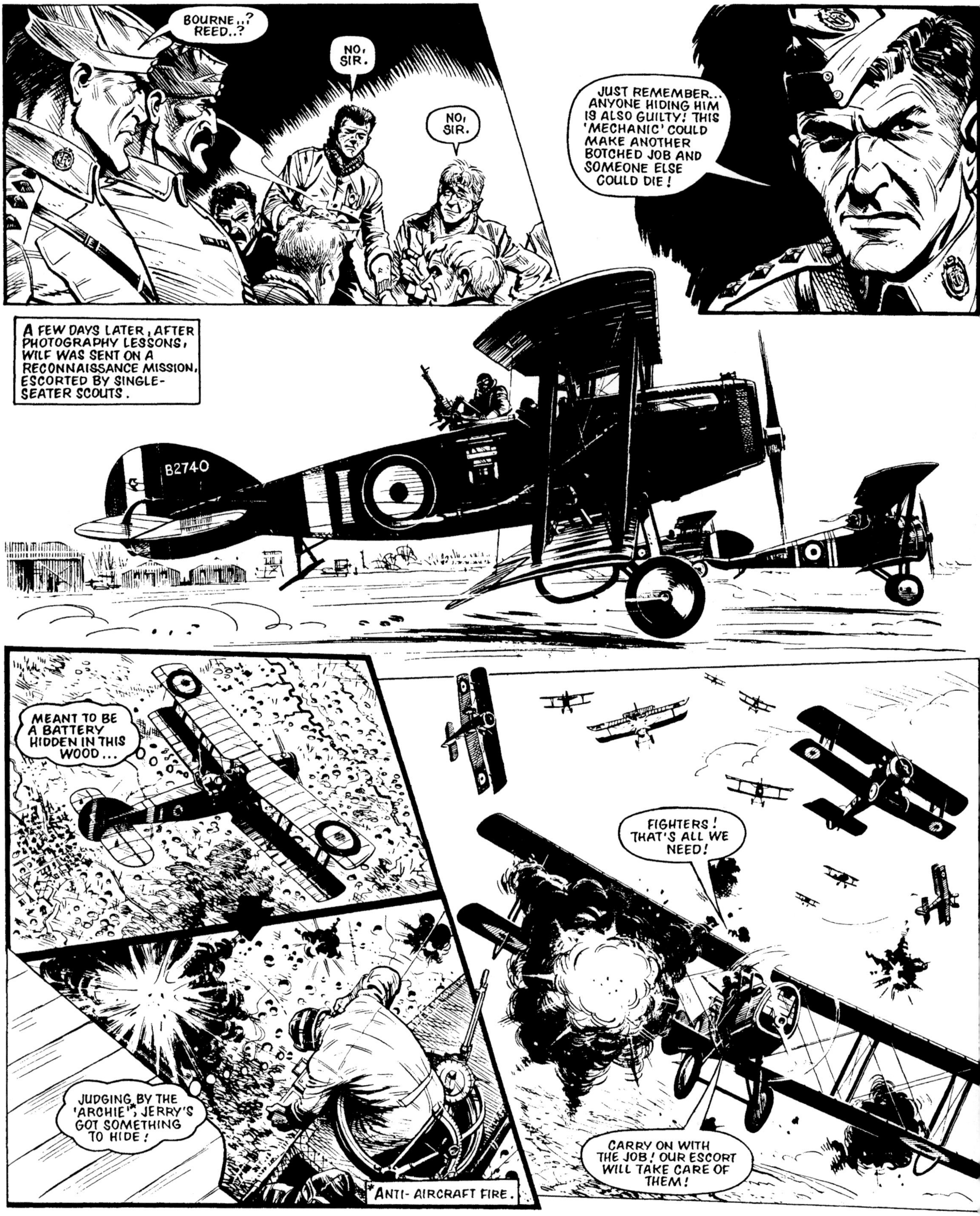
BOURNE..? REED..?
NO, SIR.
NO, SIR.
JUST REMEMBER... ANYONE HIDING HIM IS ALSO GUILTY! THIS 'MECHANIC' COULD MAKE ANOTHER BOTCHED JOB AND SOMEONE ELSE COULD DIE!
A FEW DAYS LATER, AFTER PHOTOGRAPHY LESSONS, WILF WAS SENT ON A RECONNAISSANCE MISSION, ESCORTED BY SINGLE-SEATER SCOUTS.
B2740
MEANT TO BE A BATTERY HIDDEN IN THIS WOOD...
JUDGING BY THE 'ARCHIE'*, JERRY'S GOT SOMETHING TO HIDE!
*ANTI-AIRCRAFT FIRE.
FIGHTERS! THAT'S ALL WE NEED!
CARRY ON WITH THE JOB! OUR ESCORT WILL TAKE CARE OF THEM!

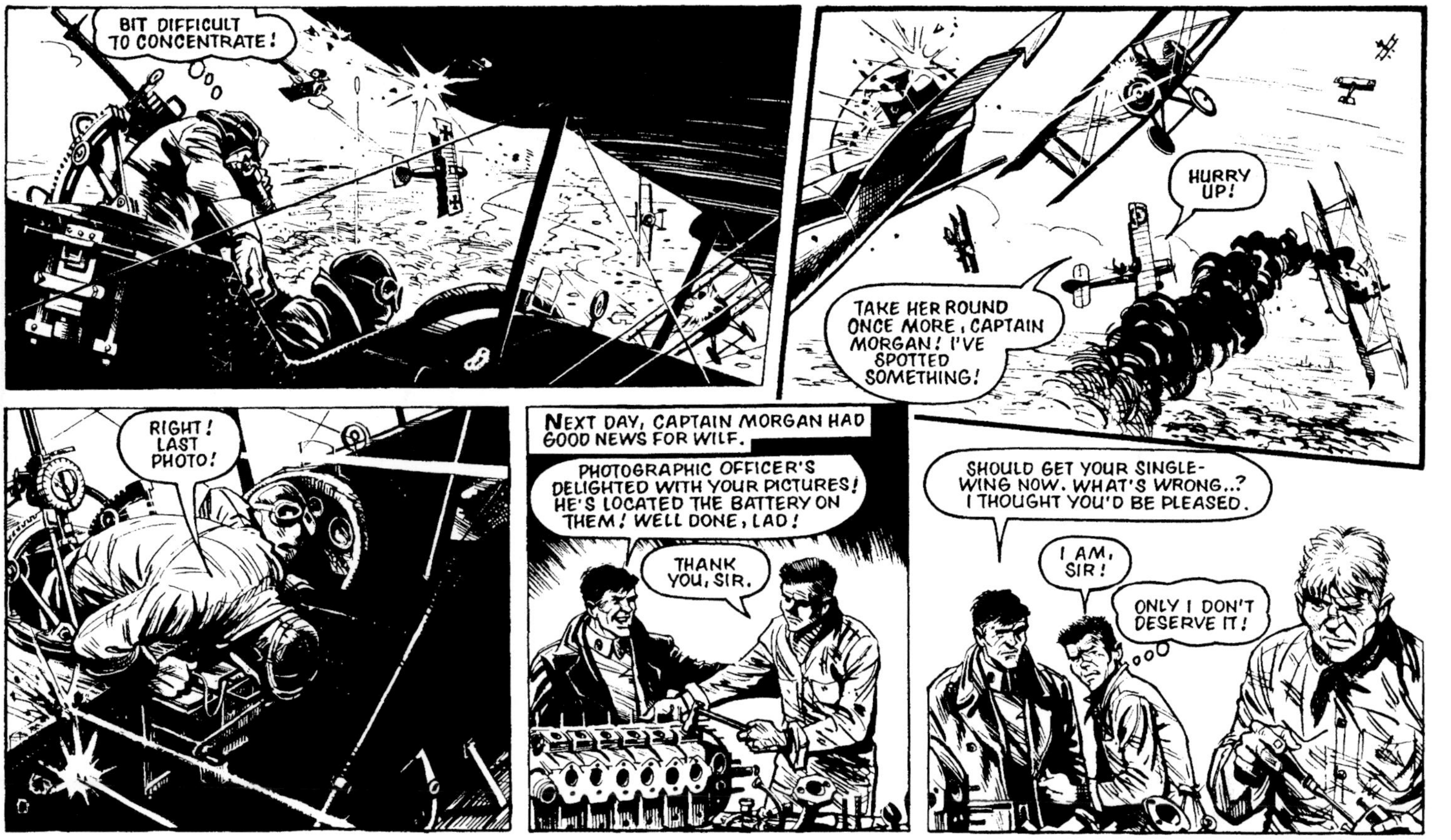
BIT DIFFICULT TO CONCENTRATE!
HURRY UP!
TAKE HER ROUND ONCE MORE, CAPTAIN MORGAN! I'VE SPOTTED SOMETHING!
RIGHT! LAST PHOTO!
NEXT DAY, CAPTAIN MORGAN HAD GOOD NEWS FOR WILF.
PHOTOGRAPHIC OFFICER'S DELIGHTED WITH YOUR PICTURES! HE'S LOCATED THE BATTERY ON THEM! WELL DONE, LAD!
THANK YOU, SIR.
SHOULD GET YOUR SINGLE-WING NOW. WHAT'S WRONG..? I THOUGHT YOU'D BE PLEASED.
I AM, SIR!
ONLY I DON'T DESERVE IT!

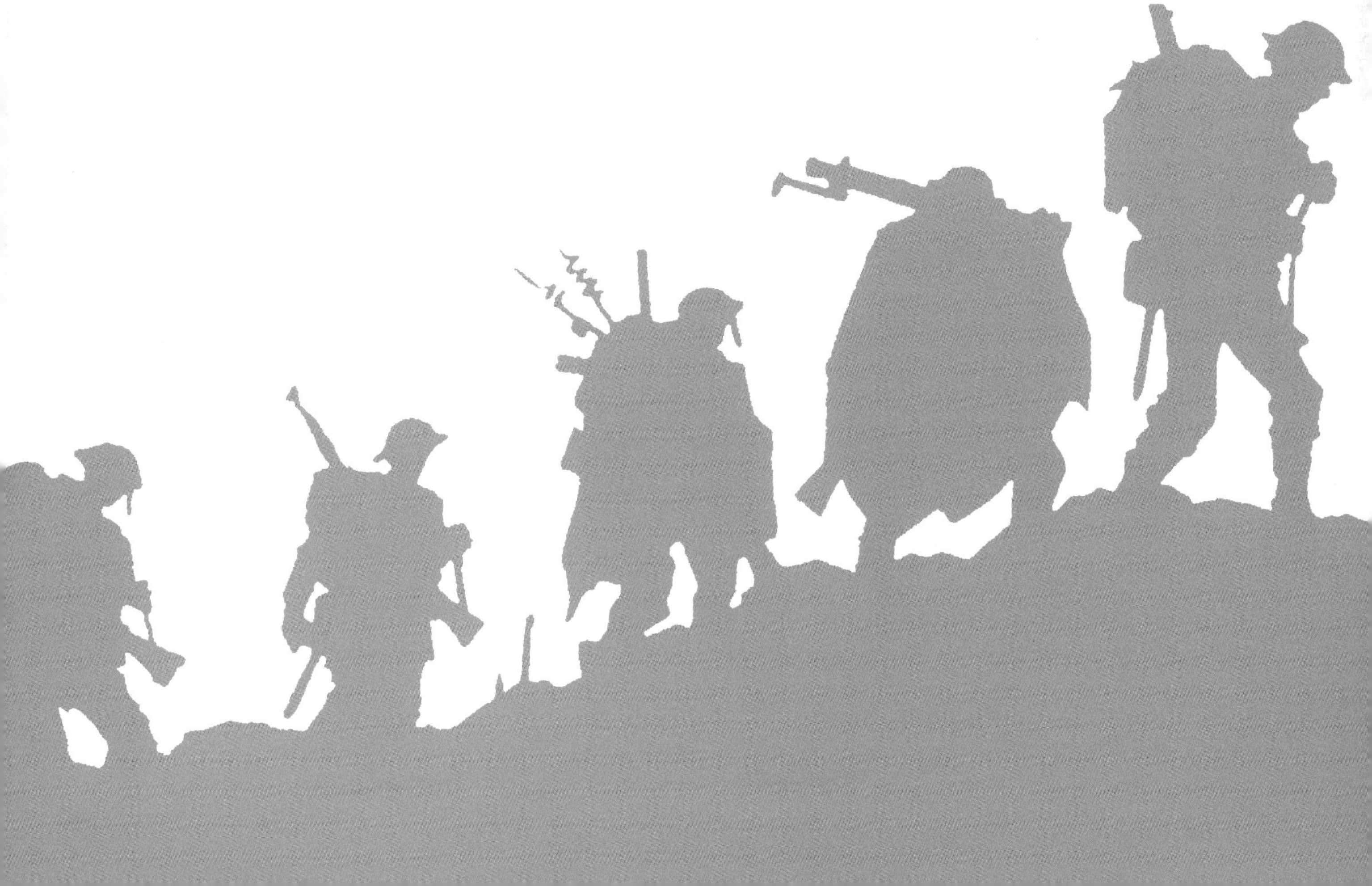

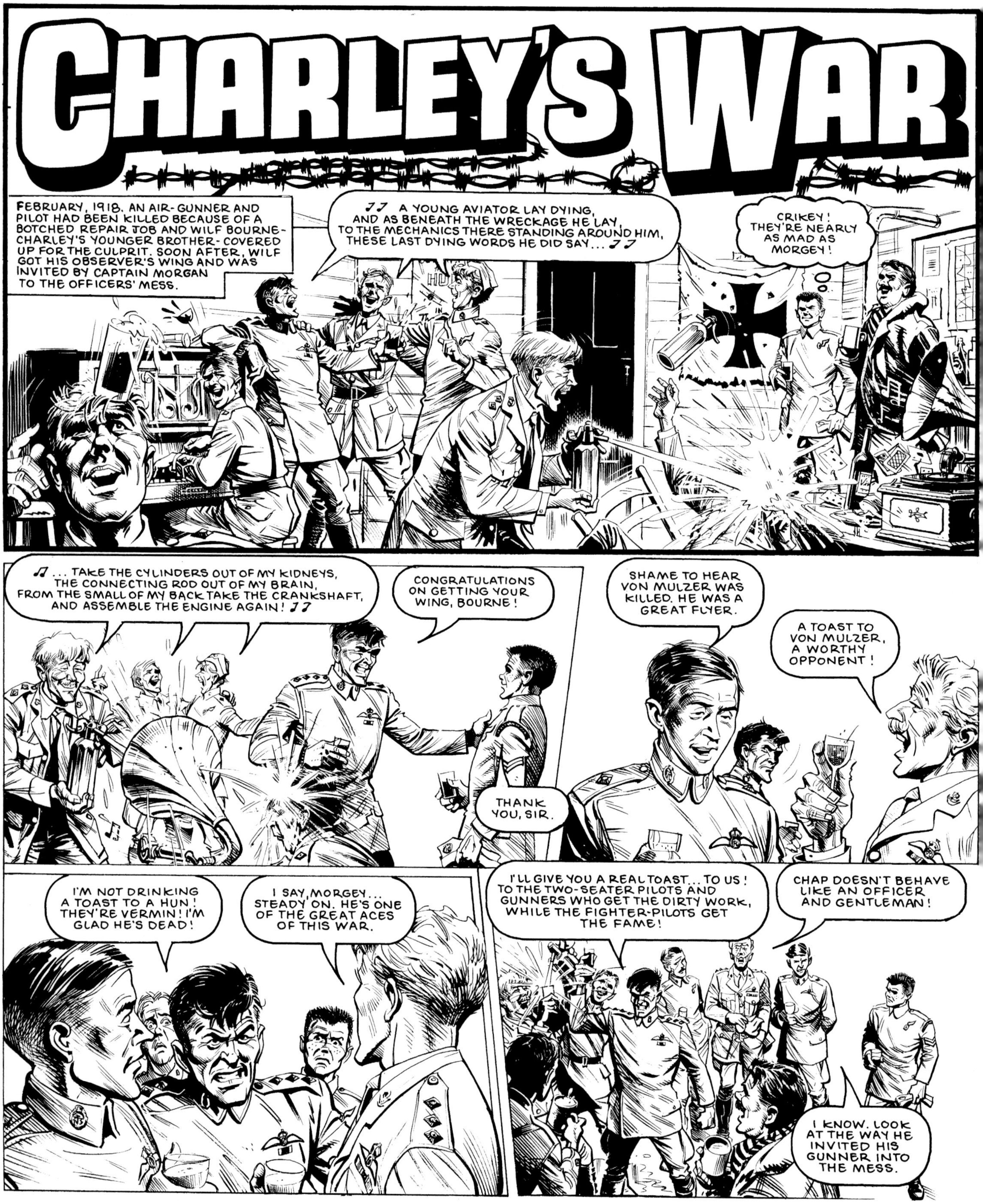
CHARLEY'S WAR
FEBRUARY, 1918. AN AIR-GUNNER AND PILOT HAD BEEN KILLED BECAUSE OF A BOTCHED REPAIR JOB AND WILF BOURNE- CHARLEY'S YOUNGER BROTHER- COVERED UP FOR THE CULPRIT. SOON AFTER, WILF GOT HIS OBSERVER'S WING AND WAS INVITED BY CAPTAIN MORGAN TO THE OFFICERS' MESS.
♫ A YOUNG AVIATOR LAY DYING, AND AS BENEATH THE WRECKAGE HE LAY, TO THE MECHANICS THERE STANDING AROUND HIM, THESE LAST DYING WORDS HE DID SAY... ♫
CRIKEY! THEY'RE NEARLY AS MAD AS MORGEY!
♫ ... TAKE THE CYLINDERS OUT OF MY KIDNEYS, THE CONNECTING ROD OUT OF MY BRAIN, FROM THE SMALL OF MY BACK TAKE THE CRANKSHAFT, AND ASSEMBLE THE ENGINE AGAIN! ♫
CONGRATULATIONS ON GETTING YOUR WING, BOURNE!
THANK YOU, SIR.
SHAME TO HEAR VON MULZER WAS KILLED. HE WAS A GREAT FLYER.
A TOAST TO VON MULZER, A WORTHY OPPONENT!
I'M NOT DRINKING A TOAST TO A HUN! THEY'RE VERMIN! I'M GLAD HE'S DEAD!
I SAY, MORGEY... STEADY ON. HE'S ONE OF THE GREAT ACES OF THIS WAR.
I'LL GIVE YOU A REAL TOAST... TO US! TO THE TWO-SEATER PILOTS AND GUNNERS WHO GET THE DIRTY WORK, WHILE THE FIGHTER-PILOTS GET THE FAME!
CHAP DOESN'T BEHAVE LIKE AN OFFICER AND GENTLEMAN!
I KNOW. LOOK AT THE WAY HE INVITED HIS GUNNER INTO THE MESS.

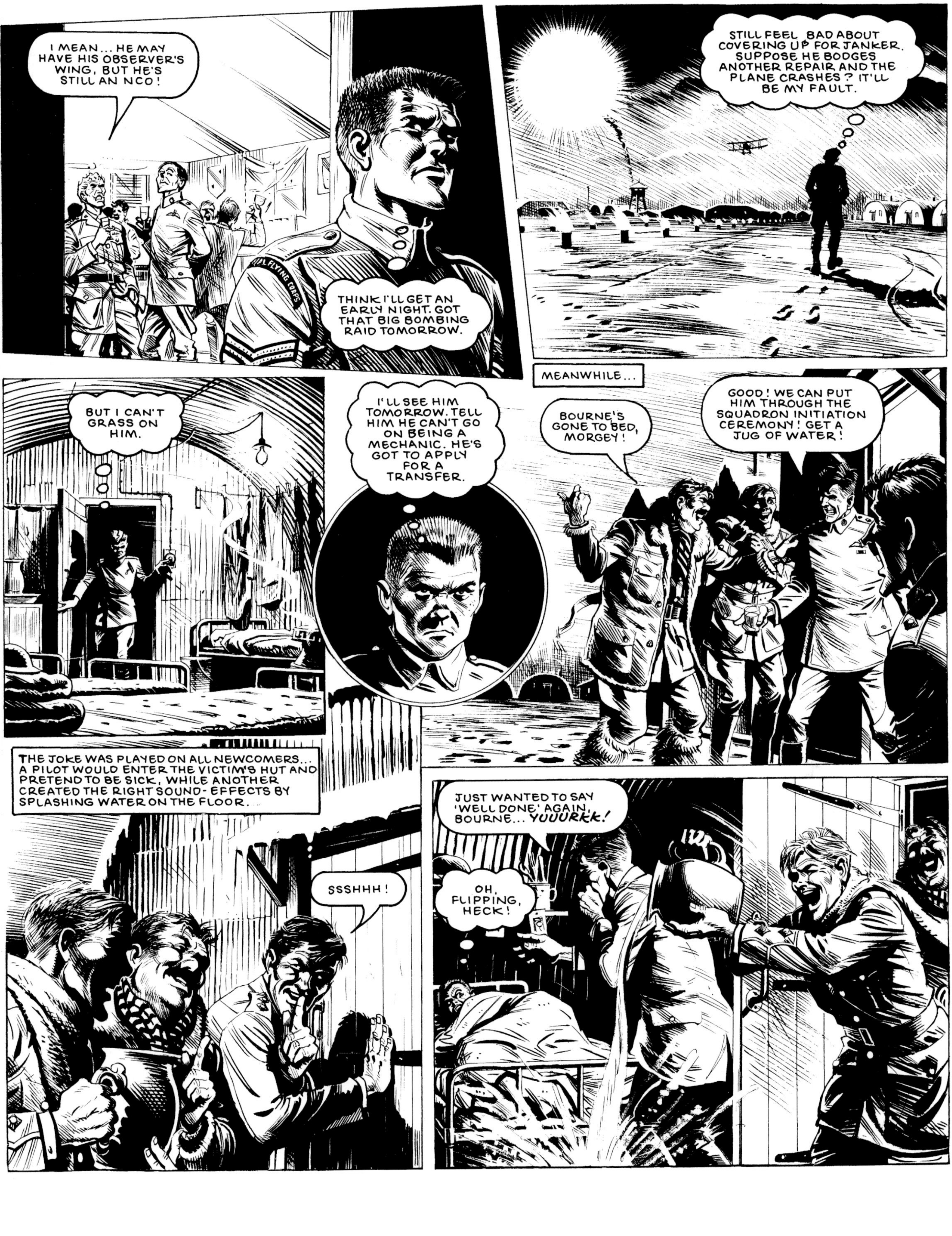
I MEAN... HE MAY HAVE HIS OBSERVER'S WING, BUT HE'S STILL AN NCO!
THINK I'LL GET AN EARLY NIGHT. GOT THAT BIG BOMBING RAID TOMORROW.
STILL FEEL BAD ABOUT COVERING UP FOR JANKER. SUPPOSE HE BODGES ANOTHER REPAIR AND THE PLANE CRASHES? IT'LL BE MY FAULT.
BUT I CAN'T GRASS ON HIM.
I'LL SEE HIM TOMORROW. TELL HIM HE CAN'T GO ON BEING A MECHANIC. HE'S GOT TO APPLY FOR A TRANSFER.
MEANWHILE...
BOURNE'S GONE TO BED, MORGEY!
GOOD! WE CAN PUT HIM THROUGH THE SQUADRON INITIATION CEREMONY! GET A JUG OF WATER!
THE JOKE WAS PLAYED ON ALL NEWCOMERS... A PILOT WOULD ENTER THE VICTIM'S HUT AND PRETEND TO BE SICK, WHILE ANOTHER CREATED THE RIGHT SOUND-EFFECTS BY SPLASHING WATER ON THE FLOOR...
SSSHHH!
JUST WANTED TO SAY 'WELL DONE' AGAIN, BOURNE... YUUURKk!
OH, FLIPPING HECK!

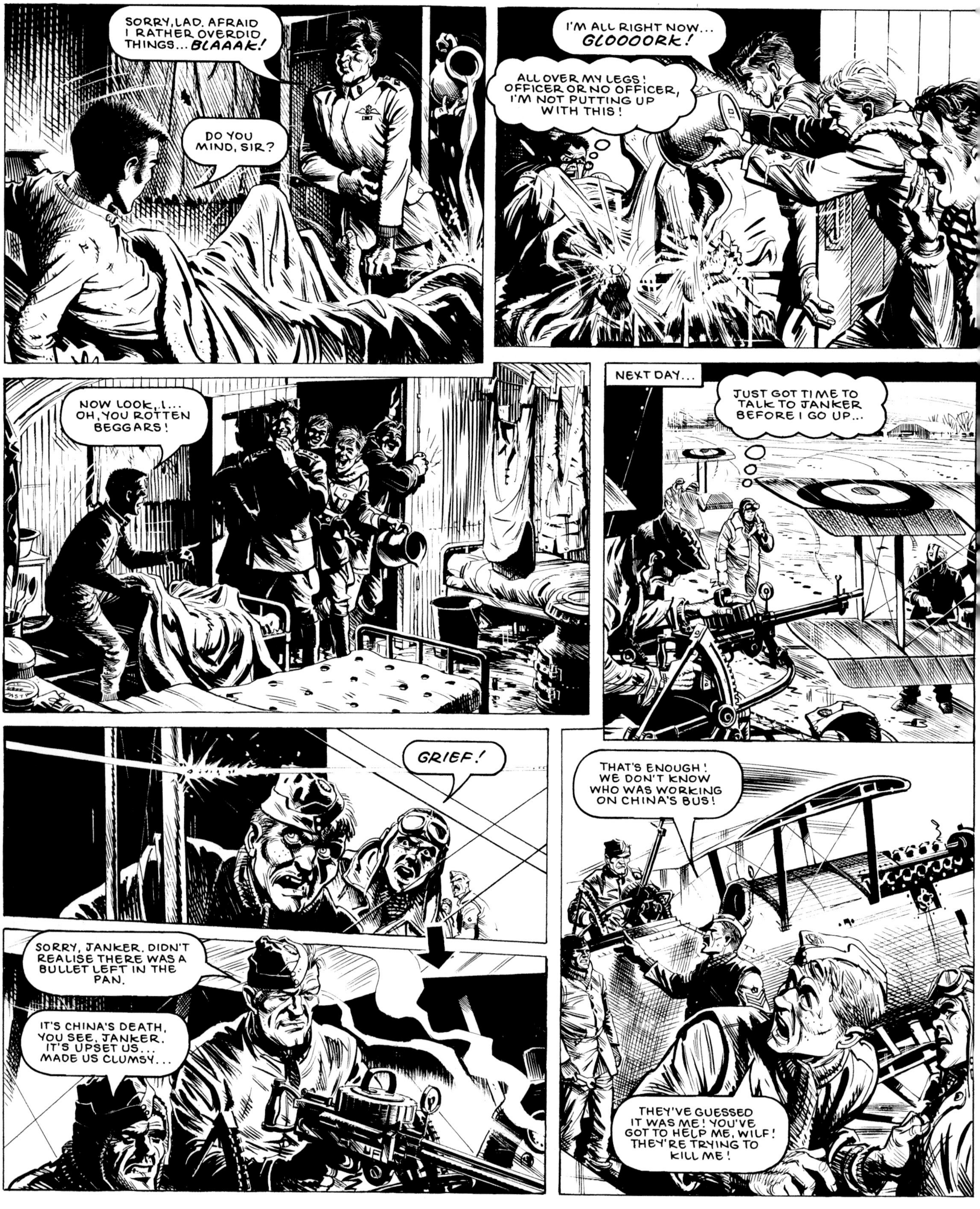
SORRY, LAD. AFRAID I RATHER OVERDID THINGS... BLAAAK!
DO YOU MIND, SIR?
I'M ALL RIGHT NOW... GLOOOORK!
ALL OVER MY LEGS! OFFICER OR NO OFFICER, I'M NOT PUTTING UP WITH THIS!
NOW LOOK, I... OH, YOU ROTTEN BEGGARS!
NEXT DAY...
JUST GOT TIME TO TALK TO JANKER BEFORE I GO UP...
GRIEF!
SORRY, JANKER. DIDN'T REALISE THERE WAS A BULLET LEFT IN THE PAN.
IT'S CHINA'S DEATH, YOU SEE, JANKER. IT'S UPSET US... MADE US CLUMSY...
THAT'S ENOUGH! WE DON'T KNOW WHO WAS WORKING ON CHINA'S BUS!
THEY'VE GUESSED IT WAS ME! YOU'VE GOT TO HELP ME, WILF! THEY'RE TRYING TO KILL ME!

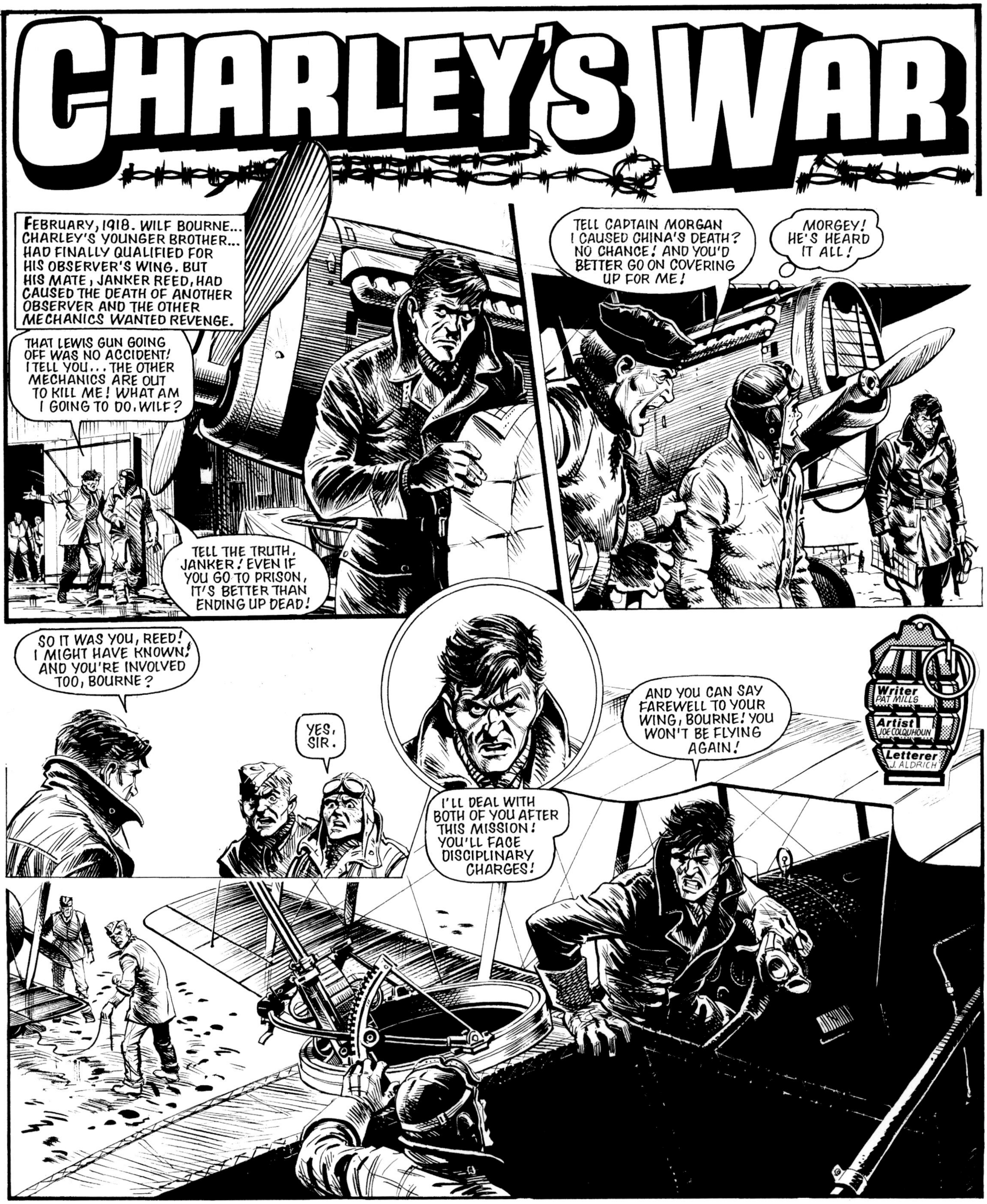
CHARLEY'S WAR
FEBRUARY, 1918. WILF BOURNE... CHARLEY'S YOUNGER BROTHER... HAD FINALLY QUALIFIED FOR HIS OBSERVER'S WING. BUT HIS MATE, JANKER REED, HAD CAUSED THE DEATH OF ANOTHER OBSERVER AND THE OTHER MECHANICS WANTED REVENGE.
THAT LEWIS GUN GOING OFF WAS NO ACCIDENT! I TELL YOU... THE OTHER MECHANICS ARE OUT TO KILL ME! WHAT AM I GOING TO DO, WILF?
TELL THE TRUTH, JANKER! EVEN IF YOU GO TO PRISON, IT'S BETTER THAN ENDING UP DEAD!
TELL CAPTAIN MORGAN I CAUSED CHINA'S DEATH? NO CHANCE! AND YOU'D BETTER GO ON COVERING UP FOR ME!
MORGEY! HE'S HEARD IT ALL!
SO IT WAS YOU, REED! I MIGHT HAVE KNOWN! AND YOU'RE INVOLVED TOO, BOURNE?
YES, SIR.
AND YOU CAN SAY FAREWELL TO YOUR WING, BOURNE! YOU WON'T BE FLYING AGAIN!
I'LL DEAL WITH BOTH OF YOU AFTER THIS MISSION! YOU'LL FACE DISCIPLINARY CHARGES!
Writer PAT MILLS
Artist JOE COLQUHOUN
Letterer J. ALDRICH

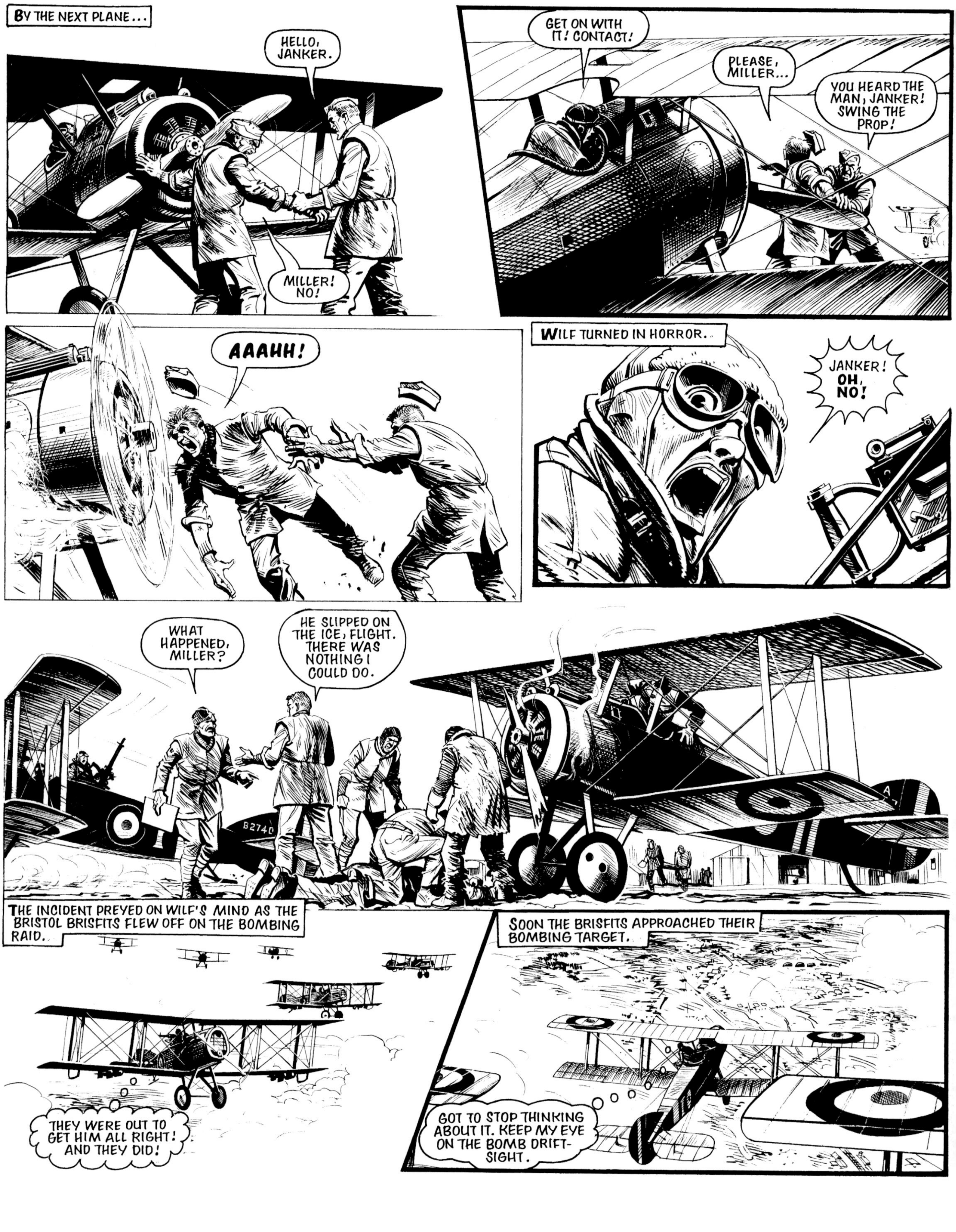
BY THE NEXT PLANE...
HELLO, JANKER.
MILLER! NO!
GET ON WITH IT! CONTACT!
PLEASE, MILLER...
YOU HEARD THE MAN, JANKER! SWING THE PROP!
AAAHH!
WILF TURNED IN HORROR.
JANKER! OH, NO!
WHAT HAPPENED, MILLER?
HE SLIPPED ON THE ICE, FLIGHT. THERE WAS NOTHING I COULD DO.
THE INCIDENT PREYED ON WILF'S MIND AS THE BRISTOL BRISFITS FLEW OFF ON THE BOMBING RAID.
THEY WERE OUT TO GET HIM ALL RIGHT! AND THEY DID!
SOON THE BRISFITS APPROACHED THEIR BOMBING TARGET.
GOT TO STOP THINKING ABOUT IT. KEEP MY EYE ON THE BOMB DRIFT-SIGHT.

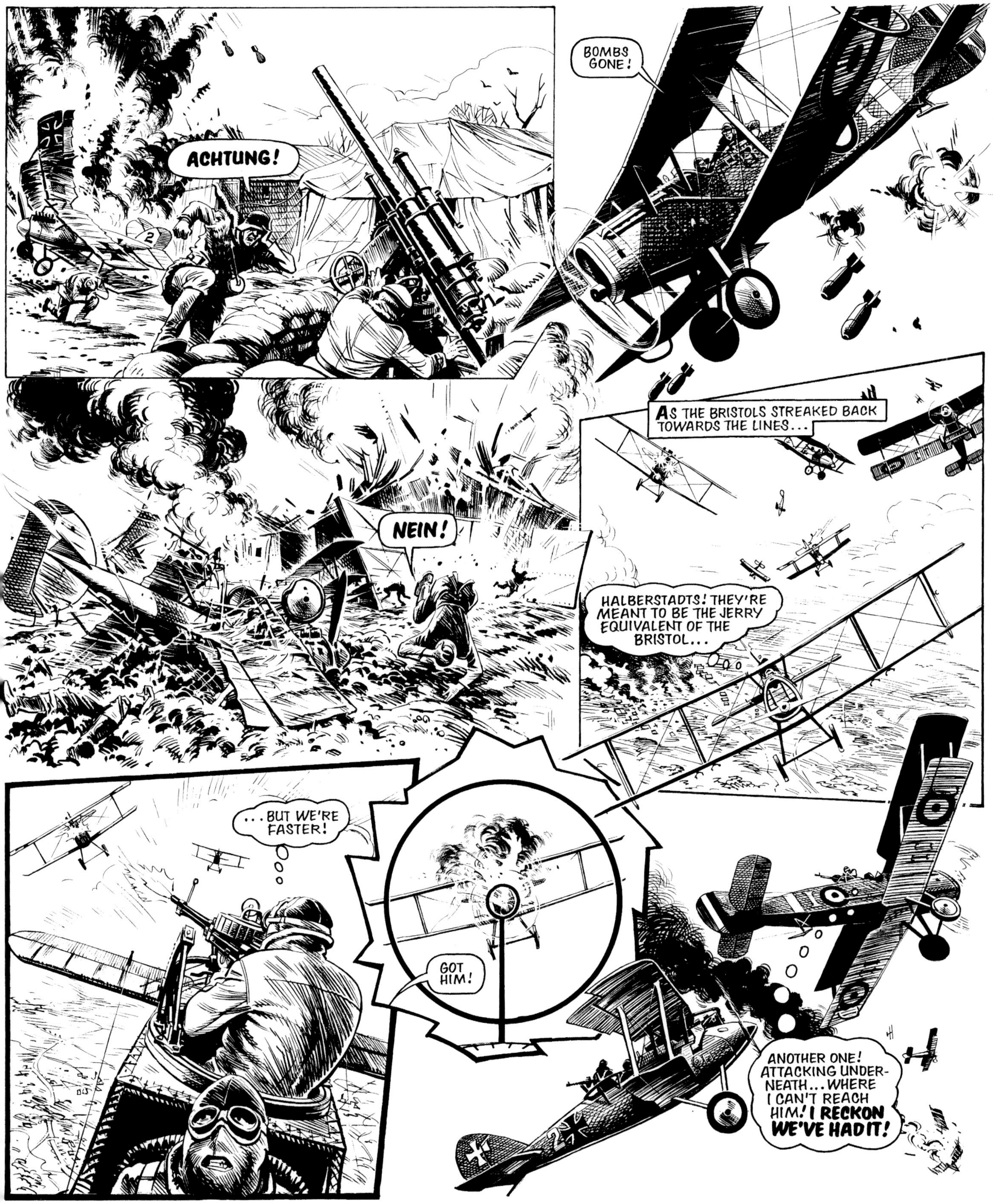
ACHTUNG!
BOMBS GONE!
NEIN!
AS THE BRISTOLS STREAKED BACK TOWARDS THE LINES...
HALBERSTADTS! THEY'RE MEANT TO BE THE JERRY EQUIVALENT OF THE BRISTOL...
...BUT WE'RE FASTER!
GOT HIM!
ANOTHER ONE! ATTACKING UNDERNEATH... WHERE I CAN'T REACH HIM! I RECKON WE'VE HAD IT!

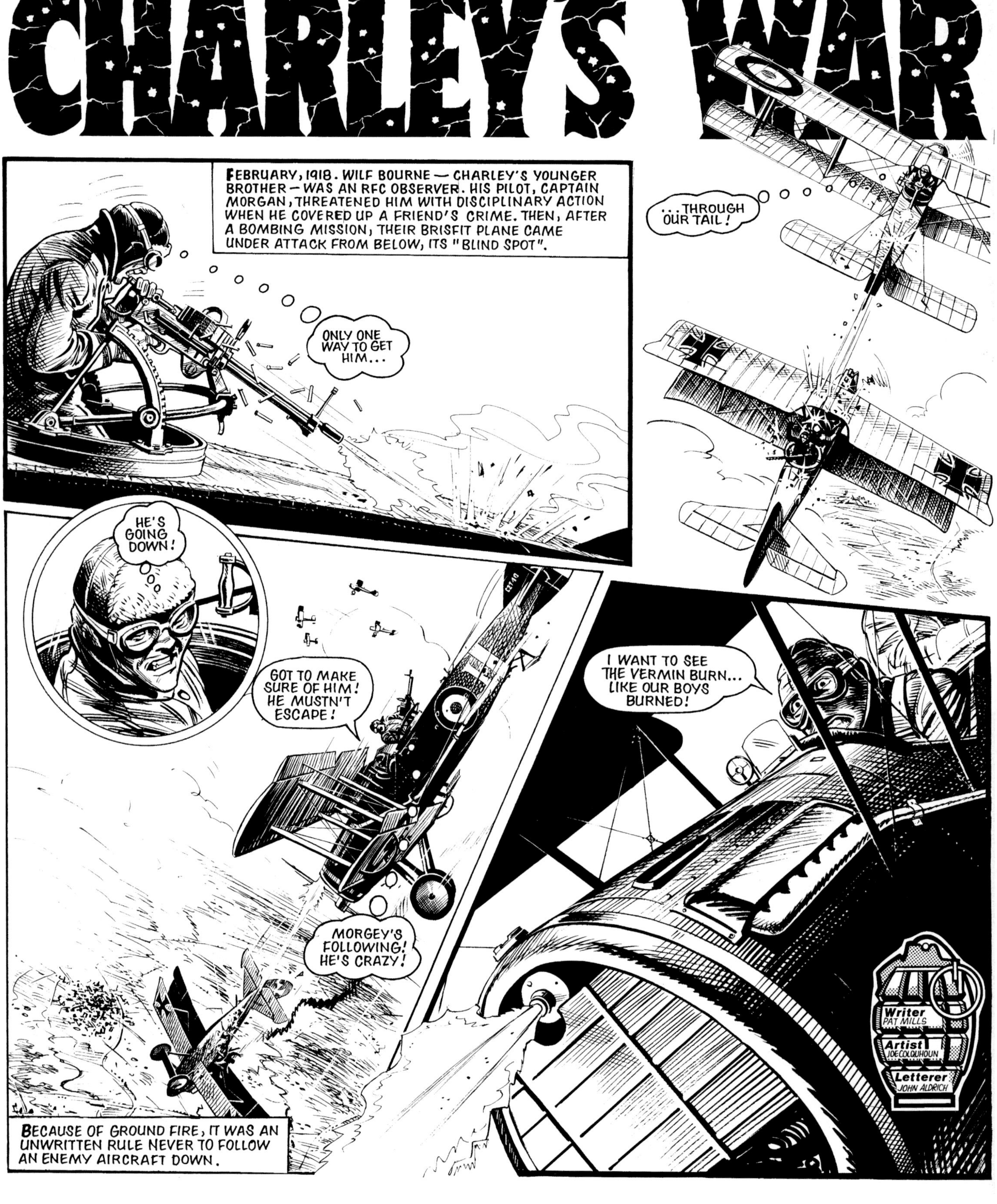
CHARLEY'S WAR
FEBRUARY, 1918. WILF BOURNE — CHARLEY'S YOUNGER BROTHER — WAS AN RFC OBSERVER. HIS PILOT, CAPTAIN MORGAN, THREATENED HIM WITH DISCIPLINARY ACTION WHEN HE COVERED UP A FRIEND'S CRIME. THEN, AFTER A BOMBING MISSION, THEIR BRISFIT PLANE CAME UNDER ATTACK FROM BELOW, ITS "BLIND SPOT".
ONLY ONE WAY TO GET HIM...
...THROUGH OUR TAIL!
HE'S GOING DOWN!
GOT TO MAKE SURE OF HIM! HE MUSTN'T ESCAPE!
MORGEY'S FOLLOWING! HE'S CRAZY!
I WANT TO SEE THE VERMIN BURN... LIKE OUR BOYS BURNED!
Writer PAT MILLS
Artist JOE COLQUHOUN
Letterer JOHN ALDRICH
BECAUSE OF GROUND FIRE, IT WAS AN UNWRITTEN RULE NEVER TO FOLLOW AN ENEMY AIRCRAFT DOWN.

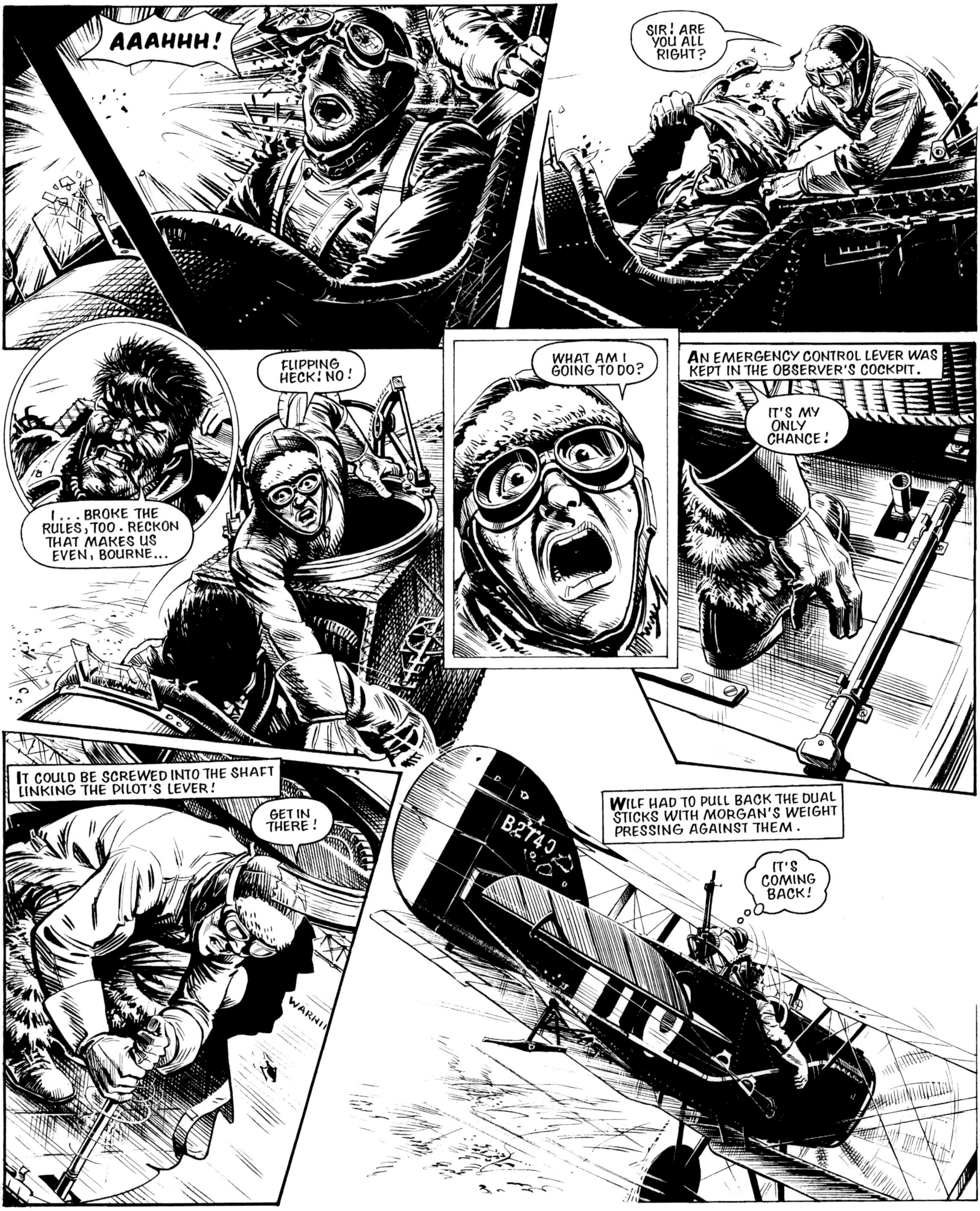
AAAHHH!
SIR! ARE YOU ALL RIGHT?
FLIPPING HECK! NO!
I... BROKE THE RULES, TOO. RECKON THAT MAKES US EVEN, BOURNE...
WHAT AM I GOING TO DO?
AN EMERGENCY CONTROL LEVER WAS KEPT IN THE OBSERVER'S COCKPIT.
IT'S MY ONLY CHANCE!
IT COULD BE SCREWED INTO THE SHAFT LINKING THE PILOT'S LEVER!
GET IN THERE!
WILF HAD TO PULL BACK THE DUAL STICKS WITH MORGAN'S WEIGHT PRESSING AGAINST THEM.
IT'S COMING BACK!

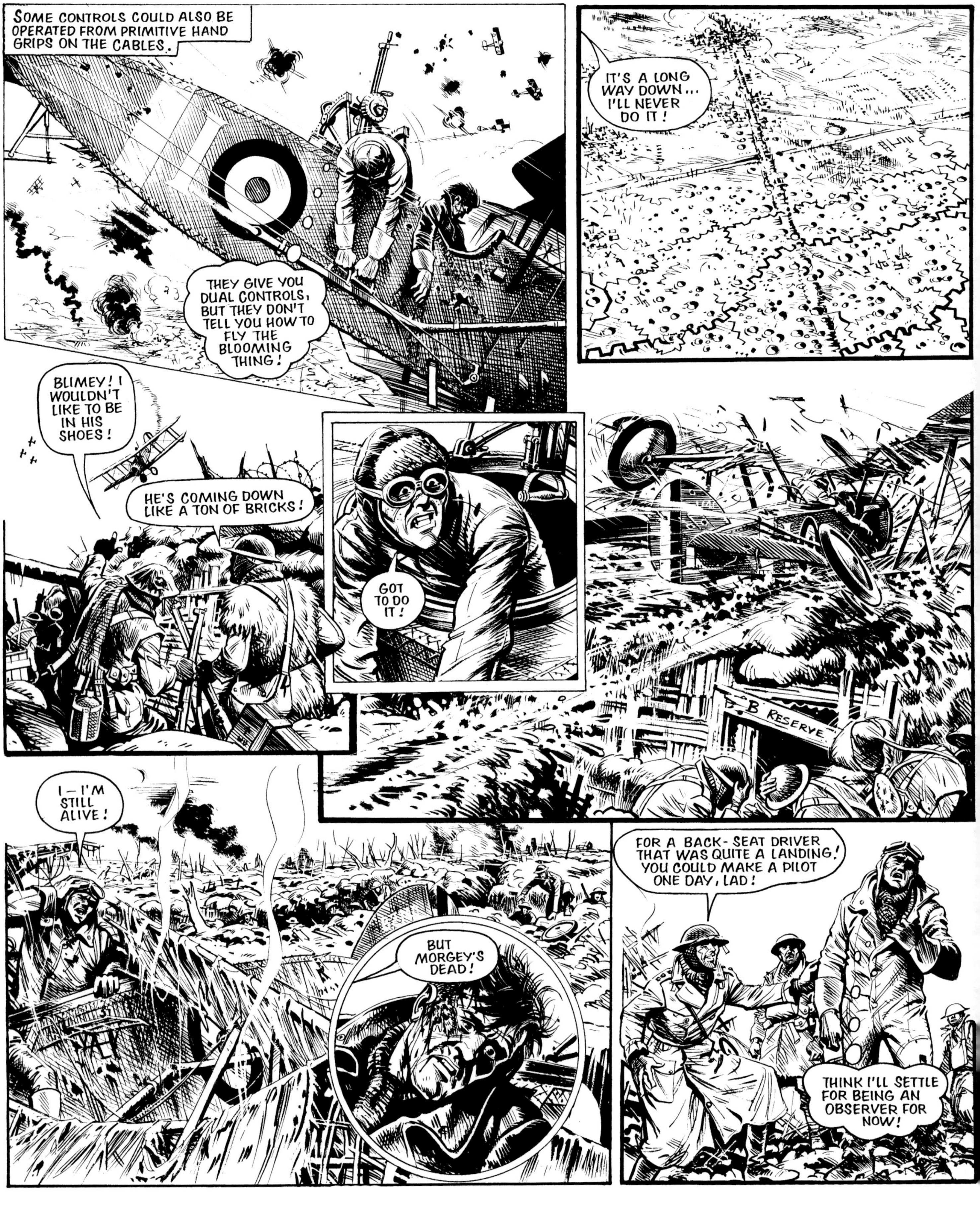
SOME CONTROLS COULD ALSO BE OPERATED FROM PRIMITIVE HAND GRIPS ON THE CABLES.
THEY GIVE YOU DUAL CONTROLS, BUT THEY DON'T TELL YOU HOW TO FLY THE BLOOMING THING!
IT'S A LONG WAY DOWN... I'LL NEVER DO IT!
BLIMEY! I WOULDN'T LIKE TO BE IN HIS SHOES!
HE'S COMING DOWN LIKE A TON OF BRICKS!
GOT TO DO IT!
B RESERVE
I-I'M STILL ALIVE!
BUT MORGEY'S DEAD!
FOR A BACK-SEAT DRIVER THAT WAS QUITE A LANDING! YOU COULD MAKE A PILOT ONE DAY, LAD!
THINK I'LL SETTLE FOR BEING AN OBSERVER FOR NOW!

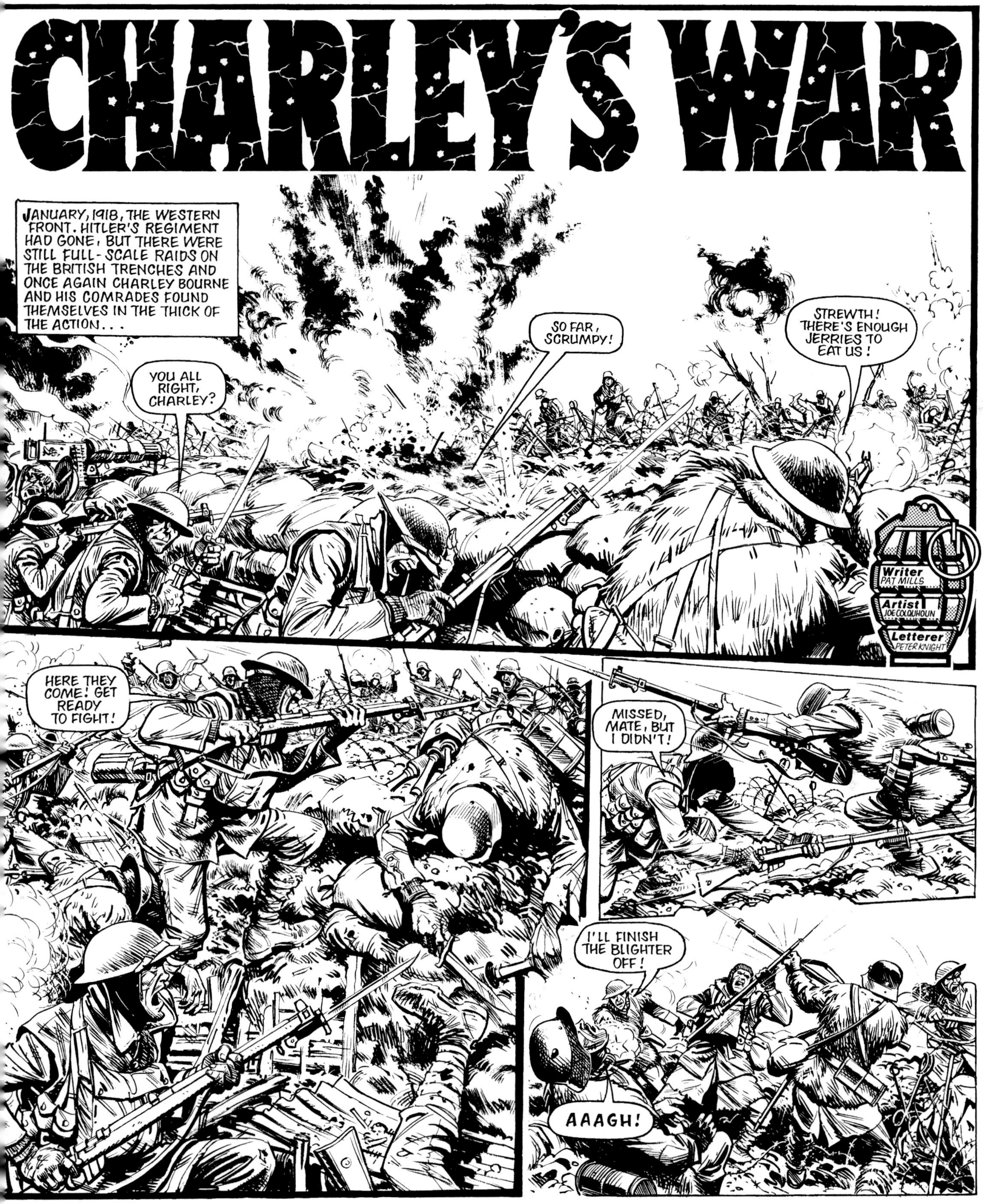
CHARLEY'S WAR
JANUARY, 1918, THE WESTERN FRONT. HITLER'S REGIMENT HAD GONE, BUT THERE WERE STILL FULL-SCALE RAIDS ON THE BRITISH TRENCHES AND ONCE AGAIN CHARLEY BOURNE AND HIS COMRADES FOUND THEMSELVES IN THE THICK OF THE ACTION...
YOU ALL RIGHT, CHARLEY?
SO FAR, SCRUMPY!
STREWTH! THERE'S ENOUGH JERRIES TO EAT US!
Writer PAT MILLS
Artist JOE COLQUHOUN
Letterer PETER KNIGHT
HERE THEY COME! GET READY TO FIGHT!
MISSED, MATE, BUT I DIDN'T!
I'LL FINISH THE BLIGHTER OFF!
AAAGH!

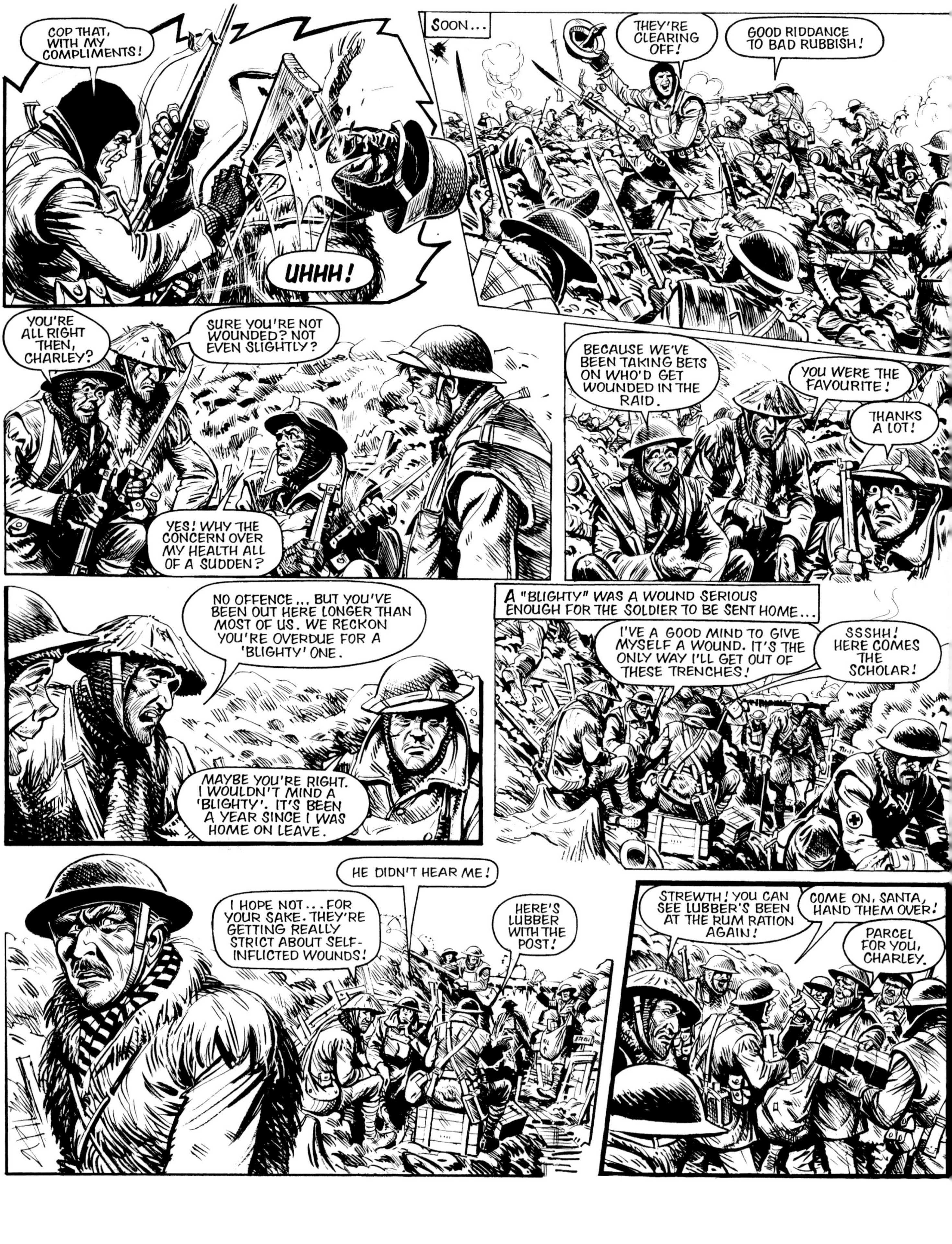
COP THAT, WITH MY COMPLIMENTS!
UHHH!
SOON...
THEY'RE CLEARING OFF!
GOOD RIDDANCE TO BAD RUBBISH!
YOU'RE ALL RIGHT THEN, CHARLEY?
SURE YOU'RE NOT WOUNDED? NOT EVEN SLIGHTLY?
YES! WHY THE CONCERN OVER MY HEALTH ALL OF A SUDDEN?
BECAUSE WE'VE BEEN TAKING BETS ON WHO'D GET WOUNDED IN THE RAID.
YOU WERE THE FAVOURITE!
THANKS A LOT!
NO OFFENCE... BUT YOU'VE BEEN OUT HERE LONGER THAN MOST OF US. WE RECKON YOU'RE OVERDUE FOR A 'BLIGHTY' ONE.
MAYBE YOU'RE RIGHT. I WOULDN'T MIND A 'BLIGHTY'. IT'S BEEN A YEAR SINCE I WAS HOME ON LEAVE.
A "BLIGHTY" WAS A WOUND SERIOUS ENOUGH FOR THE SOLDIER TO BE SENT HOME...
I'VE A GOOD MIND TO GIVE MYSELF A WOUND. IT'S THE ONLY WAY I'LL GET OUT OF THESE TRENCHES!
SSSHH! HERE COMES THE SCHOLAR!
HE DIDN'T HEAR ME!
I HOPE NOT... FOR YOUR SAKE. THEY'RE GETTING REALLY STRICT ABOUT SELF-INFLICTED WOUNDS!
HERE'S LUBBER WITH THE POST!
STREWTH! YOU CAN SEE LUBBER'S BEEN AT THE RUM RATION AGAIN!
COME ON, SANTA, HAND THEM OVER!
PARCEL FOR YOU, CHARLEY.

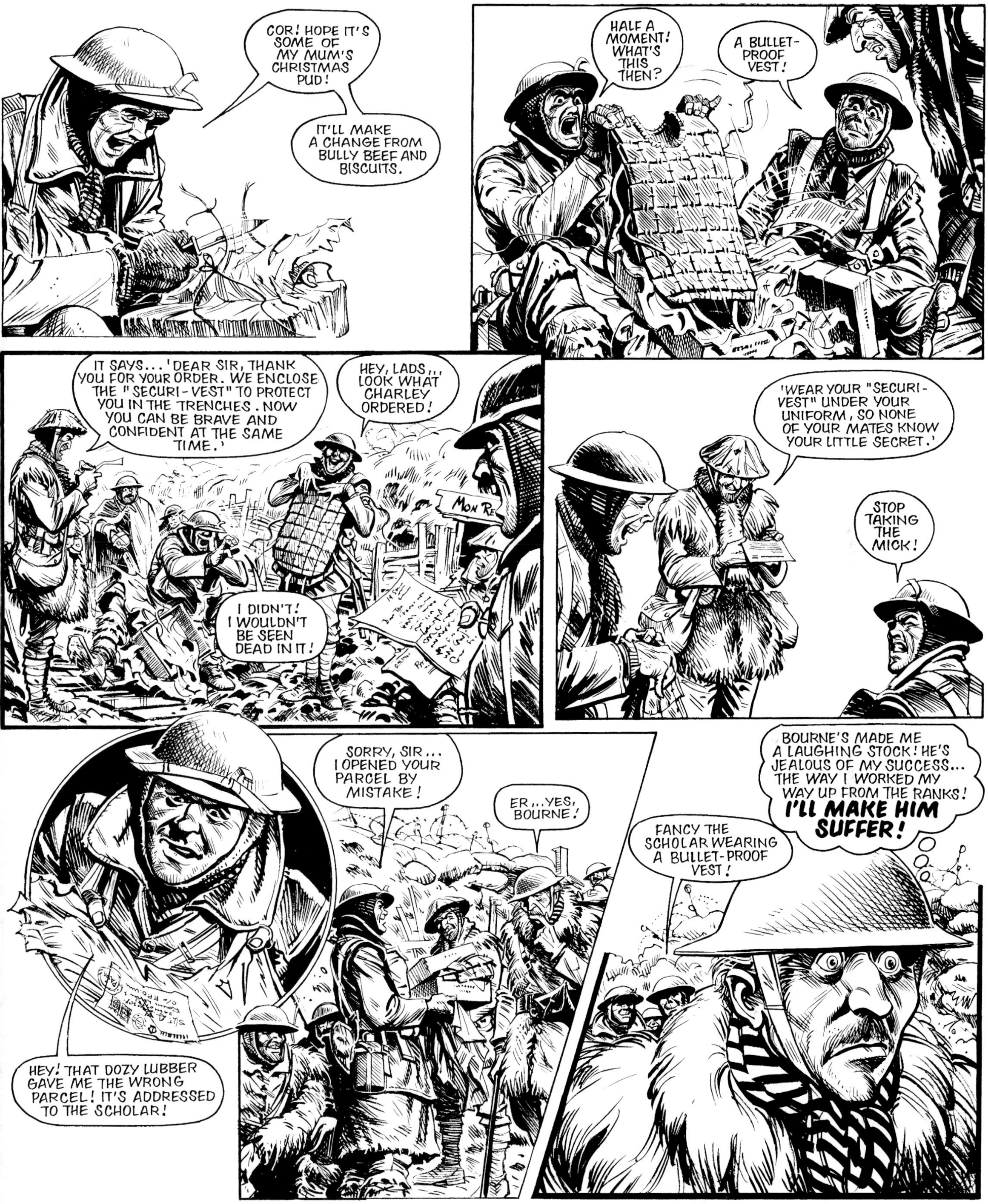
COR! HOPE IT'S SOME OF MY MUM'S CHRISTMAS PUD!
IT'LL MAKE A CHANGE FROM BULLY BEEF AND BISCUITS.
HALF A MOMENT! WHAT'S THIS THEN?
A BULLET-PROOF VEST!
IT SAYS... 'DEAR SIR, THANK YOU FOR YOUR ORDER. WE ENCLOSE THE "SECURI-VEST" TO PROTECT YOU IN THE TRENCHES. NOW YOU CAN BE BRAVE AND CONFIDENT AT THE SAME TIME.'
HEY, LADS... LOOK WHAT CHARLEY ORDERED!
MON RE
I DIDN'T! I WOULDN'T BE SEEN DEAD IN IT!
'WEAR YOUR "SECURI-VEST" UNDER YOUR UNIFORM, SO NONE OF YOUR MATES KNOW YOUR LITTLE SECRET.'
STOP TAKING THE MICK!
HEY! THAT DOZY LUBBER GAVE ME THE WRONG PARCEL! IT'S ADDRESSED TO THE SCHOLAR!
SORRY, SIR... I OPENED YOUR PARCEL BY MISTAKE!
ER... YES, BOURNE!
FANCY THE SCHOLAR WEARING A BULLET-PROOF VEST!
BOURNE'S MADE ME A LAUGHING STOCK! HE'S JEALOUS OF MY SUCCESS... THE WAY I WORKED MY WAY UP FROM THE RANKS!
**I'LL MAKE HIM SUFFER!**

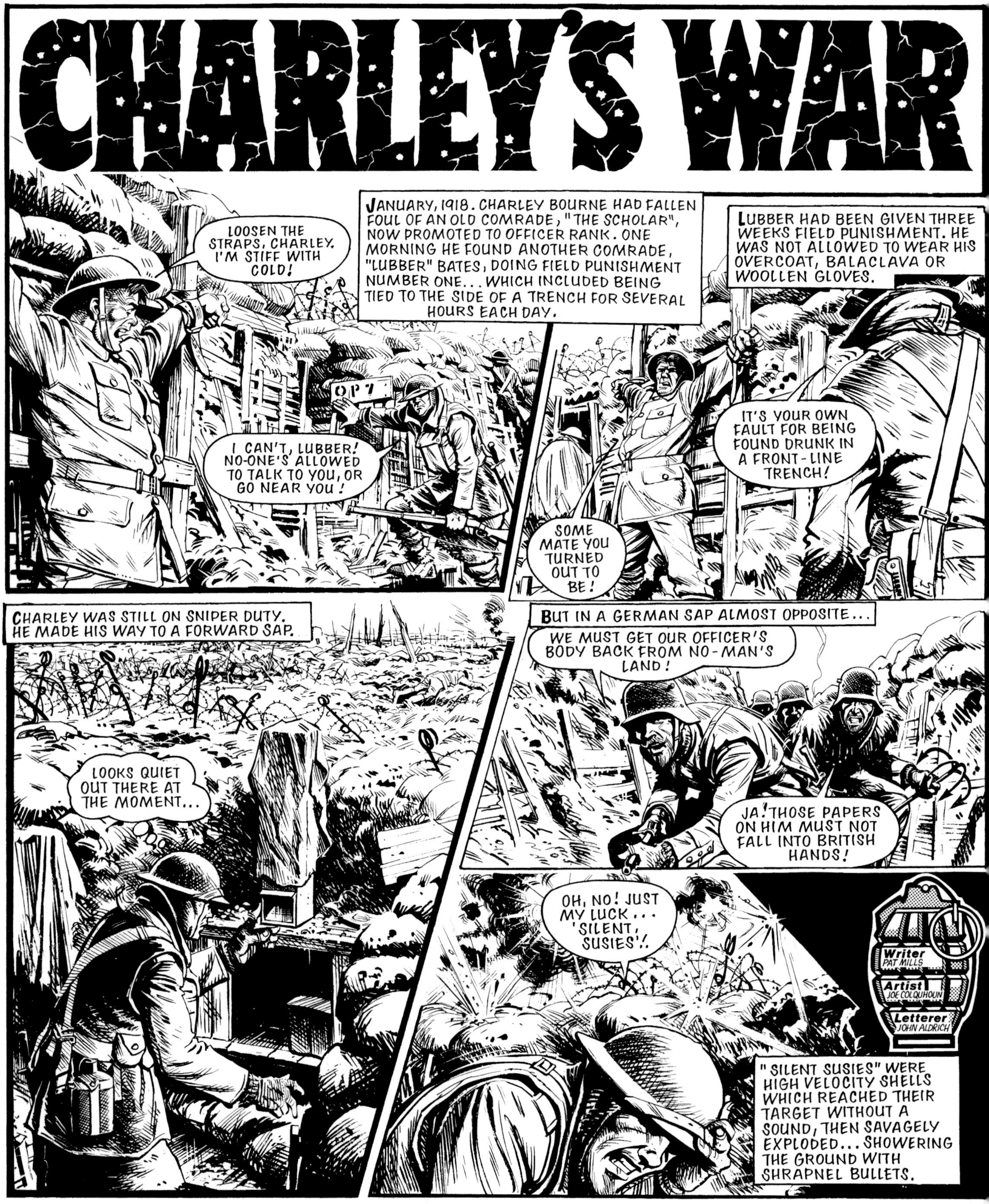
CHARLEY'S WAR
JANUARY, 1918. CHARLEY BOURNE HAD FALLEN FOUL OF AN OLD COMRADE, "THE SCHOLAR", NOW PROMOTED TO OFFICER RANK. ONE MORNING HE FOUND ANOTHER COMRADE, "LUBBER" BATES, DOING FIELD PUNISHMENT NUMBER ONE... WHICH INCLUDED BEING TIED TO THE SIDE OF A TRENCH FOR SEVERAL HOURS EACH DAY.
LOOSEN THE STRAPS, CHARLEY. I'M STIFF WITH COLD!
OP 7
I CAN'T, LUBBER! NO-ONE'S ALLOWED TO TALK TO YOU, OR GO NEAR YOU!
LUBBER HAD BEEN GIVEN THREE WEEKS FIELD PUNISHMENT. HE WAS NOT ALLOWED TO WEAR HIS OVERCOAT, BALACLAVA OR WOOLLEN GLOVES.
IT'S YOUR OWN FAULT FOR BEING FOUND DRUNK IN A FRONT-LINE TRENCH!
SOME MATE YOU TURNED OUT TO BE!
CHARLEY WAS STILL ON SNIPER DUTY. HE MADE HIS WAY TO A FORWARD SAP.
LOOKS QUIET OUT THERE AT THE MOMENT...
BUT IN A GERMAN SAP ALMOST OPPOSITE...
WE MUST GET OUR OFFICER'S BODY BACK FROM NO-MAN'S LAND!
JA! THOSE PAPERS ON HIM MUST NOT FALL INTO BRITISH HANDS!
OH, NO! JUST MY LUCK... 'SILENT, SUSIES'!
Writer PAT MILLS
Artist JOE COLQUHOUN
Letterer JOHN ALDRICH
"SILENT SUSIES" WERE HIGH VELOCITY SHELLS WHICH REACHED THEIR TARGET WITHOUT A SOUND, THEN SAVAGELY EXPLODED... SHOWERING THE GROUND WITH SHRAPNEL BULLETS.

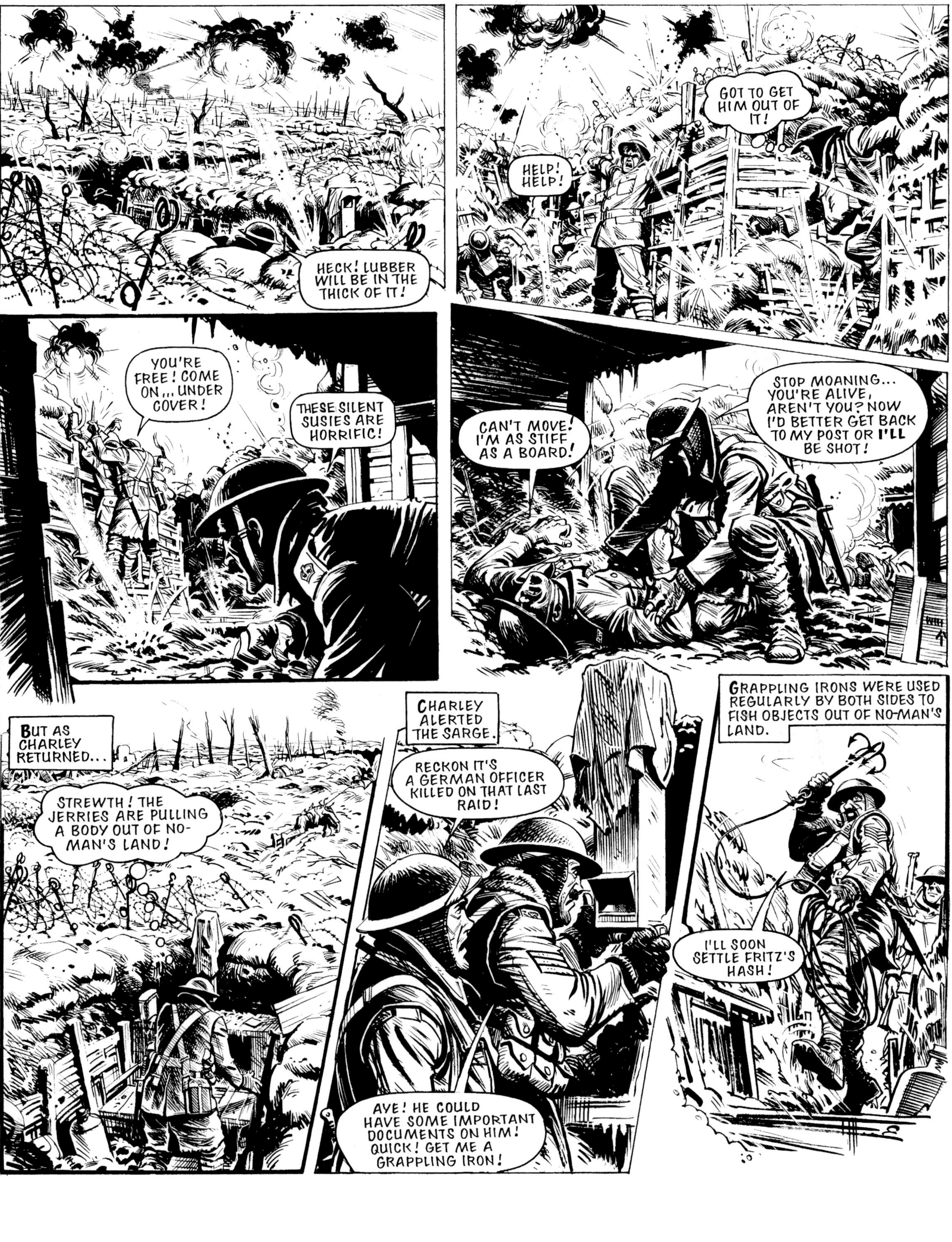
HECK! LUBBER WILL BE IN THE THICK OF IT!
HELP! HELP!
GOT TO GET HIM OUT OF IT!
YOU'RE FREE! COME ON... UNDER COVER!
THESE SILENT SUSIES ARE HORRIFIC!
CAN'T MOVE! I'M AS STIFF AS A BOARD!
STOP MOANING... YOU'RE ALIVE, AREN'T YOU? NOW I'D BETTER GET BACK TO MY POST OR I'LL BE SHOT!
BUT AS CHARLEY RETURNED...
STREWTH! THE JERRIES ARE PULLING A BODY OUT OF NO-MAN'S LAND!
CHARLEY ALERTED THE SARGE.
RECKON IT'S A GERMAN OFFICER KILLED ON THAT LAST RAID!
AYE! HE COULD HAVE SOME IMPORTANT DOCUMENTS ON HIM! QUICK! GET ME A GRAPPLING IRON!
GRAPPLING IRONS WERE USED REGULARLY BY BOTH SIDES TO FISH OBJECTS OUT OF NO-MAN'S LAND.
I'LL SOON SETTLE FRITZ'S HASH!

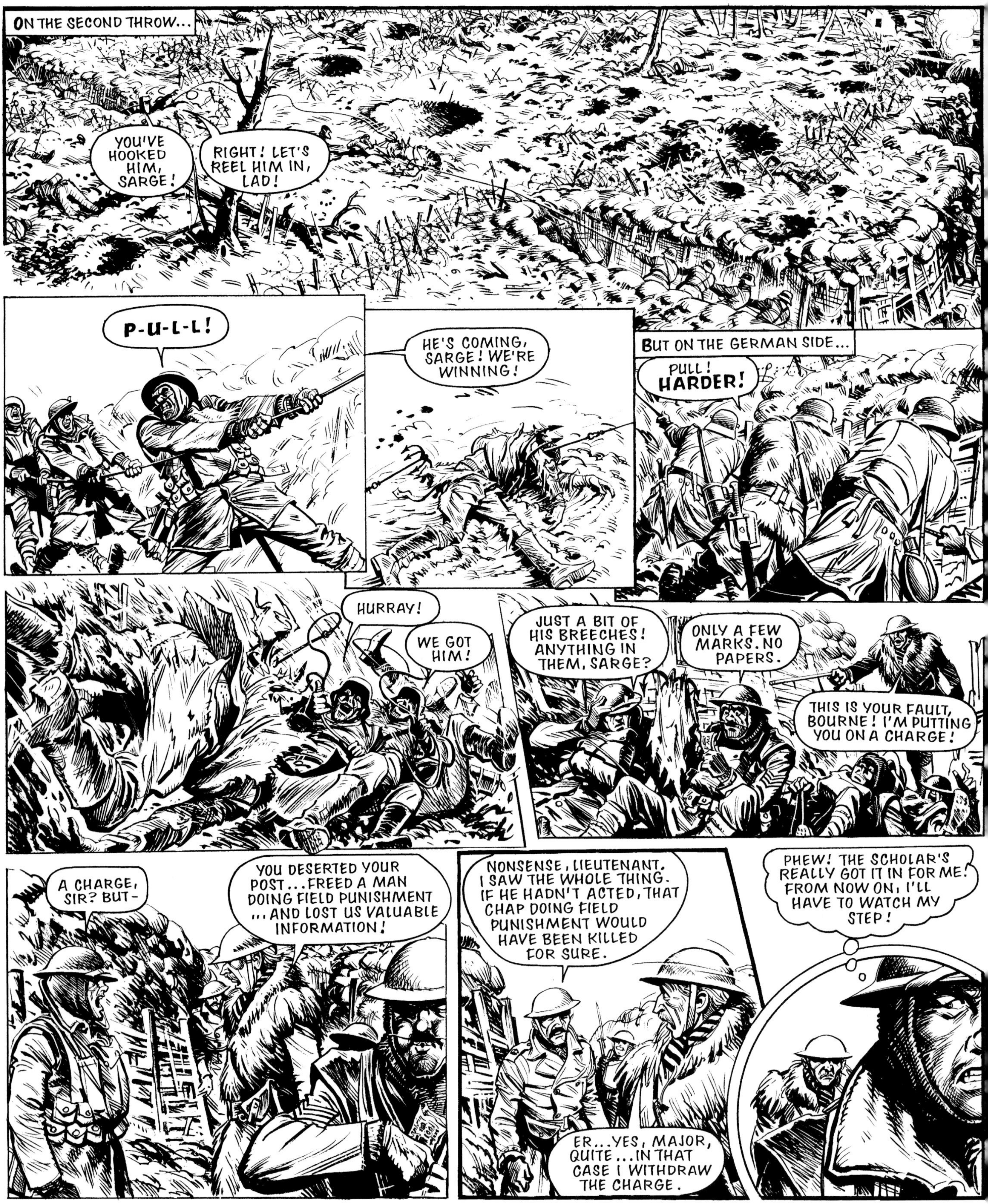

ON THE SECOND THROW...
YOU'VE HOOKED HIM, SARGE!
RIGHT! LET'S REEL HIM IN, LAD!
P-U-L-L!
HE'S COMING, SARGE! WE'RE WINNING!
BUT ON THE GERMAN SIDE...
PULL! HARDER!
HURRAY!
WE GOT HIM!
JUST A BIT OF HIS BREECHES! ANYTHING IN THEM, SARGE?
ONLY A FEW MARKS. NO PAPERS.
THIS IS YOUR FAULT, BOURNE! I'M PUTTING YOU ON A CHARGE!
A CHARGE, SIR? BUT-
YOU DESERTED YOUR POST...FREED A MAN DOING FIELD PUNISHMENT ...AND LOST US VALUABLE INFORMATION!
NONSENSE, LIEUTENANT. I SAW THE WHOLE THING. IF HE HADN'T ACTED, THAT CHAP DOING FIELD PUNISHMENT WOULD HAVE BEEN KILLED FOR SURE.
ER...YES, MAJOR, QUITE...IN THAT CASE I WITHDRAW THE CHARGE.
PHEW! THE SCHOLAR'S REALLY GOT IT IN FOR ME! FROM NOW ON, I'LL HAVE TO WATCH MY STEP!

# STRIP COMMENTARY

*by Pat Mills*

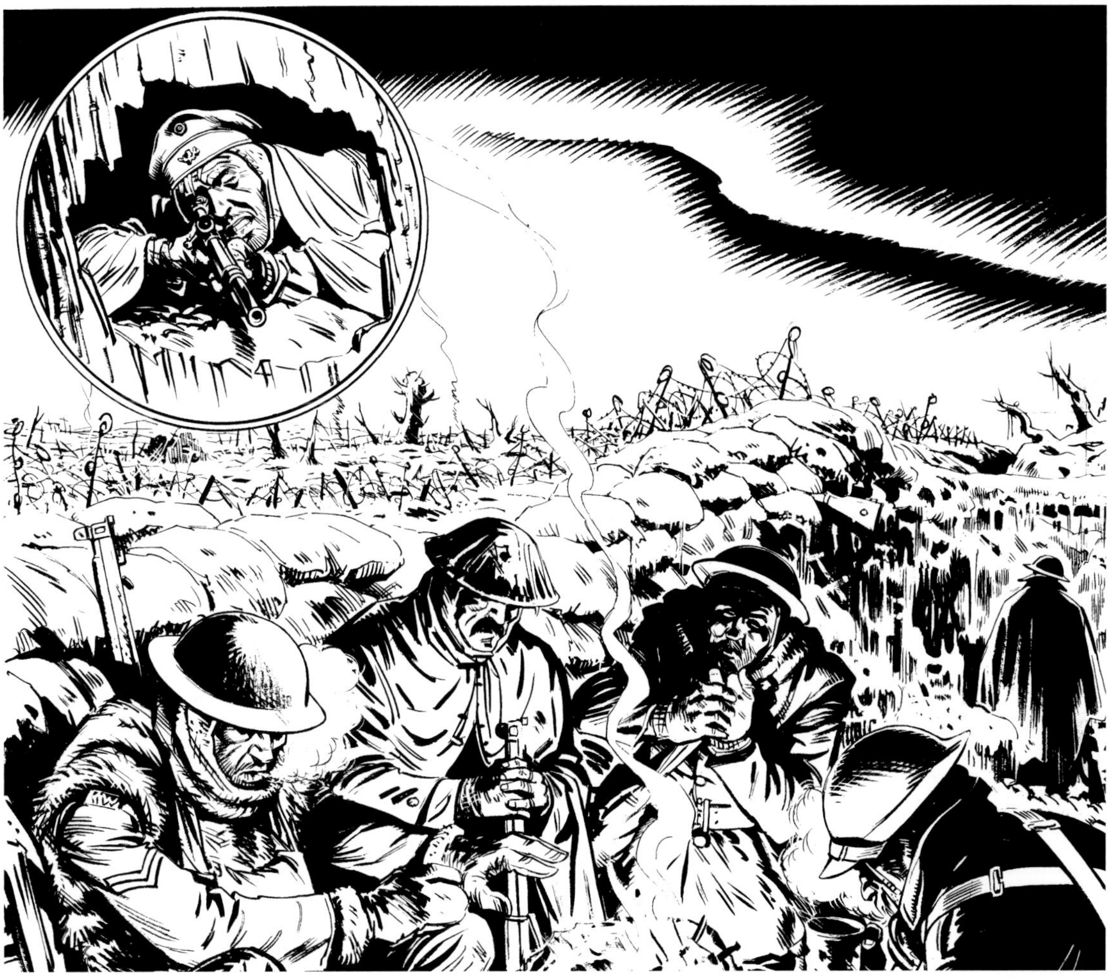

## EPISODES ONE AND TWO

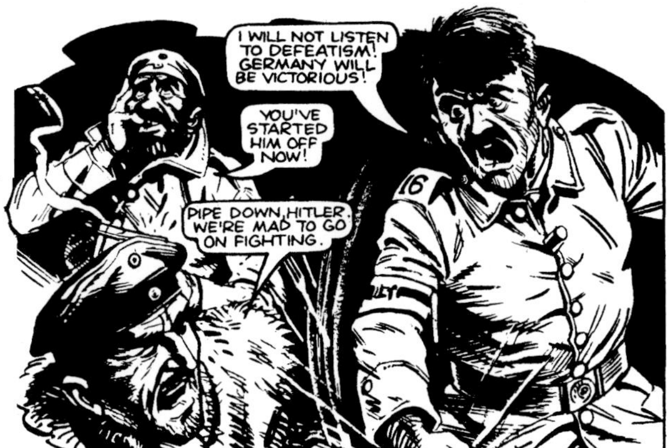

PIPE DOWN, HITLER. WE'RE MAD TO GO ON FIGHTING.
I WILL NOT LISTEN TO DEFEATISM! GERMANY WILL BE VICTORIOUS!
YOU'VE STARTED HIM OFF NOW!


A film producer recently told me that what he particularly liked about Joe's art was the way the characters in *Charley's War* were portrayed in natural and unassuming poses. It's as if they are totally unaware they are being watched by us, the reader, or that there is a "camera" (the artist) following them around, "filming" them. This is very much the case with the scenes with Hitler in the German dug-out.

This is the opposite of how heroes are portrayed in fantasy or science fiction comics. The more successful heroes are "self-conscious", invariably posing for the camera and striking iconic poses – whether it's super heroes running on one leg towards us, *2000AD*'s *Sláine* wielding an axe or Judge Dredd leaping from his motorbike. This is what that audience looks for and is therefore valid in the world of fantasy; it's interesting that the reverse is highly regarded in the world of historical realism.

## EPISODE THREE

In John Toland's biography of Hitler he quotes an eerie poem written by the Führer while he was in the trenches. It is reproduced in full below:

*I often go on bitter nights*
*To Wotan's oak in the quiet glade*
*With dark powers to weave a union*
*The runic letters the moon makes with its magic spell*
*And all who are full of impudence during the day*
*Are made small by the magic formula!*
*They draw shining steel – but instead of going into combat*
*They solidify into stalagmites.*
*So the false ones part from the real ones*
*I reach into a nest of words*
*And then give to the good and just*
*With my formula blessings and prosperity.*

Hitler's interest in the occult is well known and it would appear from this poem he was already trying to contact dark forces during World War I. I found this very chilling, especially when you consider his miraculous escapes from death in the trenches and later in World War II.

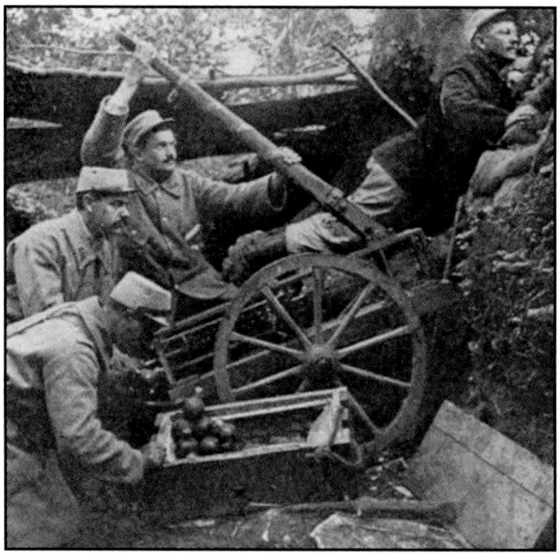

**LEFT:** An example of French Army WWI technology in action — in this image, the soldier on the right is ranging the target, whilst the crewmen man the grenade launcher.

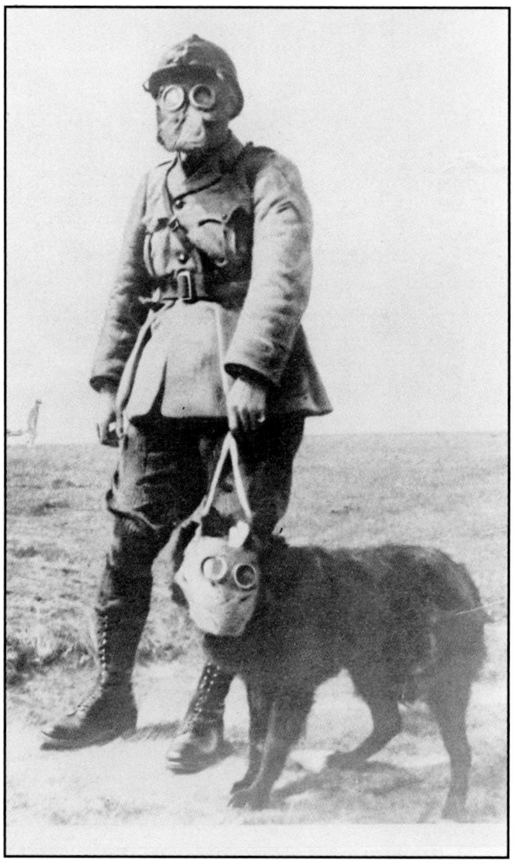

**BELOW:** A rarely seen image of a French Army dog in a gas mask.

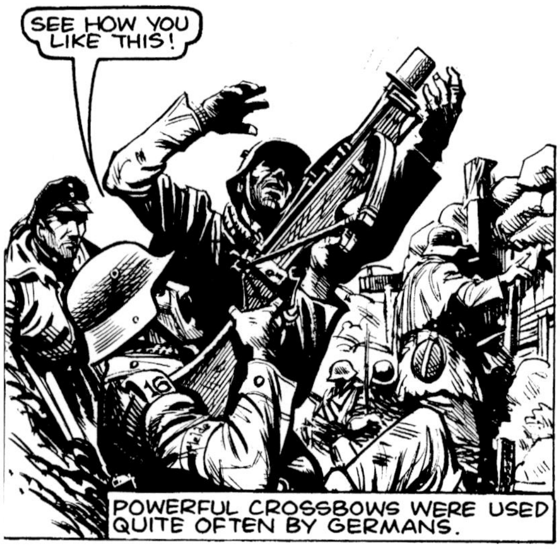
SEE HOW YOU LIKE THIS!
POWERFUL CROSSBOWS WERE USED QUITE OFTEN BY GERMANS.

## EPISODES FOUR TO SIX

I found myself sympathising with the Germans as they come under attack by the British snipers. Germans as positive figures in comics were relatively new when *Charley's War* was written. I had pioneered them in *Action* with *Hellmann of Hammer Force*, pleading with the publisher to let me include a German hero. At first he was reluctant, concerned that the British Legion might complain as well as the media who loathed comics, apart from the "educational" *Eagle*. But he eventually saw my point that this was the Seventies, and it was time we recognised the heroism of the enemy. I commissioned Gerry Finley-Day to write *Hellmann* and *Battle* ran *Fallmann, Fighter from the Skies*, about a German paratrooper – also written by Gerry, drawing on his parachute training in the Territorial Army.

Looking at episode five, I cringed at the text panel, "Powerful crossbows were used quite often by Germans." This was added by editorial and comes – once again – under the category of stating the bleeding obvious. But they are not entirely to blame; readers had previously cast doubt on the strange artefacts of World War I, such as dogs wearing gas masks. A reader cited them as an example of how stupid and unbelievable comics were. Even a soldier who served in North Africa in World War II was sceptical that snipers wore medieval armour until I showed him the photo references. An example of World War I armour can be seen on page one of episode six.

## EPISODES SEVEN AND EIGHT

The British join in the German 'Hymn of Hate'. A very British response, almost Pythonesque. You could never imagine any other nation doing it. I laughed out loud when I read this scene.

By World War II, other songs had replaced the 'Hymn of Hate' such as the German national anthem – 'Deutschland Über Alles'. According to German reader, Josef Rother, this originated as a call for a united democratic Germany, rather than for Germany to conquer all. Arguably our 'Rule Britannia' and the American 'Twilight's Last Gleaming' are more jingoistic.

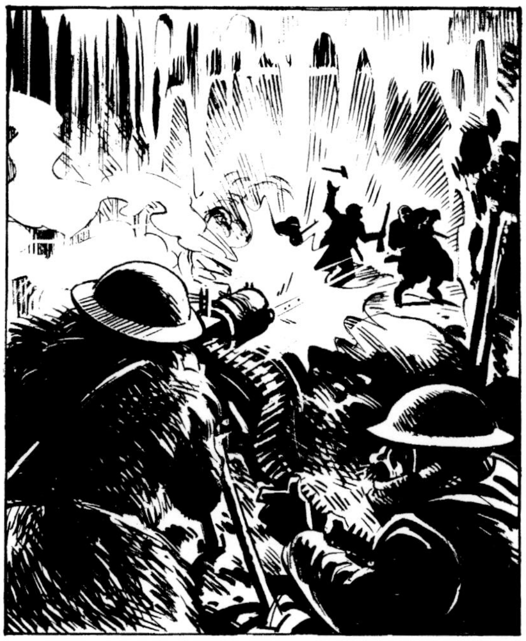

## EPISODE NINE TO ELEVEN

I noticed there were several pictures with no dialogue and I'm pleased that they work well here. It's not always the case – sometimes words are needed to understand what's going on and also to stop the page seeming empty. I'm not fond of comics, notably American super hero comics, where characters have long, unlikely, pseudo-witty conversations as they knock the stuffing out of each other. However, one artist colleague believes that words are needed with action sequences to slow the reader down, otherwise he will turn the page too quickly. I don't agree – if the pages are visually absorbing, the reader will take his time perusing them. Ideally, I'd like to see action scenes in comics written like film scenes with very little dialogue (e.g. the action scenes in *Kill Bill: Volume 2*); but it doesn't always come off. With Joe, it works every time.

## EPISODE TWELVE

The Field Punishment Number One handed out to a soldier in this episode seems cruel, medieval and barbaric. But is the treatment handed out to an American soldier in 2011, Bradley Manning, for allegedly passing information to Wikileaks any less cruel, medieval and barbaric? The untried Manning is kept awake during the day, forbidden to exercise in his cell, and forced to present himself naked to his guards.

In this episode there is a reference to Hitler staying in Liverpool before the war. This fascinating possibility was explored by Beryl Bainbridge in her novel *Young Adolf*.

## EPISODE THIRTEEN AND FOURTEEN

Episode thirteen ends with a boxing match between a German and a Tommy and Charley's question "Wouldn't it be good if wars could be settled this way?". If that seems hopelessly naïve, it's worth noting America's most decorated soldier General Smedley Butler made equally "naïve" suggestions in his book *War is a Racket*. He proposed that only soldiers should have the right to vote on whether a nation goes to war and politicians and arms manufacturers should receive the same wages as soldiers as an acknowledgement of how the latter were risking their lives.

I wish I could have explored the sinister role of arms manufacturers further. The superb TV series, *Reilly Ace of Spies*, exposes the questionable activities of Vickers boss, Baron Zaharoff, one of the most infamous "Merchants of Death". He was notorious for selling to both sides in war. In episode fourteen, Smith 70, the machine gunner, discovers his German opposite number has the same weapon: the Vickers machine gun. The profits made by these Merchants of Death were astronomical. How apt therefore that in the background the Tommies sing, "Oh, it's the same the whole world over, it's the poor gets all the blame while the rich gets all the pleasure. Oh, isn't it a bleeding shame." The luxurious Christmas menu for the officers underlines the point.

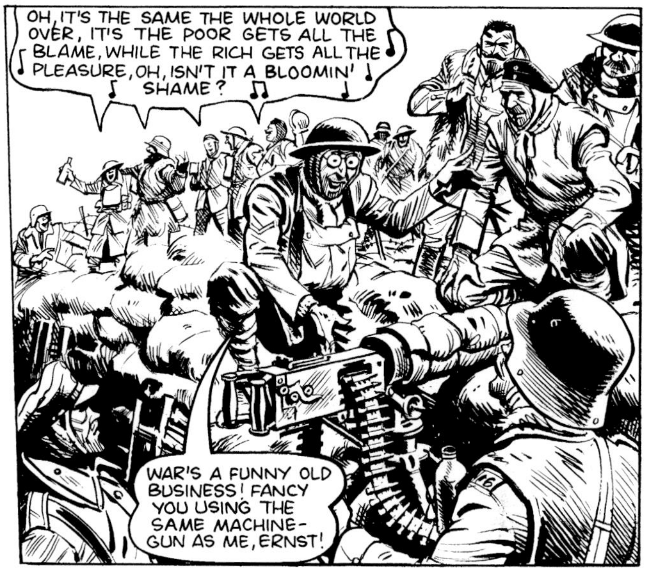
OH, IT'S THE SAME THE WHOLE WORLD OVER, IT'S THE POOR GETS ALL THE BLAME, WHILE THE RICH GETS ALL THE PLEASURE, OH, ISN'T IT A BLOOMIN' SHAME?
WAR'S A FUNNY OLD BUSINESS! FANCY YOU USING THE SAME MACHINE-GUN AS ME, ERNST!

By the way, my script originally had the authentic "ain't it a bleeding shame." Once again, a *Battle* sub-editor, obsessed with the Queen's English, has amended my dialogue.

The story of the anti-war General Butler is now the subject of a graphic novel *Devil Dog* by David Taylor and Spain Rodriguez, the celebrated underground artist.

The last page of the 'Young Hitler' story feels rather condensed. I should have taken an extra page over it or perhaps even an episode. Probably the reason I didn't was because slow or "talking heads" episodes could get negative reactions from readers and editors were therefore wary of them.

## EPISODE FIFTEEN TO SEVENTEEN

Stunning aerial detail in 'Wilf's War'. Joe benefited from having less pictures on a page in flying scenes and I think if we were doing this story today, I would be suggesting four pictures on a page or even double page spreads for "wide screen" drama to convey the complexities and the distances involved in aerial action.

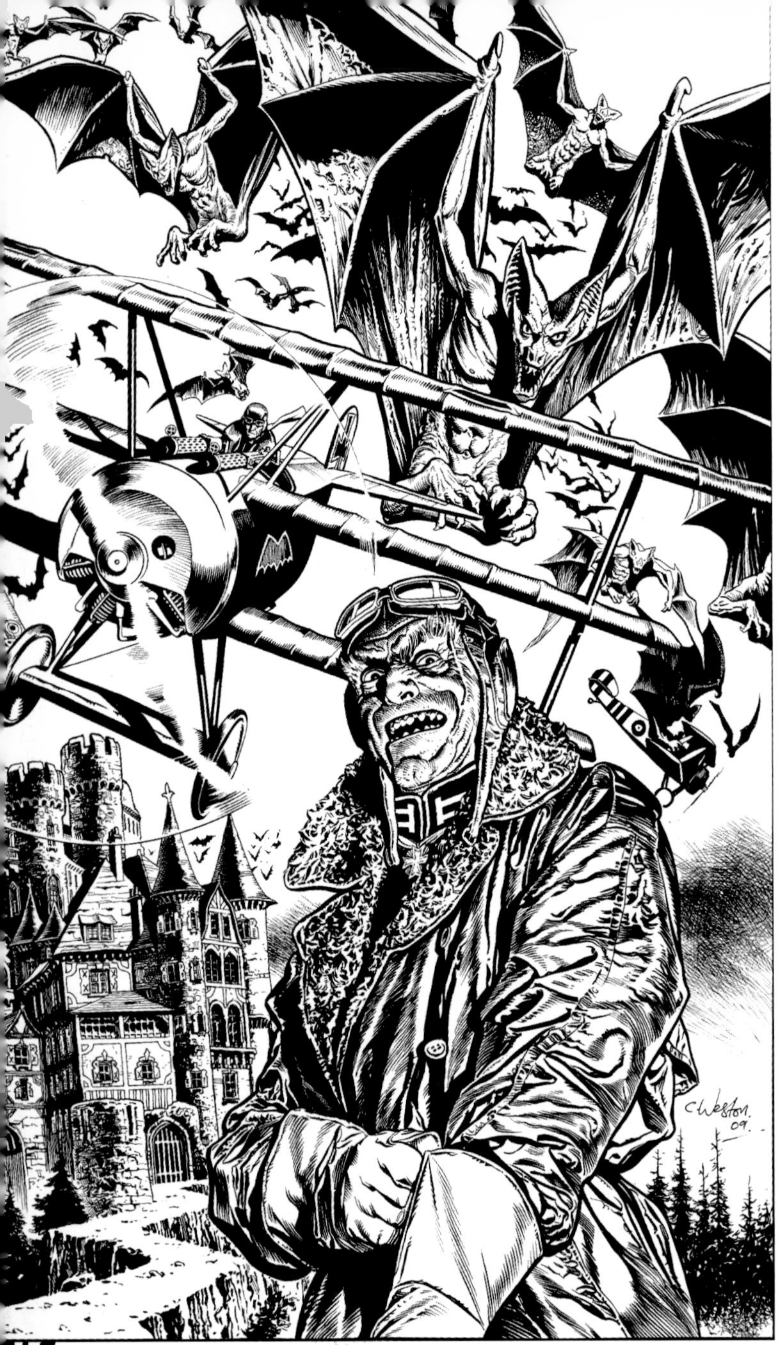

LEFT: *Black Max* (from *Thunder*) re-imagined by artist Chris Weston.

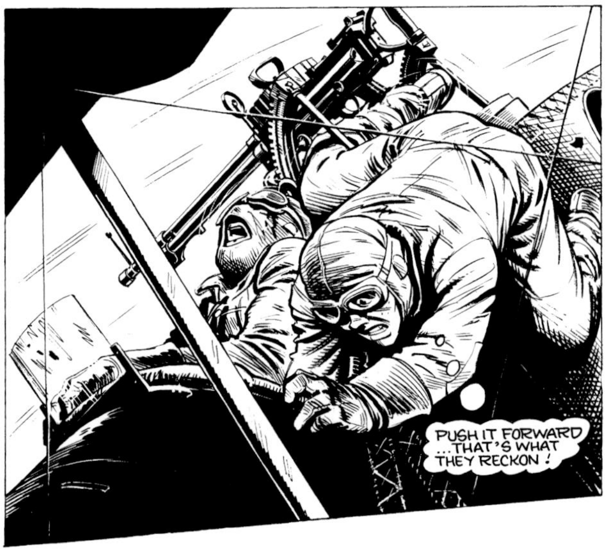
PUSH IT FORWARD ...THAT'S WHAT THEY RECKON!

Like 'Blue's Story', Charley doesn't feature in this adventure and once again the readers approved of the character "deviation" because it was in the same spirit as the trench war, showing the unsung working-class heroes of the RFC, rather than the high profile, middle and upper-class air aces.

## EPISODE EIGHTEEN TO TWENTY

I don't think there's any artist today who could draw something as visually demanding as the observer standing on the wing of a plane and directing the pilot. I'm sure the incident is authentic and the working-class subtext to the story stops it being a "ripping yarn".

## EPISODE TWENTY ONE

The attitude expressed by the mechanic is an important one and relates to the theme of ambition that runs through 'Wilf's War'. He says, "You shouldn't have tried to better yourself, Wilf. If you never try, you'll never fail. See what happens when you have ambition? Dreams? You end up as the smoke-bloke." I heard something similar from the editorial "old guard" when I was creating *Battle*, *Action* and *2000AD*. They hated and feared change, wanting comics to remain the way they had been for decades. They told me nothing worked in comics anymore and it was best to just "coast" along, not taking any chances, until such time as they were all shut down and they would receive their redundancies. I'm sure that's what inspired me to include those lines.

Wilf ignores the attempts to drag him down into a morass of complacency and is constantly pro-active, even on the ground.

## EPISODE TWENTY TWO TO TWENTY FOUR

Wilf's pilot, Captain Morgan, is a fascinating character – he reminds me of the role played by George Peppard in *The Blue Max,* a German pilot obsessed with aerial kills who will do anything to earn his "Pour le Merite", Germany's highest military honour.

I heard a rumour a year or so ago that *The Lord of the Rings* film director Peter Jackson was interested in the British comic book serial *The Black Max*. Then I discovered comic artist Chris Weston had also heard this rumour. To quote from his blog: "*The Black Max* was a strip that originated in *Thunder* weekly comic way back in October 1970. Drawn by European supremo, Alfonso Font, it featured the villainous exploits of the German air ace Von Klorr, who used his flying skills and giant bats to fight the allies in WWI. After twenty-two issues, *Thunder* folded, but *The Black Max* continued his adventures within the pages of *Lion* weekly."

The artwork on *The Black Max* was fantastic, in the same league as Joe's aerial art, although I don't recall being impressed by the stories. But it's a fun idea and, like Chris, I'd prefer giant bats to hobbits any day. I guess it's just a fanciful rumour, but if anyone knows more, do let us all know.

## EPISODE TWENTY FIVE TO TWENTY SEVEN

China's disfigured face, obscured by a mask, and the scene where a propeller cuts Jankers to pieces set me thinking once again about how much we should actually show in comics. I think we should go further – even for our original audience of boys aged 9–14 – so they are aware of the true nature of war, rather than the Hollywood glamorisation.

In General Butler's *War is a Racket* there are a grim series of photographs of the dead and wounded, including one where a soldier has lost half his face but is still alive. I truly believe if such photos were more widely shown it would make young men think twice before joining up. Of course it could never happen, because the media has a vested interest

HE'S GOING DOWN!

GOT TO MAKE SURE OF HIM! HE MUSTN'T ESCAPE!

MORGEY'S FOLLOWING! HE'S CRAZY!

BECAUSE OF GROUND FIRE, IT WAS AN UNWRITTEN RULE NEVER TO FOLLOW AN ENEMY AIRCRAFT DOWN.

technology of the past. Here, Wilf uses an emergency stick to pilot the plane, as well as moving cables by hand! I wonder if there is a name for World War I and II weird tech? For instance, 17th and 18th century weird tech is called "clock punk" (see my *Defoe* which features clockwork robots). 19th century weird tech is called "steam punk". Perhaps this is "propeller punk" or "prop punk"? Or is there another name already out there?

## EPISODE TWENTY NINE AND THIRTY

The detail on these two episodes is as mesmerising as ever. The literal tug of war for a German body, for instance. But my favourite scene is on the last page of episode thirty, in the final bank of pictures. Old Bill quietly pockets the German marks that were on the corpse. The sly expression on his face is a joy to behold!

We also see Field Punishment Number One carried out under fire. Looking again at this outrageous brutality, I recalled the words of the Great War Prime Minister Lloyd George quoted in John Pilger's moving documentary *The War You Don't See* about the shameful and dishonest reporting of the Iraq War by the media.

Nothing has changed since December 1917. Back then, Lloyd George said to the editor of the *Guardian*, "If people really knew the truth, the war would be stopped tomorrow. But of course they don't know and can't know."

With *Charley's War,* I had an opportunity to show aspects of the war that are even to this day played down, avoided or not shown to a mass audience. An unimportant "kids comic" like *Battle* was largely ignored, so I could write what I liked. In the final two volumes, we will continue to show the result: "The Great War You *Don't* See."

Today, Charley is finally reaching a wider audience than ever. A French edition is now under way; it headlined an exhibition *Comics and Conflicts* at the Imperial War Museum in August 2011; and it is also used as a teaching aid in school. Jane Colquhoun, Joe's daughter, told us that a local school has been using it over ten years to support GCSE war poets study. Perhaps we are "educational", after all! ✢

in concealing the real effects of "shock and awe", otherwise the recruiting offices would be out of business.

In fact, the media has always been hostile to war comics, believing that only *Eagle* and *Look and Learn* were educational and everything else was some kind of gratuitous penny dreadful that should be torn up or confiscated by school teachers.

When *Battle* first appeared, editor Dave Hunt was interviewed by John Craven for the BBC. *Eagle* fan Craven asked Dave why a comic like *Battle* ran stories about the Second World War when the conflict had been over for thirty years. His concern was that children were being constantly exposed to the violence, hatred and trauma of yesteryear. Dave responded by pointing out that films about the Second World War were regularly shown on daytime BBC TV. Needless to say, his reply was cut from the transmitted interview.

For another graphic novel about the true reality of war, I'd recommend the recent *Dougie's War* by Rodge Glass and Dave Turbitt. Set in our times, it's about one soldier's return from Afghanistan.

## EPISODE TWENTY EIGHT

The death of Captain Morgan. I found this very powerful and exciting. But I wish I'd written it over two episodes to really give space to the key moments in this dramatic finale to 'Wilf's War'.

Particularly because I think we're all interested in the primitive

A CHARGE, SIR? BUT—

YOU DESERTED YOUR POST...FREED A MAN DOING FIELD PUNISHMENT ...AND LOST US VALUABLE INFORMATION!

## THE ORIGINALS RESTORED

Normally, *Charley's War* is scanned from copies of the *Battle* comic, but for this volume, sixty-five pages of Joe's original art have been scanned and incorporated. The quality is outstanding and really shows what a brilliant artist Joe was. On the following page – the cover of *Battle* dated 25 June 1982 – is a case in point. Some of the detail would have been lost if it had been taken from the printed comic. Thanks to everyone who made it happen, especially Moose Harris and Joe's family for making the pages available to us.

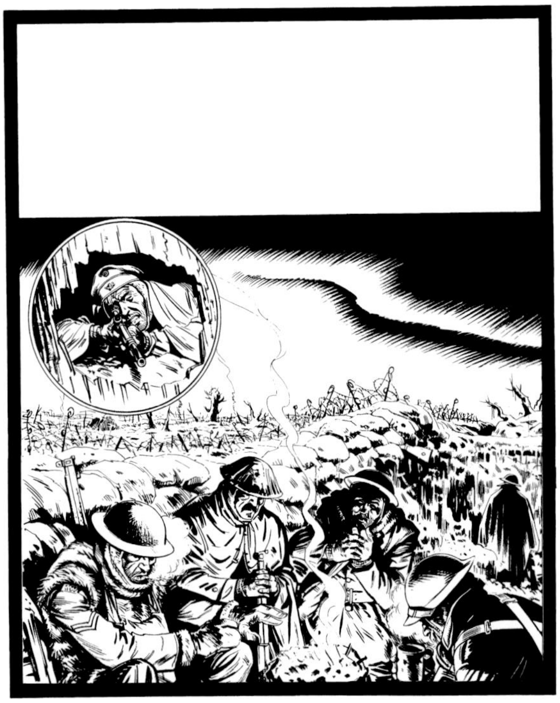

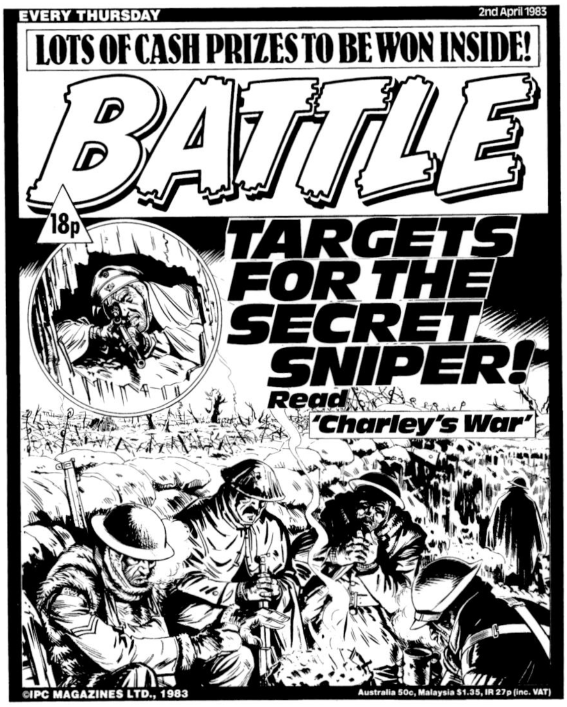
EVERY THURSDAY
2nd April 1983
LOTS OF CASH PRIZES TO BE WON INSIDE!
BATTLE
18p
TARGETS FOR THE SECRET SNIPER!
Read 'Charley's War'
©IPC MAGAZINES LTD., 1983
Australia 50c, Malaysia $1.35, IR 27p (inc. VAT)

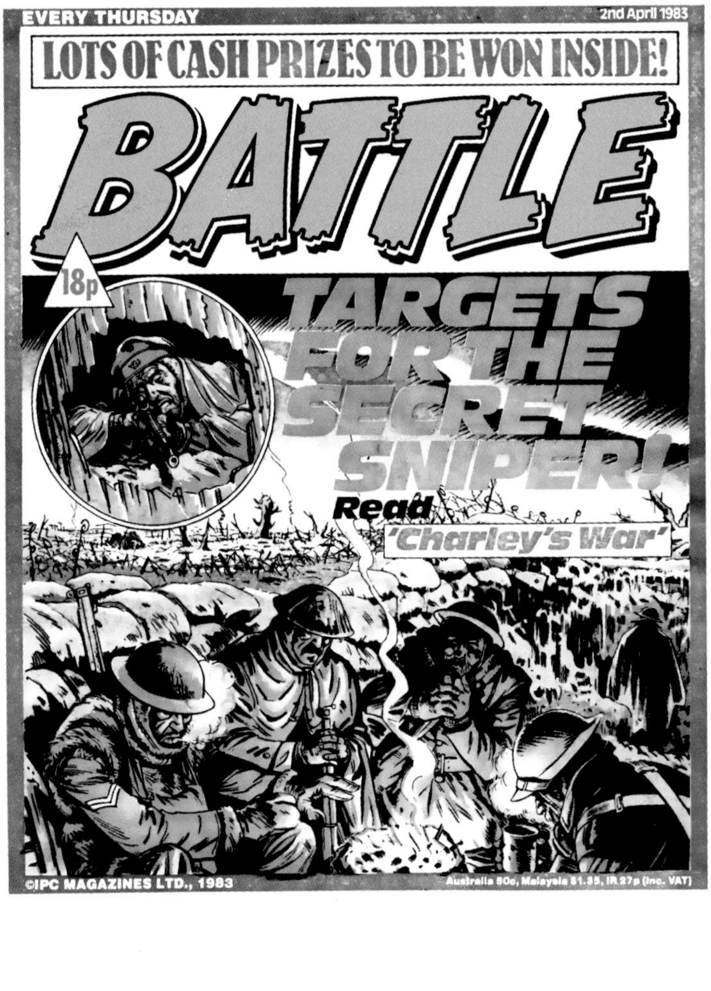
EVERY THURSDAY
2nd April 1983
LOTS OF CASH PRIZES TO BE WON INSIDE!
BATTLE
18p
TARGETS FOR THE SECRET SNIPER!
Read 'Charley's War'
©IPC MAGAZINES LTD., 1983
Australia 50c, Malaysia $1.35, IR 27p (inc. VAT)

**RIGHT:** Unusually, this *Charley's War* cover, published in April 1983, was not part of the story itself.

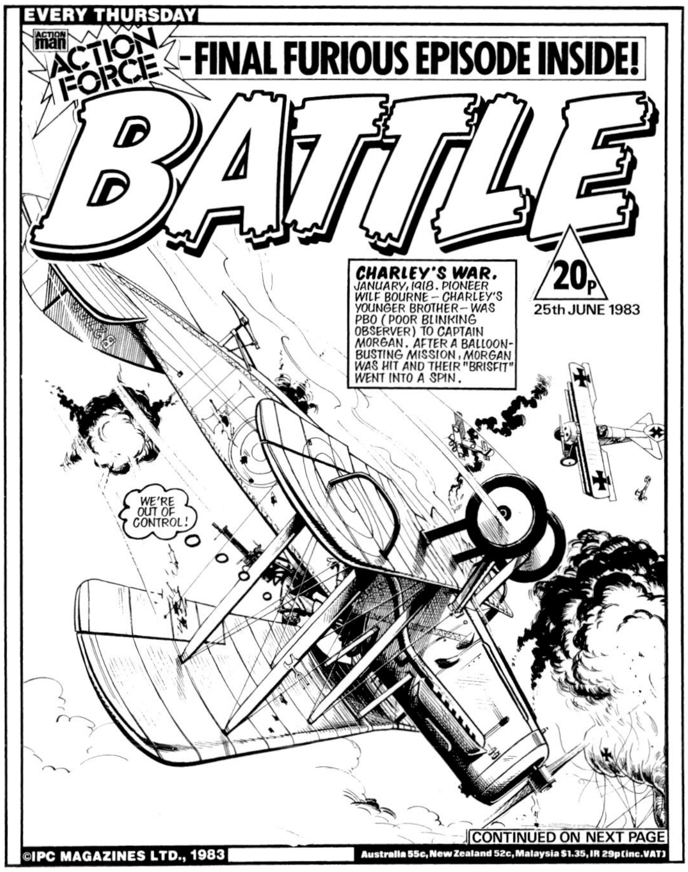
EVERY THURSDAY
ACTION man
ACTION FORCE
-FINAL FURIOUS EPISODE INSIDE!
BATTLE
20p
25th JUNE 1983
CHARLEY'S WAR.
JANUARY, 1918. PIONEER WILF BOURNE – CHARLEY'S YOUNGER BROTHER – WAS PBO (POOR BLINKING OBSERVER) TO CAPTAIN MORGAN. AFTER A BALLOON-BUSTING MISSION, MORGAN WAS HIT AND THEIR "BRISFIT" WENT INTO A SPIN.
WE'RE OUT OF CONTROL!
CONTINUED ON NEXT PAGE
©IPC MAGAZINES LTD., 1983
Australia 55c, New Zealand 52c, Malaysia $1.35, IR 29p (inc.VAT)

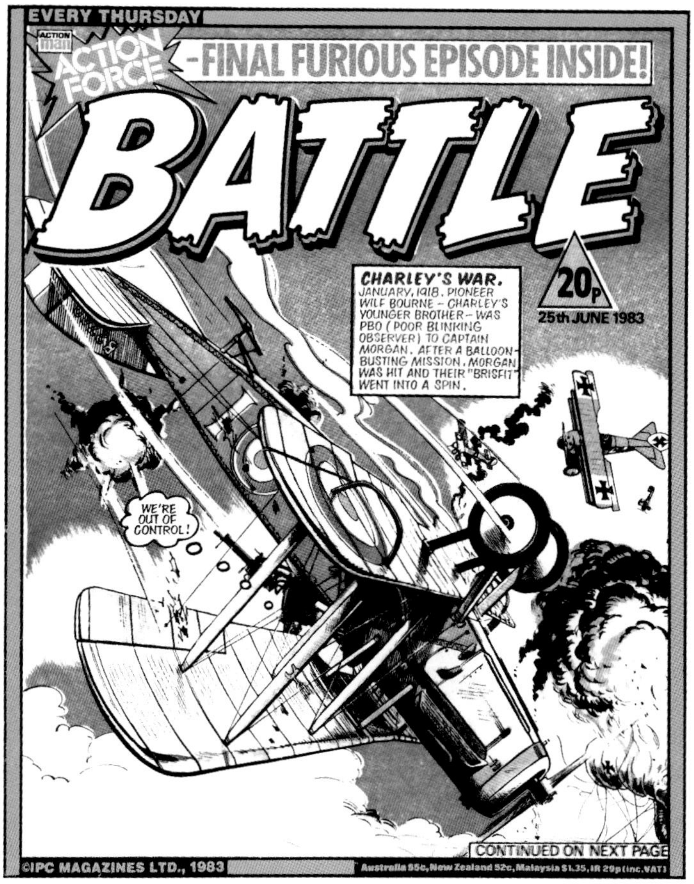
EVERY THURSDAY
ACTION man
ACTION FORCE
-FINAL FURIOUS EPISODE INSIDE!
BATTLE
20p
25th JUNE 1983
CHARLEY'S WAR.
JANUARY, 1918. PIONEER WILF BOURNE – CHARLEY'S YOUNGER BROTHER – WAS PBO (POOR BLINKING OBSERVER) TO CAPTAIN MORGAN. AFTER A BALLOON-BUSTING MISSION, MORGAN WAS HIT AND THEIR "BRISFIT" WENT INTO A SPIN.
WE'RE OUT OF CONTROL!
CONTINUED ON NEXT PAGE
©IPC MAGAZINES LTD., 1983
Australia 55c, New Zealand 52c, Malaysia $1.35, IR 29p (inc.VAT)

**LEFT:** The original uncoloured artwork for the issue. Colquhoun's wonderful linework can be seen in greater detail.

**BELOW:** Joe Colquhoun's cover for 25 June 1983 as it appeared on the newsstand.

## FURTHER READING:

*Hitler* by John Toland, Wordsworth Military Library, 1997.
ISBN: 9781853266768.

*Young Adolf* by Beryl Bainbridge, Abacus, 2003.
ISBN: 9780349116136.

*War is a Racket* by Major General Smedley Butler, Feral House, 2003.
ISBN: 9780922915866.

*Devil Dog: The Amazing True Story of the Man Who Saved America* by David Talbot, Simon and Schuster, 2010.
ISBN: 9781439109021.

*Dougie's War: A Soldier's Story* by Rodge Glass and Dave Turbitt, Freight Design, 2010.
ISBN: 9780954402488.

**Online:**

Pat Mills on Facebook
*www.facebook.com/PatMillsComics*

Paul Gravett: The Great War in Comics
*www.paulgravett.com/index.php/articles/article/ww1/*

The Museum of the Great War (French language)
*en.historial.org*

Gas Protection for Animals
*www.vlib.us/medical/gaswar/gasmasks.htm*

Chris Weston, Artist – Official Site
*www.chrisweston.co.uk*

# CLASSIC BRITISH COMICS FROM TITAN BOOKS

208 PAGES OF THRILLING FOOTBALL ACTION!
THE BEST OF ROY OF THE ROVERS
THE 1970s
WITH AN INTRODUCTION BY FRANK SKINNER
THE BUMPER BOOK OF ROY OF THE ROVERS

THE JAMES BOND
IAN FLEMING
OMNIBUS
THE JAMES BOND
IAN FLEMING
OMNIBUS002

MODESTY Blaise
THE DOUBLE AGENT
MODESTY Blaise
THE SCARLET MAIDEN


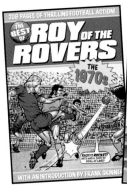

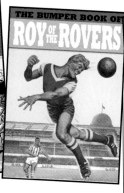

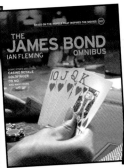

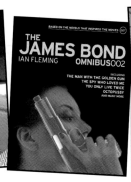

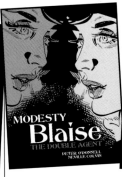

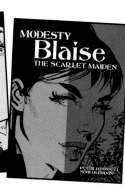

## ROY OF THE ROVERS

- The Best of Roy of the Rovers: The 1980s
- The Best of Roy of the Rovers: The 1970s
- The Bumper Book of Roy of the Rovers: Volume 1
- The Bumper Book of Roy of the Rovers: Volume 2

## THE JAMES BOND OMNIBUS

- Volume 1
- Volume 2

JAMES BOND 007
THE SPY WHO LOVED ME
IAN FLEMING
JAMES BOND 007
THE MAN WITH THE GOLDEN GUN
IAN FLEMING


## MODESTY BLAISE

- The Gabriel Set-Up
- Mister Sun
- Top Traitor
- The Black Pearl
- Bad Suki
- The Hell-Makers
- The Green-Eyed Monster
- The Puppet Master
- The Gallows Bird
- Cry Wolf
- The Inca Trail
- Death Trap
- Yellowstone Booty
- Green Cobra
- The Lady Killers
- The Scarlet Maiden
- Death In Slow Motion
- Sweet Caroline
- The Double Agent

DAN DARE
PILOT OF THE FUTURE
THE PHANTOM FLEET
DAN DARE
PILOT OF THE FUTURE
ROGUE PLANET


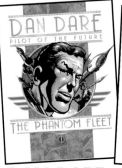

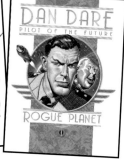

## DAN DARE

- Voyage to Venus Part 1
- Voyage to Venus Part 2
- The Red Moon Mystery
- Marooned on Mercury
- Operation Saturn Part 1
- Operation Saturn Part 2
- Prisoners of Space
- The Man From Nowhere
- Rogue Planet
- Reign of the Robots
- The Phantom Fleet
- Safari In Space
- Trip to Trouble

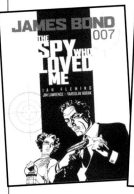

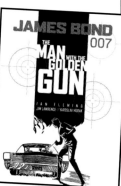

## JAMES BOND

- Casino Royale
- Dr No
- Goldfinger
- On Her Majesty's Secret Service
- The Man with the Golden Gun
- Octopussy
- The Spy Who Loved Me
- Colonel Sun
- The Golden Ghost
- Trouble Spot
- The Phoenix Project
- The Paradise Plot
- Polestar
- Death Wing
- Shark Bait
- The Girl Machine

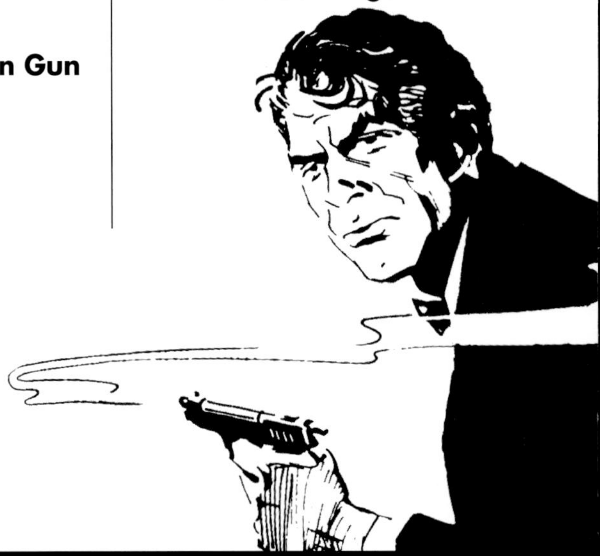

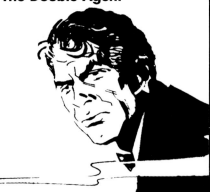

**FOR MORE INFORMATION ON THESE TITLES — AND MUCH, MUCH MORE — CHECK OUT OUR WEBSITE AT WWW.TITANBOOKS.COM!**

# THE BATTLE CONTINUES!

**FOLLOW YOUR FAVOURITE CHARACTERS' ADVENTURES IN THESE ALL-NEW REPRINT COLLECTIONS!**

FALCON'S FIRST FLIGHT
JOHNNY RED
INTRODUCTION BY GARTH ENNIS
TOM TULLY ★ JOE COLQUHOUN

DARKIE'S MOB
JOHN WAGNER
MIKE WESTERN
INTRODUCTION BY GARTH ENNIS
THE SECRET WAR OF JOE DARKIE


**PLUS**

# RAT PACK

**AND**

# MAJOR EAZY

## MORE TITLES COMING SOON!

**WWW.TITANBOOKS.COM**

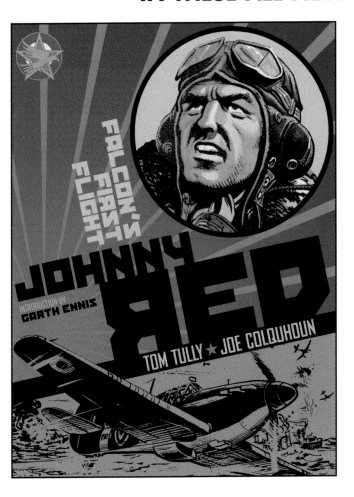

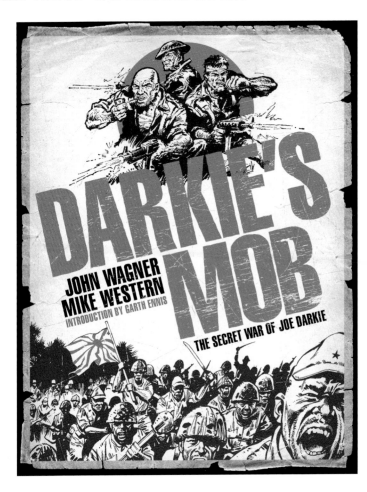

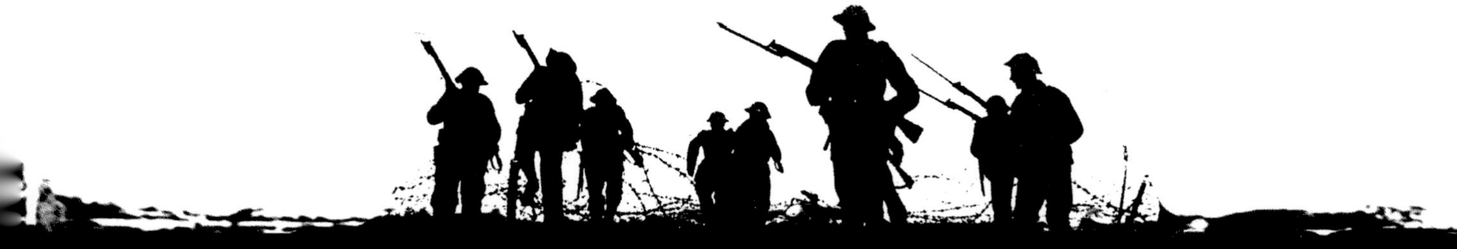

# ALSO AVAILABLE FROM TITAN BOOKS

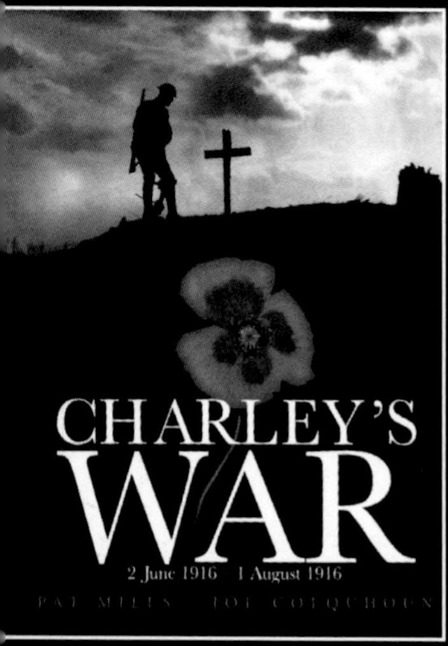
CHARLEY'S WAR
2 June 1916 – 1 August 1916
PAT MILLS JOE COLQUHOUN

ISBN: 9781840236279

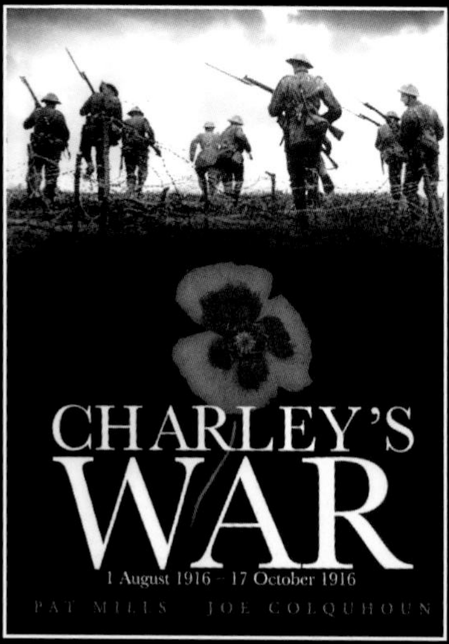
CHARLEY'S WAR
1 August 1916 – 17 October 1916
PAT MILLS JOE COLQUHOUN

ISBN: 9781840239294

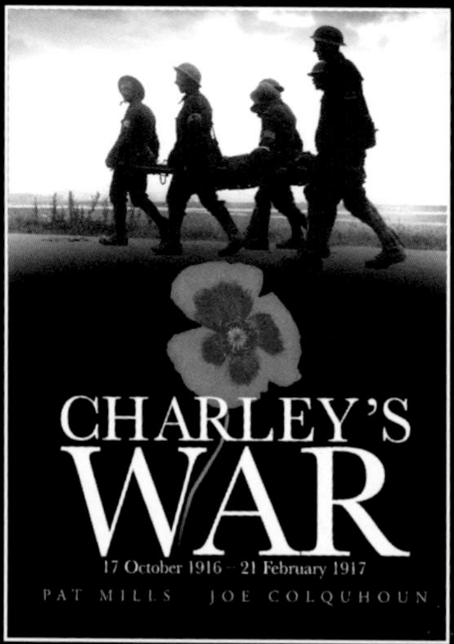
CHARLEY'S WAR
17 October 1916 – 21 February 1917
PAT MILLS JOE COLQUHOUN

ISBN: 9781845762704

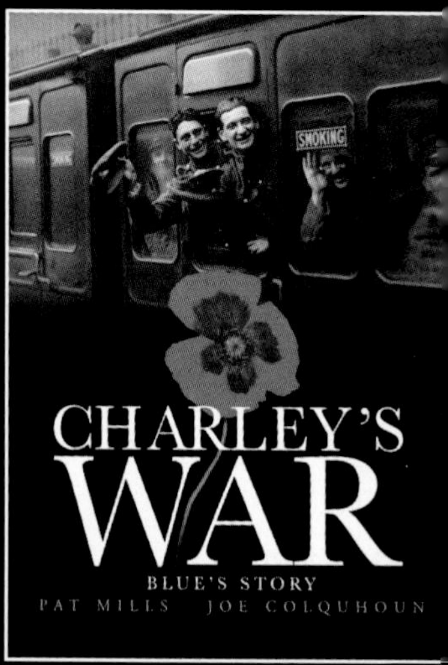
SMOKING
CHARLEY'S WAR
BLUE'S STORY
PAT MILLS JOE COLQUHOUN

ISBN: 9781845763237

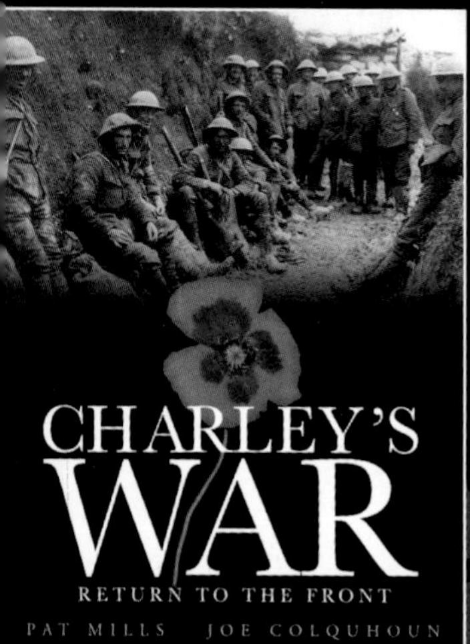
CHARLEY'S WAR
RETURN TO THE FRONT
PAT MILLS JOE COLQUHOUN

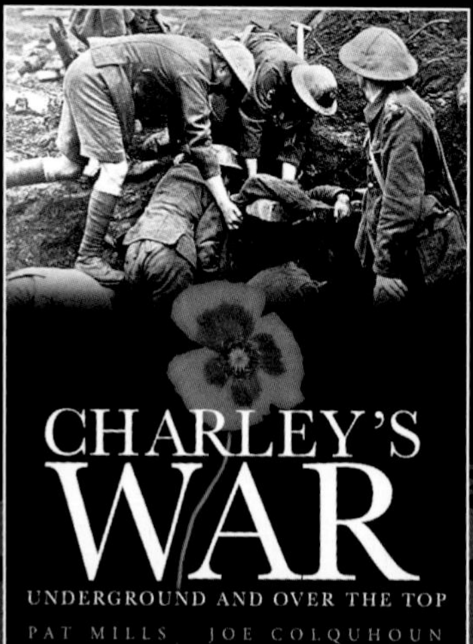
CHARLEY'S WAR
UNDERGROUND AND OVER THE TOP
PAT MILLS JOE COLQUHOUN

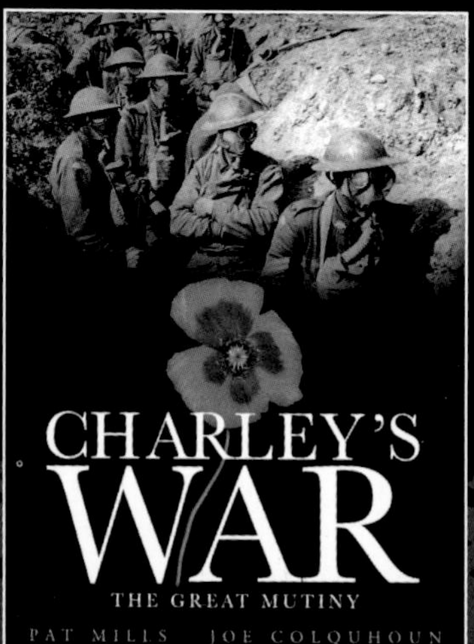
CHARLEY'S WAR
THE GREAT MUTINY
PAT MILLS JOE COLQUHOUN

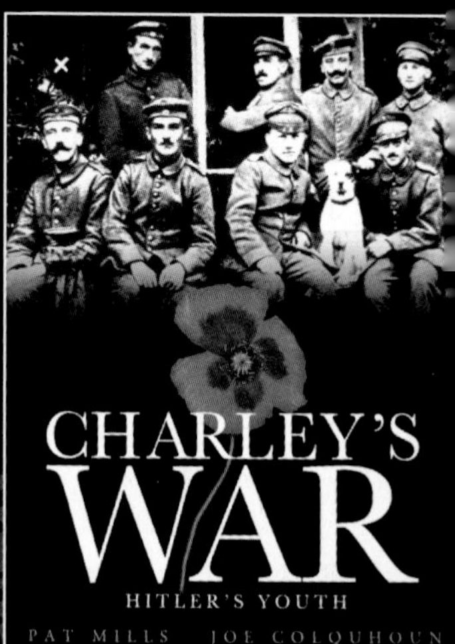
CHARLEY'S WAR
HITLER'S YOUTH
PAT MILLS JOE COLQUHOUN

ISBN: 9780857682994